Psycholinguistic Approaches to Instructed Second Language Acquisition

Full details of all our publications can be found on http://www.multilingual-matters.com, or by writing to Multilingual Matters, St Nicholas House, 31-34 High Street, Bristol, BS1 2AW, UK.

Psycholinguistic Approaches to Instructed Second Language Acquisition

Linking Theory, Findings and Practice

Daniel R. Walter

MULTILINGUAL MATTERS
Bristol • Jackson

DOI https://doi.org/10.21832/WALTER8755
Library of Congress Cataloging in Publication Data
A catalog record for this book is available from the Library of Congress.
Names: Walter, Daniel (Linguist), author.
Title: Psycholinguistic Approaches to Instructed Second Language Acquisition:
   Linking Theory, Findings and Practice/Daniel R. Walter.
Description: Bristol; Jackson: Multilingual Matters, [2023] | Includes bibliographical
   references. | Summary: "This book applies a psycholinguistic perspective to
   instructed second language acquisition, bridging the gap between research and
   teaching practices. It re-envisions the explicit and implicit learning divide as
   a continuum of consciousness, explores the pedagogical applications of SLA
   findings and offers practical suggestions for instructors"—Provided by publisher.
Identifiers: LCCN 2022054410 (print) | LCCN 2022054411 (ebook) |
   ISBN 9781788928755 (hardback) | ISBN 9781788928748 (paperback) |
   ISBN 9781788928762 (pdf) | ISBN 9781788928779 (epub)
Subjects: LCSH: Language and languages—Study and teaching—Psychological
   aspects. | Second language acquisition.
Classification: LCC P53.7 .W35 2023 (print) | LCC P53.7 (ebook) |
   DDC 18.0071—dc23/eng/20230303
LC record available at https://lccn.loc.gov/2022054410
LC ebook record available at https://lccn.loc.gov/2022054411

British Library Cataloguing in Publication Data
A catalogue entry for this book is available from the British Library.

ISBN-13: 978-1-78892-875-5 (hbk)
ISBN-13: 978-1-78892-874-8 (pbk)

Multilingual Matters
UK: St Nicholas House, 31-34 High Street, Bristol, BS1 2AW, UK.
USA: Ingram, Jackson, TN, USA.

Website: www.multilingual-matters.com
Twitter: Multi_Ling_Mat
Facebook: https://www.facebook.com/multilingualmatters
Blog: www.channelviewpublications.wordpress.com

Copyright © 2023 Daniel R. Walter.

All rights reserved. No part of this work may be reproduced in any form or by any means without permission in writing from the publisher.

The policy of Multilingual Matters/Channel View Publications is to use papers that are natural, renewable and recyclable products, made from wood grown in sustainable forests. In the manufacturing process of our books, and to further support our policy, preference is given to printers that have FSC and PEFC Chain of Custody certification. The FSC and/or PEFC logos will appear on those books where full certification has been granted to the printer concerned.

Typeset by Deanta Global Publishing Services, Chennai, India.

Contents

Acknowledgements		vii
Introduction		1
1	Instructed SLA: A (Modern) History	7
	ISLA Before SLA Existed	7
	Non-Western Language Teaching Traditions and Practices	21
	The Genesis of (I)SLA	25
	Recent 'Turns' in SLA and Their Impact on Instruction	28
	The Future of (I)SLA: A Closer Relationship between Researchers, Theorists and Educators	39
2	The Conscious|Unconscious Divide	41
	Behind the Scenes: Automatic Psycholinguistic Processes and Mechanisms of Learning	41
	Center Stage: Volition and Consciousness	50
	Conclusion	57
3	Re-envisioning a Conscious–Unconscious Continuum	60
	Dynamic Attention	61
	Conscious–Subconscious Fluctuation and Interaction	68
	Conclusion: A Continuum of Activity	71
4	The Conscious Continuum in Individual Development	73
	The Initial State	75
	Beyond the Four Skills: A Proposed Trajectory of Individual Language Learning	88
	Early Active Learning: The Search for Systematicity	92
	Early Acquisition	93
	Growing Proficiency	96
	Budding Multilingualism	105
	Native-Like Proficiency or Advanced Multilingualism?	106

		Individual Development and the Conscious–Unconscious Continuum	114
5		Psycholinguistic Processes in the Classroom	117
		The Second/Foreign Language Classroom as a Complex Social Environment	118
		Classroom Place and Space	119
		Artifacts We Learn By	126
		People in the L2 Classroom Community	130
		Structural and Systematic Influences	137
		Classroom Context Effects on Consciousness and Learning	143
6		Curricular and Pedagogical Recommendations	144
		Designing a Curriculum	145
		Daily Instruction	152
		L2 Skills and Knowledge	158
		Assessment	170
		Building a Language Learning Community to Support Multilingual Identity Development	171
		Putting It All Together	175
		More than Methods: The Art in L2 Teaching	177
		Conclusion: A Robust Language Learning Experience	178
		References	179
		Index	205

Acknowledgements

For all of my German teachers and professors who inspired my love of languages and language learning, especially Herr Deible and Frau Stein.

And for Brian MacWhinney and Adam van Compernolle, whose work inspired this book.

Introduction

This book links advances in psycholinguistic approaches to second language acquisition (SLA) with curricular design and classroom-based practices. It is the result of efforts to bridge two strands of research: one largely lab based and individual, focusing on attempts at isolating variables and limiting outside noise and interference, and the other participatory and interactional, playing out in the lived experiences of millions of teachers and students every day. In the majority of psycholinguistic publications, the focus is either on the unfolding of microgenetic, cognitive processes in a controlled setting, the development of some psycholinguistic process within an individual over time or a comparison between groups of learners at different stages of development. It is rare to read discussions of a psycholinguistic experiment that includes the context of the actual classrooms where the subject learned their second language (L2) or the implications of the study back into the classroom. For those studies that do discuss teaching applications, it is unusual for the implementation to be described in a way that is feasible in the L2 language classroom and for teachers with little time for or training in interpreting the results of experimental studies. This book repairs these missing links by directly connecting what we know about SLA and learning from a psycholinguistic perspective with pedagogical considerations and curricular design decisions.

This book also contributes to SLA psycholinguistics research itself, which is usually studied as two separate areas, by reimagining two distinct research paradigms as a continuum of consciousness. On the one side, researchers and educators engage with explicit instruction that uses the conscious mind of the language learner to instruct various aspects of vocabulary, grammar and strategies for language learning. These include traditional cognitive SLA methods as well as those that fall under the auspices of other theoretical approaches to SLA, such as sociocultural theory, that involve psycholinguistic processes, but which are not frequently discussed in the same vein as SLA research or across researchers from these separate theoretical paradigms. On the other side, researchers and educators focus on implicit learning and automated processes.

While both areas of research are essential for advancing knowledge about SLA, there is a need for more explicit dialogue between researchers from these two camps, especially when it comes to relating findings in clearly stated terms. Indeed, if one of the goals of SLA is to increase the efficacy of language instruction, one cannot come without the other. This book proposes that, for instructed SLA (ISLA), we are studying a single continuum of psycholinguistic processes that can be leveraged to increase the effectiveness of language instruction.

This book re-envisions the findings of psycholinguistic approaches to SLA in a meaningful way for ISLA. Included is a concise but encompassing picture of the diverse, complex and interconnected mental faculties and mechanisms involved in learning an L2. This understanding is applied to both the individual learner and the L2 classroom across the curriculum, from learners' first encounter with a second/additional language to advanced stages of proficiency. From the perspective of a continuum along conscious and unconscious language learning processes, this book provides practical suggestions for L2 teachers and researchers, as well as a way to understand the role of both conscious and unconscious processes throughout the course of learner development and throughout the curriculum.

The emergence of SLA, as with any newly established discipline, inevitably carried with it epistemologies, standards of proof, theories, methodologies and assumptions from its root fields. Therefore, it is imperative that we are aware of the role that these fields played in the formation of ISLA. It is also necessary to attend to advances in other related fields, such as cognitive science, that may alter some of the base assumptions made during the establishment of ISLA. In many ways, this book is a deliberate attempt at joining the advances in ISLA to the advances made in these parental and partnering fields.

ISLA is a term that has evolved from Western philosophical and scientific traditions. Thus, a large portion of the book, including much of the prior research cited, as well as the development of a curricular approach, is centered around a Western conceptualization of instruction. To account for this perspective discrepancy, L2 instruction methodologies from around the world are included and the author is aware and explicit in the assumptions made throughout the book, particularly the chapter on curricular design. While some specifics for understanding and implementing instructional design may not be suitable for all languages, language learners or language classrooms, the general theory built around specific rationalizations and realizations of methodology are sufficiently adaptable to be broadly informative for an array of language instructors and learning contexts.

It is also important here to clearly outline the theoretical perspective taken in this book, and how the author's conceptualizations of language learning, psycholinguistics, pedagogy and instruction have impacted the way the book is structured. Learning an L2 is a complex task grounded in social, cognitive, physical and physiological realities. These different layers play intertwining roles in the development, maintenance and change of language as a dynamic social, cultural and psychological phenomenon. Any complete theory of SLA must account for the ubiquity of language learning across human history, as well as the wide variation across geographical and temporal space. One of the most complete frameworks that takes many of these aspects into consideration was proposed by the Douglas Fir Group. One particular section of the Douglas Fir Group's conceptualization of the nature of language that the author calls attention to is

> [l]anguage learning is a complex, ongoing, multifaceted phenomenon that involves the dynamic and variable interplay among a range of individual neurobiological mechanisms and cognitive capacities and L2 learners' diverse experiences in their multilingual worlds occurring over their life spans and along three interrelated levels of social activity: the micro level of social action and interaction, the meso level of sociocultural institutions and communities, and the macro level of ideological structures. (The Douglas Fir Group, 2016: 36)

Two important implications can be made from the Douglas Fir Group's conceptualization: (1) the nature of language and (2) the importance of both a biological and cultural basis for understanding psycholinguistics.

First, language cannot be defined by its structure at a single moment in time. Static instances of language exist in both cultural artifacts, such as books and text messages, and within individuals at a particular moment in time, but the perception that a language exists in this way, that it can be defined and constrained to a static object, cannot be true. Language exists in its use, be that passive or productive, internal (self-talk) or external. The continual encounters of an individual with familiar and unfamiliar language structures across time can change the organization of the system itself. These encounters with other language structures come upon larger social and cultural issues, such as ideologies of 'correct' and 'incorrect' language use. This inability to pin down a language in a static way that is anything more than a snapshot of a particular confluence of time, space, people and culture is fundamental to the nature of language.

The second part of the Douglas Fir Group's conceptualization that is necessary to unpack for this book, is that language is based on cultural, social and historical processes grounded in underlying 'neurobiological mechanisms and cognitive capacities'. This is the key factor that distinguishes psycholinguistics from the more general field of linguistics. Psycholinguists are required to acknowledge that language, in all of its abstraction and levels of representation and reproduction, is based on a physical system of interconnected neurons that display common, although not necessarily universal, regions of functionality, represented in various structures of gray matter that are thoroughly interconnected through white matter tracks, and that these pathways of connectivity have been formed, informed and trained by the cultural forces at play on both small and grand scales of language in use. Thus, the perspective taken in this book regarding instruction and learning always acknowledges the importance of neurobiologically plausible foundations for higher-order psychological and cognitive processes, as well as the cultural and social environment in which learners, and their instructors, find themselves.

The final term outlined in the preface is *instruction*. While seemingly simple, a closer inspection reveals how nebulous this term is, and that one's understanding of the concept of instruction is reliant on one's own cultural and educational experiences, which do not necessarily overlap from one classroom to the next, let alone one culture to another. The first chapter of the book expands on the ways that instruction has been defined and what it typically means within ISLA as an academic discipline. Suffice to say here that, in order to make this book applicable to K-12 and higher education teachers and researchers, the focus is primarily on a Western, language classroom setting. However, where possible, attempts are made to draw parallels to other modes of instruction, including one-on-one tutoring, self-guided learning, computer-assisted language learning and other alternative learning experiences.

Book Outline

Chapter 1 discusses the appearance of ISLA as a unique area of study. An outline is provided of the rather long history of humans' attempts, successes and struggles with learning the language(s) of other humans, including initial attempts to formally study and teach foreign languages, which moved much of the experience of learning another language from an immersive to a didactic relationship. The chapter then moves on to explain how changes in instructional methods came about or diverged from new findings in SLA. Relevant changes within the field of SLA as well as others, such as linguistics, educational psychology, developmental psychology, psycholinguistics and cognitive science, are discussed. The chapter concludes with how SLA and language instruction began to separate the consciousness of the learner from unconscious, psycholinguistic processes.

Chapter 2 expands on the current state of psycholinguistic approaches to instruction and what is known about the psycholinguistic processes involved in learning an L2. Two major camps of research – those examining implicit and automatic learning processes and those examining the role of conscious thought and explicit instruction – are described. In doing so, an outline is provided of the research goals and motivations of these camps, and it is shown how the questions, theories, research agendas and methods used by these groups served to further separate these two research areas.

Chapter 3 dissolves the discrete boundary between conscious and unconscious activity in SLA. Rather than dividing these seemingly distinct processes, the chapter re-envisions them on a continuum of consciousness. On this continuum, activities normally associated with conscious functions such as goal orientation or grammar learning become unconscious activities over time, and vice versa; activities normally associated with unconscious functions such as parsing words from a continuous speech stream or first language transfer come to the conscious forefront for direct reflection by learners. This book's primary contribution to SLA itself is that the spotlight of consciousness and the obscurity of the unconscious operate in conjunction with each other, and that the boundary between the two is overexaggerated, especially when it comes to the learner's mental processes in real time in the classroom.

Chapter 4 describes how a re-envisioned continuum of psycholinguistic processes plays out across the language learning experience of an individual. The chapter focuses on how the multitude of language learning-related processes and skills (e.g. vocabulary learning, auditory and visual processing, production, planning, proceduralization and automatization) play out across multiple time spans and within single moments. By highlighting how the types of activities undertaken in the conscious and unconscious mind shift over the course of a learner's development, a progression of learning is devised that is applied in Chapter 6 toward building an L2 curriculum.

Chapter 5 moves from the individual to the L2 classroom. An outline is provided of how the L2 classroom is itself a complex, dynamic space in which multiple sources of information unite through a community of practice involved with the common goal of language learning, albeit to different ends and for different purposes. Included are discussions of space, people, cultural and educational artifacts, and institutional environments, as they affect both the L2 classroom and the activities that take place within it.

Chapter 6 shows how the psycholinguistic processes and teaching techniques described in the previous chapters can be used to design a curriculum that supports the needs of students throughout the language learning curriculum and across multiple years of study. Within this broad-scale curriculum, changes in learners' proficiency, along with gains in metalinguistic knowledge growth, push learners through increasingly complex tasks, while simultaneously maintaining an awareness of balancing cognitive processing demands. The chapter then reflects on how to assess learner development within this framework for those looking to understand best practices for assessing L2 development across modalities, tasks and developmental stages. Finally, a concise recap via a framework to think about the design of L2 curricula and teaching practices with the developmental needs of students, as individuals and as a class, is provided.

1 Instructed SLA: A (Modern) History

Instructed second language acquisition (ISLA), at least as it is conceptualized in this era of linguistics, is a relatively new field of study, under the relatively new umbrella fields of applied linguistics and second language acquisition (SLA). In fact, the words *instructed* and *SLA* did not appear next to each other as a unified term in linguistic pedagogical literature until 1985 (Long, 1985). The unification of ISLA as a meaningful unit was an important reconceptualization of and response to other movements within SLA in the latter 20th and early 21st century and brought with it many assumptions about the process of language learning, which are explored later in this chapter.

However, this does not mean that there has not been a long and rich history of the study of second language (L2) instruction and foreign language learning. For this reason, the chapter begins with an overview of what language instruction consisted of in previous centuries, up to and including the formalization of SLA as an independent framework in applied linguistics and linguistics as a whole. The chapter then moves on to the specifics of late 20th- and early 21st-century and current-day conceptualizations of ISLA in order to position it within and distinct from other areas of SLA and applied linguistics. Along the way, different topics relevant to the following chapters are connected, such as methodologies, reasons for instruction and goals and motivations for language learning and teaching. The chapter concludes with a description of where ISLA stands today as its own subfield within SLA, as well as the role of ISLA in the future of applied linguistics, language pedagogy and related fields.

ISLA Before SLA Existed

ISLA, conceptualized as an interest in the practices of students and teachers in the L2 classroom, has been essential to intercultural communication for as long as humans have interacted with other humans who speak different languages. Long before SLA became its own field of study, there was still much interest in teaching and learning other languages. Be it trade, religion or some other purpose, learning and teaching other languages have been an important part of global cultural history. As Musumeci (2009: 43) muses, 'One can easily imagine that second-language learning has been going on since people with different language systems first encountered one another on the savannahs of Africa, in the Mesopotamian valley, and on the plains of northern Europe'. As such, it is important to understand the similarities and differences that exist between the lived experiences of those teaching and learning languages across time.

Language instruction in medieval Europe

Despite the aforementioned imagined ubiquity of formal and especially informal language teaching, actual records of language instruction do not appear until much more recent human history, and if we are conceptualizing ISLA in terms of teacher–student interactions within a classroom, the earliest records of such are not traceable until medieval times. Bischoff's (1961) article 'The Study of Foreign Languages in the Middle Ages' provides a good starting point, although, interestingly, he leaves out much of the study of Latin, because, as he notes, it does not fit into the category of either 'living' or 'dead' languages of study because of its importance to Christianity and mission work. He begins his history of language study with an increasing interest in 12th-century French language resulting from the converging factors of 'the Crusades, the superiority of French chivalrous culture, the attraction exerted on tradesmen by the by fairs of Champagne' (Bischoff, 1961: 210). This was also enhanced by its use as the language of literature. From there, he indicates the importance of learning 'Italian, Catalan, and Greek' in the Mediterranean for trade, and eventually German as well, as they too entered the region.

In terms of language study, Bischoff (1961) points out that, 'Texts illustrating language studies are preserved rather unequally', which muddles a clear understanding of what was available in terms of materials, and there is little textual information about 'how' languages were taught. That being said, textual artifacts that hint at methods and philosophies related to language teaching do exist, such as 'schoolbooks for the study of French', 'vocabularies and patterns of conversation for Flemish-speaking as well as for French-speaking people', 'Spanish and Arabic translations of Latin manuscripts' (Bischoff, 1961: 211). The 'first strictly medieval grammar, the Old High German "grammatica patrii sermonis"' (Bischoff, 1961: 212) was contracted by Charlemagne. Other translations and grammars were commonly found for Greek, Hebrew and many other languages. These texts provide evidence that scholars of these languages were interested in both explaining the grammar of other languages, albeit often within the paradigm of Latin grammar (e.g. Old

High German grammar), and providing usage-based language, such as vernacular vocabularies and patterns of conversation, as these became important resources for tradesmen, pilgrims and all other manner of travelers from the 12th and 13th centuries onward.

However, before we advance too much further into the future, it is important, for the same reasons Bischoff (1961) mostly excluded it from his analysis, that we turn to Latin. As one of the most widely taught languages in medieval Europe and its corollaries, it held a unique status among other languages in medieval Europe. In fact, it is expounded upon in its own chapter in Long and Doughty's (2011) *The Handbook of Language Teaching*. In this chapter, Musumeci (2009) reviews the history of the teaching of Latin from the Middle Ages to the 20th century, as it was often viewed as a lingua franca with special roles in both academic and religious contexts. Musumeci (2009) even makes a comparison between the role of Latin in the (Western) medieval world and English's contemporary role in global communication and trade. An important note from this chapter is the author's repeated emphasis of the ebb and flow of trends in language learning and teaching methods. For centuries, core concepts and questions about best practices, learning outcomes and the nature of language itself have been debated within the realm and on the periphery of language education. The terminology used today to talk about language-related concepts, such as universal grammar (UG), which will be discussed in the following chapters, were also topics of discussion in medieval times, albeit under different names or with different meanings (see Fredborg, 1980; Thomas, 1995).

There are several reasons for the importance of Latin and its role in language education in the Western tradition, and yet there was a lack of everyday use which made its acquisition more of an academic endeavor than an everyday language. As Musumeci (2009) notes, students had many of the same complaints as students today. Namely, that they find limited application for particular languages outside of the classroom. In medieval Europe, despite Latin's presence in institutions, everyday conversations were conducted in those languages spoken by the public. Reforms that attempted to force students to communicate in Latin outside of class failed. From early on, then, we can see that motivation, utility and language beliefs have always played a part in L2 learning.

Later, this chapter describes the strong shift in SLA to focus on the learner, but it is important to establish here that prior to this turn, the focus of language pedagogy was on the teacher and how they conducted their courses, rather than the various linguistic, psychological and social processes that the learner was undertaking. As Musumeci (2009) points out, over the course of time and space, teaching even within a single language discipline is not monolithic, and even texts that prescribe certain methods of instruction do not necessarily reflect what was happening in classrooms across the European continent. However, we can point to a few different methods that may have been employed and reflect on what we might call them today. In a review of 12th-century teaching practices of teaching Latin as an L2, Murphy (1980: 174) argues that 'European schoolmasters had evolved an effective, commonly-used mode of instruction utilizing the best elements of ancient, patristic, insular, and Carolingian programs. At the heart of the system was a sequence of Christian (or Christianized) progymnasmata'. In other words, a set of common rhetorical practices were used to teach the basic principles of Latin focused on texts that also served to support the education and evangelism of Christianity. Initially, as Murphy (1980: 174) details, 'Both dialectic and rhetoric were elementary subjects along with grammar until the burgeoning university structure preempted dialectic and displaced rhetoric to leave grammar the basic subject for elementary education'. This point reflects quite nicely the division we see in many of the current approaches to language instruction regarding the role of grammar. While rule learning was championed for much of the latter 20th century, early 21st-century proponents of communicative language teaching, as well as other rhetoric-based approaches like multiliteracies, have questioned the place of rule instruction and the primacy of grammar in language teaching practices.

The question of teaching rules versus usage leads to other questions, namely what did and did not count as grammar. Interestingly, Murphy (1980) points out that various modes of instruction beyond rules were in place. For example, an early emphasis was placed on phonetics and the sounds of Latin. It seems that teachers have always been confronted with decisions about what is important for their learners to be able to do with the language. This would have naturally impacted what and how they taught. These questions lead us directly to why people were learning these languages, and the necessary types of language, speech acts and intercultural and interpersonal competencies they would need to fulfill their reason for pursuing knowledge of or fluency in a particular language.

Teaching language as a means to an end

Language instruction is frequently associated with a means to complete some type of social, interpersonal or academic objective. In this section, we explore distinctive human activities that have motivated the teaching and learning of particular languages to achieve the goals set forth by institutions, communities and individuals. First, I cover language teaching for the purposes of evangelizing or spreading the word of God. This includes the instruction of languages to target populations to enable those populations to read and communicate in the language of the evangelists, as well as instruction of other languages for evangelists to communicate in the language(s) of target populations. Next, I look at how language teaching has impacted the global economy and international trade. The proliferation of international trade, especially with the evolution of lingua francas, has led to many languages being positioned with privileged statuses in the global economy. This has special implications as a result of the development of global English, and with it English as a foreign language/English as a second language/teaching English to speakers of other languages (EFL/ESL/TESOL) institutions, as well as training and testing in the latter half of the 20th and into the 21st century. Next, I investigate how language teaching acts as a means to educational access. Here, language is envisioned as both a pathway into educational opportunities, as well as a barrier or doorway to knowledge itself. And finally, I explore how language teaching is also a means to preserve cultural heritage. Through weekend language programs and heritage language (HL) courses, these practices serve to sustain family and community ties in an increasingly globalized world where the physical and cultural space between family members continues to increase. These four motivators are certainly not the only ones, but they serve as examples to help us understand how large societal factors motivate the instruction of certain languages and deter the acquisition of others.

Teaching the words of god(s)

Missionary work and evangelizing have deep historical roots, and those performing this work didn't just bring their religion with them. They also brought their traditions, their culture and, of course, their language(s). The Crusades are a prime example of this. What this language contact initiated is not within the scope of this book, and what, if any, language instruction was provided, certainly did not resemble anything like the 21st-century language classroom. However, questions about the role of one language versus another for evangelizing and then continued religious study are important to understand as these historical processes have shaped and continue to shape our current world. Bischoff (1961) presents two different views that played out in tandem with one another. On the one hand,

> Missionary practice demanded in the first place the study of the vernacular languages if the missionary did not content himself with the mediation of an interpreter. Besides preaching, it was indispensable to translate at least parts of the Bible, the liturgy and catechisms, Creed and confessions, and in fact quite a number of languages became recorded in script for the first time in this way and in such texts. (Bischoff, 1961: 223)

Thus, the introduction of religion to people who spoke other languages inevitably produced texts (both physical and oral) to be learned, studied and dispersed. On the other hand,

> for practical, institutional, and liturgical reasons, it seemed desirable that the Christianized nations should become familiar with Latin as

the language of the Roman Catholic Church, and in the countries situated on the northern and eastern edge of the Latin Christian world this was achieved. After the conquest of Constantinople in 1204, and again in the fourteenth century, plans were made for the reunification of the Church, and some radical theorists like a certain Dominican Adam even considered the extirpation of Greek language and script; but such plans were moderated in view of the fact that Greek had been one of the sacred languages of the inscription on Christ's Cross. (Bischoff, 1961: 223)

Language ideologies clearly played a part in the power dynamics between those doing the evangelizing and those being evangelized. Even those rulers who promoted learning other languages felt pressure to preserve Latin as a religious language. In one example, Bischoff (1961: 212) describes the case of 'The indefatigable Catalan Raymundus Lullus (Ramon Lull)' who was 'known to have insisted more than anybody else on the study of the languages required for active missions; but even he in his utopian missionary romance Blanquerna gave the advice that Latin should be made the universal world language so that definitely all language barriers and language difficulties should vanish once and for all'.

More recent attempts at evangelizing have replaced the invading army of soldiers with an invading army of teachers. As missions continued over time, other languages like English became the language of salvation. Missionaries traveled to other countries where English or other Western languages were not spoken and imposed their language on the local populations. These practices show the omnipresent ideology that the language of the places where the missionaries came from was the language of religion. While there is little doubt that at least some, if not most of these newcomers picked up tidbits, portions or even significant amounts of the language or languages taught in their new location, it is preferable to keep the deep discussion of religion and religious texts centered around the language of the missionaries. Using their own languages, missionaries and later priests, pastors and other religious figure heads ensured that they retained their power as the ones delivering the message of their religion, thereby maintaining religious and social power over the local populations.

Advances in cultural understanding have not stopped the pursuit of such missions, but they have affected the way in which religion is instructed. Stronger efforts have been made to teach missionaries the languages of their target populations, and the Bible and other religious texts have been translated into multiple languages. As a prime example, Brigham Young University (BYU), a private Mormon university that works with thousands of students each year either preparing to go or returning from across the globe on missions, has one of the most well-recognized and highly praised foreign language instruction programs in the United States. This testament is reinforced by both external and internal statements about BYU. In its rankings for foreign languages and linguistics, College Factual (2021) ranks BYU third overall, just behind Gallaudet University in Washington, DC and Columbia University in New York City, and it produces the third highest number of graduates with a degree in a foreign language, behind the University of California at Los Angeles and the University of Wisconsin at Madison (The Chronicle of Higher Education, 2021). From US News and World Report (2021): 'Provo is also home to the Missionary Training Center, where students of the Latter-day Saints faith can enroll to learn and grow before serving at least 18 months around the world. Known for its excellence in language education, BYU regularly offers courses in 62 different languages. About 65 percent of students speak a second language'. The statistic that 65% of students attending BYU speak an L2 should be staggering to anyone with even an intuition about the number of bi/multilingual students attending US universities. While there is no national average statistic for the percentage of students at the average US university who speak an L2, the fact that 'Only 7 percent of college students in America are enrolled in a language course' (Friedman, 2015: n.p.) should give some indication.

Not only does BYU have a depth of student engagement, but its breadth is also quite astounding in terms of its ubiquity across programs and the sheer number of languages taught. According to Brigham Young University (2022), its 'Center for Language Studies provides strategic planning and assessment services for the College of Humanities, oversees special-purpose language resource centers, supports 12 departmental major and minor language programs, and provides instruction in 40+ additional languages'. This connection with language learning was emphasized by Spencer W. Kimball, the twelfth president of the Church of Jesus Christ of Latter-day Saints, whose 1975 quote 'BYU should become the acknowledged language capital of the world', is eminently displayed on BYU's Center for Language Studies' 'About' page. In addition, the language of mission work is easily visible within the language used to describe the center: 'The Center for Language Studies, housed within the BYU College of Humanities, strives to fulfill the university's mission of "Enter to learn. Go forth to serve."' The Center strives to maintain the core competencies valued by the BYU College of Humanities, especially Cultural Literacy and Language Proficiency, but simultaneously acts as a support structure for mission work.

Language learning for religious purposes has been and continues to be an important part of the educational curriculum for other religions as well. Arabic is the holy language of the Quran and for those people living in countries where Arabic is not the language of everyday communication, or if Arabic is not one of the primary languages spoken in the home, educational programs seeking to support Muslim religious teaching have language acquisition as an integral part. According to Hamidah (2019):

> In the religious context, every Muslim is obliged to learn Arabic as much as he can to help him do the prayer. To understand the Qu'ran and Hadith, and to master in Islamic studies, he has to learn Arabic, and so does those who teach Islamic lessons in the school, Arabic teachers and other Muslim academics. Parents should pay special intention to their children's Arabic skill so that the language will remain sustainable. (Hamidah, 2019: n.p.)

This is also essential for those seeking to study Islam, as

> Across the centuries, the Arabic language has always been the backbone of Islamic sciences due to its epistemological relation. Not only Al-Quran and Prophet Muhammad's traditions, but the main epistemological sources for Islamic sciences were also revealed in Arabic, both too, have been engrossed with Arabic metaphors and semantics. Thus, a sufficient command of Arabic language or at least, certain degree of competency in understanding certain Arabic terminologies and grammar are expected for one to mastering Islamic studies. (Mat & Abas, 2016: n.p.)

Similarly, for those of the Jewish faith, learning Hebrew is often required. In many traditions, such as Hasidic Judaism, Hebrew continues to be the language of the Old Testament and Talmud, even though other languages, including Yiddish, may be the language used for everyday communication. Even in instances where Hebrew is the language of everyday communication, it is still seen by many to be a 'religious language'. For example, many 'Ultraorthodox' Jews in Israel will not speak it outside of religious contexts (Keane, 1997).

All this is to say that, as Kramsch (1998: 3) puts it, 'Through all its verbal and non-verbal aspects, language embodies cultural reality'. Religion is either associated with or directly tied to a particular language or language practices, which means that the instruction and proliferation of 'religious languages' may be seen as necessary to maintain religious understanding among a secular, global community of practitioners. As such, language instruction and SLA become essential features of religious education in maintaining norms, power structures and contiguity across time and space.

For specific purposes, in this case religion, language teaching is both a practice that is significantly pressured by powerful, external institutions to produce outcomes, as well as a practice that, through extra attention, receives more commitment and support than we typically see in K-12 and post-secondary language classrooms. These beliefs about the connection between language, religion and spirituality are supported by actionable goals set by religious leaders and those educators in charge of instructing

L2s, and in turn motivate L2 learning in significant ways that not only support learners but also have direct effects on their language learning outcomes and developmental trajectories.

Language learning for economic purposes

Like religion, the economic endeavors of people throughout history have led them to encounters with speakers of other languages. These encounters have resulted in a variety of linguistic, social and cultural phenomena, including the development of pidgins and creoles, where speakers of one or multiple languages are forced to either learn, ignore or compromise with speakers of another language. The language one chooses to use, or is coerced to use, can often signal the real or perceived power dynamic between two parties. This is exemplified by the quote attributed to former German Chancellor Willy Brandt on international trade: 'If I'm selling to you, I speak your language. If I'm buying, dann müssen Sie Deutsch sprechen!'. The implication here is that if you are in possession of something I want, I am in the position of less power and should try to accommodate you as best as possible, and vice versa.

The power dynamics of multi-language interactions can have significant impacts not only on how parties view each other, but also on the outcomes of negotiations and trade. For example, the inability to clearly express oneself in another language during high-stakes business meetings can have serious repercussions and cause misunderstandings about what was agreed upon. According to the Giang (2012), citing a survey of 572 US senior executives, nearly half of the respondents 'admitted that misunderstandings and "messages lost in translation" have halted major international business deals for their company' and '64 percent of [surveyed senior executives] said poor communication skills have negatively affected their plans to expand internationally'. Culture, as it is embedded in language itself, and part of the L2 learning experience, is also noted as an issue of misunderstandings. A recent statistic from the US Committee on Economic Development estimates that America is losing over $2 billion annually due to cultural miscommunication (interpreting) (McCulloch, 2019). International corporations pay significant amounts of money for translators and language courses for their employees to mitigate and hopefully avoid these situations. In fact, the global market size of the language services industry grew from $23.5 billion in 2009 to $49.6 billion in 2019, with growth estimated to continue to $56.18 billion by the end of fiscal year 2021 (Statista, 2022).

Globalization has affected not only which languages and populations US businesses interact with internationally, but also the languages spoken by participants in US domestic markets. According to New American Economy (2017: 2) 'Over the past five years, demand for bilingual workers in the United States more than doubled. In 2010, there were roughly 240,000 job postings aimed at bilingual workers; by 2015, that figure had ballooned to approximately 630,000. Employers seek bilingual workers for both low- and high-skilled positions'. Clearly, there are opportunities for bilingual work across the spectrum of employment and educational training.

The changing dynamics of international relations, migration and US domestic demographics continually alter which languages are desirable for jobs located in the United States. Nationally, 'Employers are increasingly looking for workers who can speak Chinese, Spanish, and Arabic. Employers posted more than three times more jobs for Chinese speakers in 2015 than they had just five years earlier. During the same time period, the number of U.S. job ads listing Spanish or Arabic as a desired skill increased by roughly 150 percent' (New American Economy, 2017: 2). These patterns also differ at the state level due to the idiosyncratic migrations of various populations to different locations in the United States. For example, 'Some states have particularly high demand for bilingual workers. Despite being home to 12.4 percent of the overall U.S. working-age population, California accounted for 19.4 percent of all job ads seeking bilingual workers. Arizona displayed similar trends—accounting for just 2 percent of working-age adults, but 4 percent of bilingual job listings'. On the other hand, 'Seven states—including Colorado, Oregon, and Texas—had considerably higher demand for bilingual speakers than would be expected based on their share of the working-age population overall' (New American Economy, 2017: 2). These regional effects can in part be explained by language enclaves (Bauer *et al.*, 2005), but where international companies decide to set up headquarters and offices in the United States, population density (Blake & Walter, 2020) and educational access (Leite & Cook, 2015) are also part of the equation.

These global and local factors have created a need and a desire for better language education in the United States, especially in languages needed for highly compensated positions. Money is an amazing motivator and when language learning is either part of the pathway toward or the barrier against it, it seems multiple stakeholders (e.g. governments, businesses and educational institutions) have paid renewed attention to language instruction, although admittedly, it still feels like we are far from where we need to be in the United States.

But now we must confront the global elephant in the room: English. The globalization of English, its ubiquity in corporate workplaces around the globe and its seemingly accepted domination of multilateral trade, politics, science and beyond have had two very important implications. First, it has negatively affected the motivation of the populations of English-speaking countries, like the United States, to value and invest in foreign[1] language instruction. Second, it has ballooned the interest in learning and using English beyond any capacity of those countries who claim it as an official language to control its growth and evolution. While learners and teachers may still have a preferred target English dialect, like 'American', 'British/UK' or 'Australian', the use of English by such a broad and diverse population of speakers has resulted in the emergence of global English and multiple World Englishes. While there is far too much to unpack here about the good, the bad and the ugly of English's global omnipresence, one thing is clear: many view knowledge of English as a requirement for international business and many businesses operating within multiple countries, even if they don't operate in an English-speaking country, are increasingly making the move toward English as the preferred language of communication within their company (Borzykowski, 2017). The global economy is a prodigious motivator for language learning and teaching, which is a billion-dollar industry in its own right.

Not only do economic factors put pressure on educational systems to provide solid learning outcomes that enable international, intercultural communication, but language learning and teaching on conclusion of PreK-12 or post-secondary schooling are also essential to understand, if ISLA is interested in the instruction of L2s in a broad sense. Especially in a new era of app-based and online learning, informed practices from ISLA could enhance learning outcomes and increase workers' comfort as part of linguistically, geographically and culturally diverse teams.

Teaching language to access education and knowledge

Another important motivator for language learning is the knowledge a language has been used to encode. In reality, this seems to have two poles. Around one pole are languages such as English, in which vast amounts of knowledge and educational resources exist, and large-scale educational operations funded by governments, educational institutions and the like are actively trying to promote the learning of these languages. In fact, UNESCO (2016) reported that 40% of the global population accesses education in a language other than their first language (L1).[2] This means that language acts as a barrier for students whose first or dominant languages do not align with those languages that have been prioritized by the broader international community, of which English is a prime example. As Flowerdew (1999: 124) states, since 1990, it has been increasingly recognized that 'English is the dominant language for publication and academic research'. This claim is backed up by empirical evidence provided by Jin (2020: 60), citing Curry and Lillis (2018), who reports that 'It is estimated that by 2016, around 87% of the Science Citation Index (SCI) journals were published in English'. This has significant impacts on the scientific community and those who are aspiring to join it. This is especially true 'in countries where English is not the native language, especially developing countries' because 'publishing in high-impact-factor journals is often required for promotion or even graduation' (Benson *et al.*, 2010: 189). Thus, extensive English proficiency is required both for the production and the consumption of knowledge. As

Meneghini and Packer (2007: 113) explain, 'scientific English has become a communication tool in a less erudite world, consisting of those who want to learn about and pass on knowledge'.

However, there is another pole around which languages congregate with regard to knowledge access, and these are languages that are scarce, maybe even not yet discovered. In these cases, cultural knowledge of a people has been kept a secret from the rest of the world because very few people even have the vocabulary or multilingual skills to express it. For anyone who has seen the documentary *The Linguists* (Kramer *et al.*, 2008), this is evident from their search for and discovery of speakers of Kallawaya, a language passed down in a ritualized fashion between male medical healers in Bolivia (LivingTongues.org). An immense amount of knowledge about different medicinal plants and their uses is stored within the Kallawaya language and it is estimated that only 100 or so speakers of this language exist today (LivingTongues.org). The extinction of this language would eliminate this vast knowledge that could be very useful to the broader medical and pharmacological community.

Currently, the impetus for the instruction of Kallawaya is based on heritage, which we will turn to in the following section, for the purposes of not only language learning and instruction, but also career prospects. Fathers teach this language to their sons or other men interested in becoming healers as part of the initiation into the practice, and with it comes the knowledge stored within it. While this instruction starkly contrasts with the opposite pole of languages, with their armies of teachers and materials, this language is still taught as an L2. How could this very intimate type of L2 instruction inform our practices of the importance of clear career, cultural and personal connections to the languages we teach?

Language teaching for heritage purposes

The final general purpose we will explore here is that of cultural transmission and familial relationship maintenance through HL learning and instruction. According to the Center for Applied Linguistics (CAL) (Kelleher, 2010), 'The term "HL" is used to identify languages other than the dominant language (or languages) in a given social context'. And importantly for this book, as CAL is a US-based institution, they continue that 'In the United States, English is the de facto dominant language (not an "official" language, but the primary language used in government, education, and public communication); thus, any language other than English can be considered a "HL" for speakers of that language' (Kelleher, 2010: n.p.). Kelleher goes on to emphasize that there is some familiarity with language:

> These languages are not 'foreign' to particular individuals or communities; instead, they are familiar in a variety of ways. Some people may be

able to speak, read, and write the language; others may only speak or understand when spoken to. Some may not understand the language but are part of a family or community where the language is spoken. The term 'heritage' language can be used to describe any of these connections between a non-dominant language and a person, a family, or community. (Kelleher, 2010: n.p.)

The impact that heritage has on the motivation to teach and to learn those languages is complex. Intergenerational beliefs about the purpose of language, language as a marker of identity, the perception of their language(s) and its use in a context in which it is a minority language and even its utility for future generations are all factors that can promote or diminish HL instruction. These factors lead to varying outcomes for HL learners, with the norm being familial and conversational use, while lacking highly developed literacy skills in their HL (Tse, 2001). Trying to distill a single theory to explain how HL as a purpose for instruction influences decisions to pursue the learning of a language, the development of teaching programs and materials and the decisions made within those classrooms by administrators, teachers, parents and students would merit its own manuscript. Rather, here I would like to simply point to a few perspectives on why HL teaching is promoted by different stakeholder groups, in different contexts and with different dominant/HL interactions.

Parents (and, in general, guardians and family members) have strong beliefs about whether their children should be learning the HL of the family and have a lot of power to decide for their children how and how much their children engage with the language. In doing so, they directly and indirectly influence the beliefs of their children about the relevance of the HL, and what goal their children should be striving toward. Studies in a US context have shown that there is a diversity of opinion among migrant populations, as one might expect. In a meta-analysis, Liang (2018) reviewed 17 studies (7 Chinese, 5 Korean, 2 Spanish, 1 Japanese, 1 Eastern European and 1 multi-language study with Arabic, Chinese, Spanish and Hebrew) that used various qualitative, mixed and quantitative methods in the United States and Canada. These studies focused on parental and familial HL perspectives and behaviors. The review showed parents' overall positive view that their child or children should learn their HL. From parents' responses, the author identified four important clusters for promoting HL: (1) communication and cohesion, (2) employment and economics, (3) ethnic and cultural identity and (4) intellectual benefits (Liang, 2018: 70–73). This general positive trend is confirmed in many other studies in the North American context (for Korean: Brown, 2011; Cho *et al.*, 1997; Kwon, 2017; Lee, 2002; Park & Sarkar, 2007; for Chinese: Zhang, 2020; Zhang & Slaughter-Defoe, 2009; for Japanese: Hashimoto & Lee, 2011; Kwon, 2017; for Hungarian: Szilagyi & Szecsi,

2020; for Russian: Kagan, 2010). Each of these studies shows how intersections of language, geography, speaker density and family affect both the beliefs about the importance of HL learning and maintenance and the practices. For example, if we compare the studies investigating Hungarian versus Chinese, we find that both populations state that connections to family heritage and with parents are positive reasons why parents support HL learning (Szilagyi & Szecsi, 2020; Zhang & Slaughter-Defoe, 2009), but if we look at the state of the two languages in the United States, we can see stark differences in the total number of speakers, community language use, educational resources and the perspectives of non-speakers.

These differences are why I have, to this point, mostly avoided Spanish in the US context (and French in Canadian contexts). The number of speakers, the role of Spanish as a HL versus an L1 and differing perceptions on the use of Spanish in the United States all make it a unique case, and a perfect point to turn from parent and familial beliefs and practices to HL learners themselves. In a study on Spanish as a HL for college Latinxs, Oh and Au (2005) cite the fact that Latinx speakers have a higher level of HL maintenance than any other HL speaker group, but that a majority of adolescents prefer to speak English over Spanish. Despite the positive response to teaching their children Spanish as a HL, the perspectives of Spanish HL learners show a mismatch between their parents' positivity and their own beliefs. To access student voices more directly, Ducar (2008) surveyed 152 heritage speakers of Spanish in HL Spanish classes. The results provide more detail on what students want from their HL courses and their beliefs about their importance. For instance, students in this study indicated a preference for Mexican or Mexican-American Spanish as the language of study, which would be quite different from what L2 learners encounter in a typical Spanish course which often adopts either a standardized version of Spanish or multiple Spanish varieties.

Spanish is not the only language in which generational divides emerge. In a study on community college HL speakers' reasons for discontinuing the study of their HL, Nagano et al. (2019) report on data from 1756 students spanning 36 different HLs. The authors found that in this context, only about 55% of HL speakers continue with their language, with the other 45% opting for a different language. The reasons for this vary, from their HL not being offered at their institution to job opportunities and career skills they believe another language will help them access.

HL loss can and does occur earlier in life as well. In a study focusing on the loss of language for Ghanaian immigrants in Calgary, Canada, Quarmyne (2018) reports on the same factors so important to the positivity and transmission of other HLs described above (e.g. family, economic relevance and educational resources). In this instance, the lack of or the negative impact of these features has led to significant intergenerational language loss.

Outside of the North American context these issues of HL learning are also at play, but the geopolitical and historical factors make any analysis from my own (US) perspective, somewhat superficial. However, it is important to at least mention that the factors listed above can be seen as broadly universal, in spite of the challenges that each unique place, time and inter-lingual and intercultural context presents. Some such phenomena include Chinese HL loss in Argentina (Ho *et al.*, 2010) versus Chinese HL resilience in Indonesia (Lie, 2017), reintroducing Gaelic in Ireland (Armstrong, 2013), parents' role in HL maintenance in Malaysia (Zamri & Azman, 2020), the role of policy on Polish as a HL in Melbourne, Australia (Romanowski, 2021) and Albanian parents' perspectives on teaching their HL in Greece (Gkaintartzi *et al.*, 2016).

Summary: Social motivators for language learning and teaching

Each of the four factors reviewed here (religion, economics, education and heritage) plays an important role in forming learners' motivations for learning another language. Learners bring these beliefs and motivations into the language classroom, influencing the L2 classroom in myriad ways through interactions, communications and encounters with peers, teachers, community and family members and administrators. In later chapters, we will take a deeper dive into how these factors interact psychologically within a learner and socially within a classroom. However, it is important to emphasize here that these motivators and beliefs are all part of the people who make up and take part in our complex classroom environment.

Non-Western Language Teaching Traditions and Practices

As stated in the introduction to this book, although its focus is on ISLA, an academic field with origins mostly in Western scientific and pedagogical traditions, there is a need to also look at how language instruction is and has been carried out in non-Western contexts, as this can both mirror and inform the types of activities, behaviors and methods that US-based language teachers employ in their classrooms. In this section, there are obvious connections to some of the previous language learning motivators (religion, economics, education and heritage). One reason for this is that many of the cultural expectations for what is supposed to be part of a language class have influenced the practices of various language programs. For example, the parents and instructors of HL programs bring with them expectations from their own language classes, and therefore these practices are part and parcel of US language teaching curricula today. Religious figures decide what is important to teach about a language and its use during and for religious practices. And migrant and refugee parents who want the best for their children have strong preferences about whether it is important to learn the language of their new country.

The learning of the Quran is an excellent example, as it has sparked a number of methods to help L2 speakers of Arabic, and in turn centered the Quran as a unique tool for language instruction in its own right. Parvini (2017, n.p.) describes the Quran as being 'considered the most important text in Arabic and is located in the top of literature and eloquence of Arabic Language because it involves verses with different articulations and such a tempo that captures the heart of the listener and stays in his mind'. Because of this, Parvini (2017: n.p.) argues, 'teaching Quranic listening skills can help in teaching Arabic listening skills'. The memorizing of an essential text of Arabic literary and cultural studies is connected directly to the hundreds of years of religious practice teaching students to memorize the Quran. The relationship between memorization techniques, mastery of the Arabic language and understanding of the Quran is also emphasized by Ikhwanuddin and Hashim (2014), who detail the role of Arabic comprehension skills in order to understand the Quran beyond the transferrable phonetic and phonological skills emphasized by Parvini (2017). Methods tied directly to religious practices are further outlined by the methodological description given by Aziz *et al.* (2016):

> Islamic Education, namely: First, Field of Al-Quran Recitation and Memorization. The proposed methods for this field are talaqqi musyafahah, tikrar, hafazan, and tasmi'. Second, Field of Aqidah. Under this particular field, the proposed techniques are discussion, workshops, brainstorming, reflection, and teaching with computer. Third, Field of Ibadah. For this field, the proposed methods are discussion, brainstorming, practical, simulation, collaboration, and co-operative learning. Fourth, Field of Akhlak and Morality. The suggested teaching techniques under this field are lectures, discussions, simulations, forum, future studies, contextual teaching, reflection, and group activities. (Aziz *et al.*, 2016: 757)

Here, teaching styles developed for the purposes of defining Islamic education have been clearly analyzed and defined according to a broad array of teaching and learning activities. Other researchers interpret the teaching of the Quran and the pedagogical practices associated with it through Western terminology. For example, Faryadi (2007) discusses the teaching of Arabic as a foreign language in Malaysian settings through the lens of a constructivist paradigm, which promotes learning as a method of personal discovery, diverse thinking and problem-solving. Whatever the term given, the motivation to learn the Quran and the methods developed over time to help learners who speak Arabic as an L2 have been sharpened to help students achieve the goal set for them by members of their religious and cultural communities.

Not only do specific goals, like memorization, drive instruction, but so also do geopolitical and cross-cultural interactions. In an ethnographic study of the people in the northern Mandara mountains and surrounding area, Moore *et al.* (2004) reports on two very different groups of language speakers. The Wandala people control the plain throughout and around the mountains, while the Montagnard groups control the mountains. The Montagnards grow up in a multilingual environment and many of them speak five or six languages. Contrastively, the Wandala people 'do not share the montagnards' multilingual norm' (Moore *et al.*, 2004: 6). For the Wandala, learning other languages means learning them as an L2, which requires instruction in a skill with which they are not familiar.

As part of their study, Moore *et al.* (2004) collected the opinions on L2 learning expressed by four participants, two Wandala and two Montagnards, who wanted to or were pursuing competency in another language (for religious purposes or trade with the Montagnards). These participants indicated that language learning was through listening in on conversations with higher proficiency speakers or seeking private help from a friend, although only the two Montagnards in the study had pursued the private lesson option. These private lessons consist of question and answer sessions where learners can ask what something means or how to say something. In addition, the Montagnards had other strategies for language learning, including planning and rehearsing, monitoring errors, reflecting on own language use and directing attention to problematic language features, and guessing at meanings in context (Moore *et al.*, 2004). The difference in approach between the two groups begs the question of whether the tradition of being multilingual and the practices honed through years of cultural experience have made the Montagnards natural L2 learners. And vice versa, whether the lack of cultural multilingualism for the Wandala has hindered the cultural development of their L2 learning strategies.

An interesting phenomenon that Moore *et al.* (2004) make note of is the acquisition of multiple L2/third languages (L3s) at the same time. This falls somewhat outside of the focus of most SLA research, and even third language acquisition (L3A) research, which is even more in its infancy than SLA, despite its ubiquity in many parts of the world. For example, in Africa, multilingualism from an early age is common. In a study on multilingualism and theories of SLA in Africa, Bokamba (2018) created a questionnaire focusing on four categories of multilingualism and language acquisition:

(1) The number of languages the participants speak.
(2) How, when and where they learned these languages.
(3) Self-assessed proficiency in each language.
(4) The tasks they use for each language, with whom and for what purposes.

The results of this survey showed, importantly, that multilingualism comes in many forms, not only across individuals, but also within the individual. As Bokamba (2018: 436) indicates, there are 'multiple pathways through which Africans develop functional fluency in several languages throughout their lives'. Many of the participants in this study have a solid multilingualism base through their everyday lives and learned earlier languages in a 'natural' setting, whereas other languages are only started in secondary school.

In comparing the two studies by Moore *et al.* (2004) and Bokamba (2018), the idea of a multilingual basis for a future L2 learner is of extreme interest to many in the United States and could influence US policy if researchers could clearly establish whether early multilingual programming could change beliefs around a majority monolingual US population and reduce counterproductive public beliefs on the supremacy of English. From a psycholinguistic perspective, there is much to learn from studying the ontogenetic language learning phases and practices that differ starkly from the majority of monolingual speakers' experiences.

While many populations around the world have their own histories of language learning, the influence of SLA and L2 pedagogical theory from the Americas and Europe has crept into the practices, or at least the views of language teachers around the world. Teachers, administrators and program developers interpret the findings from empirical studies and the theories behind them within their own cultural context (Burnaby & Sun, 1989). This can lead not only to connections between theories and their own practices, as noted in the discussion of the audiolingual method (ALM) and its preference in cultures that emphasize memorization in the learning process, but also to confrontations.

One of most exported trends in foreign language pedagogy since the 1970s has been the communicative approach, or communicative language teaching. While this term has become somewhat of a catch-all for a number of methods (Spada, 2007), there is general agreement that the emphasis of the approach is on meaning making and practical application of real-world language through communicative interactions and activities. Despite its rather long history and relevance, as well as its exportation all over the world through conferences, instructional design seminars and efficacy studies (with Viet [2008] going so far as to call its reach imperialistic), teachers in non-Western contexts often find conflict with this style of teaching. This is evident in a study on Chinese teachers' willingness to adopt communicative language teaching practices by Yu (2001), who points to the traditional dominance of the analytic grammar-translation approach in Chinese foreign language classrooms as a hurdle. Yu goes on to argue that it would require an immense amount of training to get teachers to feel comfortable enough to change their teaching style. In another study on Chinese teachers' views on Western language teaching, Burnaby and Sun (1989) place a higher emphasis on the constraints of teaching English in China that do not allow for many of the proposed methods, like the communicative approach, pursued by teachers in Western contexts. They specifically discuss class size, in-class time and the goals of the learners as barriers for the implementation of more communicative practices. They also discuss pressure at administrative and governmental levels on 'elitist' rather than 'egalitarian' approaches to teaching. This resistance to communicative language teaching has been reported in multiple studies on L2 teaching in China (Hu, 2002; Ouyang, 2003; Rao, 2013) as well as in other countries, e.g. Libya (Abu Khattala, 2014), Turkey (Ozsevik, 2010), Vietnam (Viet, 2008) and Iran (Vaezi & Abbaspour, 2014).

Other cultural mismatches from Western traditions also permeate global language teaching practices. Some examples include Sonaiya's (2002) discussion of the autonomous language learning method in Africa, and Hidri and Coombe's (2016) examination of how foreign language education is evaluated in the Middle East and Africa. These studies make it clear that SLA theory and Western language pedagogy have encroached upon and invaded, for better or worse, the global network of language teaching.

This could have been through the spread of English itself in its new role as a global language or the scientific prestige of empirical and theoretical papers acting as proponents for these methods, or a combination of the two. In any case, communicative language teaching is part of most language teachers' vocabulary. Whether they adopt it or not is a different story; they are still aware of it. Unfortunately, this knowledge transfer does not seem to be very multidirectional. Western traditions are exported, but we are not importing, at least not visibly, many or really any methods from these other cultures with equally lengthy histories of language teaching. To this day, there has been little presence of non-Western forms of instruction, and any work that has been done has not been sufficiently elevated within our field to have made much of an impact. It may be time for ISLA to take a closer look at what other instructional paradigms exist and if any of them might benefit our current preferred approaches to language instruction, while considering unique contextual affordances and constraints in a Western context.

The Genesis of (I)SLA

After millennia of language instruction and teaching, in the broadest of senses, and hundreds of years of classroom language instruction, the practices and outcomes of learners in the foreign/second language classroom finally combined with 20th-century foci on individual language development. This section outlines the genesis of SLA as its own field of study, and the multiple theoretical and practical changes that eventually led to instructed SLA receiving its own special attention.

Language instruction in the advent of behaviorism

In the middle part of the 20th century, behaviorism was king. It seemed that much of the behavior observable in the animal (and human) world could be described as resulting from stimulus–response patterns. As more behaviors came to be viewed through this lens, it seemed that this framework could be applied to all human actions, eventually including linguistic behaviors. In his book *Verbal Behavior*, Skinner (1957: 2) proposed a stimulus–response account of human linguistic behavior, albeit slightly different in that linguistic behavior is a 'behavior which is effective only through the mediation of other persons'. A person is hungry, so they ask for food. Producing the utterance does not fulfill the need. However, the use of language is reinforced by the need or want being fulfilled by a mediating entity. And so, language learning itself could be viewed as learning linguistic phrases to understand and respond to various verbal stimuli.

This had significant implications for language teaching. The most well-known method resulting from behaviorist theories was the audio-lingual method (ALM). The appeal of the ALM relies heavily on memorization, which is ubiquitous in teaching methods used in many non-Western countries, and therefore it makes logical sense that teachers in these contexts find the tenets of the ALM aligned with their cultural norms related to teaching.

As a method rooted in behaviorism, the ALM and its counterpart, the oral-situational approach (Boyadzhieva, 2014), are essentially framed as a stimulus–response activity, where the goal is to memorize entire phrases that will either answer questions posed to you, or get you what you want, be it a real-world object or a response from an interlocutor. The ALM was also influenced at the same time by 'structural approaches to linguistic description (Fries, 1952) and the Contrastive Analysis Hypothesis of Second Language Acquisition (Lado & Fries, 1957)' (Robinson & Ellis, 2008: 492). The ALM has a number of components, but generally learners are asked to memorize a dialogue and drill grammatical structures. The emphasis is on speaking and listening, supported by visual aids, rather than writing and reading. Errors in pronunciation and grammar are immediately corrected by the teacher, but actual explanations of grammar are minimal, if provided at all. The general idea is to see language development as the formation of habits and behaviors that can easily be recalled by the learner when they encounter stimuli in the real world. These encounters with language elicit a learned verbal response. For example, in the classroom, the teacher leads the learner through a conversation between a barista and a customer. There is no discussion about what formal form to use or when modals can change the tone of the interaction. The learners receive a pre-composed script delivered orally by the teacher with visual aids. Then, the learners are asked to repeat small, then increasingly larger sections and the teacher listens for errors, correcting anything that deviates from the script.

There are obvious initial advantages to using this method, at least from a teacher's perspective. Since there is a clear 'correct' answer, it is easy to assess learners. However, there are many drawbacks as well. For instance, students are not given opportunities to reflect on language (à la Swain's [2006] 'languaging') and investigate how different forms result in different interactional sequences. The critique against the ALM also includes the fact that learners cannot be guaranteed that they will encounter the exact language provided in their dialogues when they go out into the real world. While the coffee shop scenario presented to students might begin with a greeting, like 'Hello' or 'How are you today?', in real life, the barista might say 'What can I do for you', 'Welcome to Dancing Goats Coffee' or even 'I like your tie!' This variability ultimately limits the effectiveness of the ALM, as one would need to form a habit for every possible linguistic stimulus, which would present an untenable challenge.

As the supremacy of behaviorism began to decline with its growing critiques and the advent of the cognitive revolution, the focus of language researchers shifted sharply from the language teacher to the processes and mechanisms of learning in the individual. And with this sea-change, SLA, as its own field of study, emerged.

The formalization of SLA

At its emergence, SLA was cobbled together from an amalgamation of practitioners and researchers who found common ground around a united theme. In his first-person position paper on the history of SLA, Ellis (2021: 190) notes that, 'like so many other SLA researchers... [his] initial interest in L2 acquisition was rooted in [his] practical concern to make language teaching effective'. Others, inspired by Chomsky's challenge to behaviorism and his proposition of UG, contributed theories on linguistics and psychological language development. According to Larsen-Freeman (2018), the following two foundational papers established SLA as a field. Corder (1967) reformulated the idea of learner mistakes as 'errors' and brought forth the idea that these errors could inform us about what is happening developmentally within a learner, while Selinker's (1972) idea of interlanguage questioned the psychological development of an L2 in conjunction with and overlaid on an already established L1.

These two ideas supercharged inquiry into SLA and forefronted individuals' cognitive processes. Indeed, Gass (1993), citing Grabe and Kaplan (1992), echoes this point: '[SLA] was originally a subarea of applied linguistics, contributing basically to language teaching, but as the interlanguage hypothesis emerged, SLA moved to independence from both applied linguistics and generative theory'. This independence allowed perspectives from researchers with other theories and constructs to enter the conversation, which has been both beneficial and diminutive for SLA. Beneficial because SLA can and has acted as a testing ground for a wide variety of theories, epistemologies and methodologies in which to interact and challenge each other. Diminutive in that many researchers from our 'source fields' see a unidirectional influence from their work to SLA, but not always from SLA back to their source field (Gass, 1993).

While there is still much work to do to shake the perspective that SLA is not a source field for new knowledge that can contribute to other fields, the benefit of a wide array of accepted and workable theories has shaped the course of SLA's path. Ellis' (2021) recent review of the history of SLA laid out five phases through which SLA has passed. In the first phase (1960s and 1970s) proposed by Ellis (2021), L1 acquisition (L1A) heavily influenced SLA research. During this time, researchers produced a series of order of acquisition studies, which identified similar patterns in the acquisition of forms across learners. In the second phase, which Ellis (2021) labels 'the expansion period' (1980s), researchers considered a wider array of theories and phenomena, including language transfer, linguistic universals and UG, pragmatics, and input and interaction. Phases 3–5, according to Ellis (2021), include the cognitive revolution, the social turn, complex dynamic systems theory (CDST) and the multilingual turn, respectively. The following sections review each of these 'turns' and their relevance for ISLA.

Recent 'Turns' in SLA and Their Impact on Instruction

The following subsections describe major theoretical turns in the field of SLA and their implications for and on language teaching. Each of these changes had significant impacts on people's understanding of how language learning occurs and thus what the role of the instructor should be in facilitating language acquisition.

The cognitive revolution and language teaching

The cognitive revolution was, in large part, due to two major forces working in tandem. On the one hand, there was significant dissatisfaction, especially in the reinvigorated field of linguistics, with behaviorist accounts of language learning and use. On the other hand, cognitive psychology and its related fields began to provide alternatives. Chomsky (2013) provided a decidedly poignant case against behaviorist theories of language in his lengthy response to Skinner's (1957) *Verbal Behavior*. Patterns visible in children's linguistic behaviors did not seem to match the stimulus–response learning style proposed for other types of behaviors in other species. Children produced phrases that they had never heard, resulting in the poverty of the stimulus argument, which asserts that a human language system must underly child language acquisition that allows them to produce previously unheard utterances (for a full history of the term 'universal grammar', see Thomas [2002]).

These dissatisfactions with verbal behavior, as interpreted by Chomsky and others, led to a new way of thinking about language as a complex symbolic system. This dovetailed well with the burgeoning field of cognitive science. Additionally, mathematical descriptions of language and the assumption of a UG[3] (Chomsky, 1986; Montague, 1970) accounted for the fact that any human could learn any human language. These innatist models of language learning eventually had a significant impact on the way teachers and pedagogues thought about how L2s should be instructed.

However, as Seuren (2004) notes, linguistics and its subfields did not follow through with all of the advances in cognitive science simultaneously. While Chomsky had a significant impact on the emergence of cognitive science in the decline of behaviorism (Miller, 2003), his focus on the random ability of the mind to generate an innumerable array of possible sentences diverted attention from other linguistic analyses of language use and therein relevant issues of language instruction, such as semantics and pragmatics. Seuren (2004) summarizes Chomsky's unique focus on grammar and the 'linguistic wars' in the following way:

> the man who was so prominently instrumental in demolishing behaviorism and who subsequently became the most influential figure in linguistics shirked from drawing the consequences of his anti-behaviorism and continued to be distrustful of all things mental, as if behaviorism had never ceased to exist. Chomsky never developed a feel for or interest in semantics. His theory of grammar, in the various guises it assumed over the years, has not so far managed to establish an organic link with a proper theory of meaning. Nor has it ever changed its representation of grammar as a random sentence generator. The notion of a grammar as a formal mediating device between thoughts and sentences was steadfastly rejected, although that is the notion one expects if the mental, cognitive character of grammar is taken seriously. Moreover, Chomsky's ideas regarding the question of the psychological plausibility of such a randomly generating grammatical model never reached any degree of clarity or precision but kept vacillating in inconsistent ways. (Seuren, 2004: 70)

With the relatively neglected importance of linguistics and language teaching in context, combined with the dominant belief of innate mechanisms for language learning, language instruction was turned on its head. This resulted in two methods of language instruction: one with a greater focus on grammar, and the other with a greater focus on inductive rule learning and an even greater avoidance of explicit instruction of grammar, respectively: cognitive code learning (CCL) and the Silent Way (Boyadzhieva, 2014).

CCL, as Tamura (1981: 65) describes it, is rooted in 'gestalt psychology and transformation linguistics'. For teachers, this meant 'grammar does not need explicit explanations; correction of mistakes is ineffective and almost did not take place in the classroom. The grammatical rules should be established deductively and aimed at building up the learners' experiences similarly to the processes characterizing first language acquisition' (Boyadzhieva, 2014: 781). Tamura (1981) cites a report by Demirezen (2014) on the changes to a French curriculum that moved from an audio-lingual approach to a CCL approach. The major changes were as follows:

- More time spent on grammar explanations.
- Repetition exercises cycled through a variety of patterns, rather than only one.
- Speaking–writing sequence was reordered to a writing–speaking sequence.
- A great emphasis on writing.

Through quite opposing views on the role of grammatical knowledge, the Silent Way became one of the most well-known methods during this period. The most frequently cited origin of the Silent Way comes from Gattegno (2010: 27) (first published in 1972). In the foreword, the author notes that the word 'silent' in the name refers to the teacher's ability to say less and less over the course of the method as students begin to say more and more. The essence of the method is that teaching is subordinate to learning. Gattegno (2010: 27) describes this as a way of 'letting the learners learn while the teacher stops interfering or sidetracking'. In Gattegno (2010: 30), the reader can find a complete set of materials needed to enable the method, which includes everything from colored wooden rods and phonetic and vocabulary charts, to texts, anthologies and films. In Stevick's (1974) review of Gattegno's (2010) second edition of the book, he notes that many language teachers at the time found this method a 'bizarre way of learning and teaching'. After many years of working with this method, Stevick (1976, 1980) eventually became a major proponent of the Silent Way, publishing a number of books promoting it and its ethos.

Other research on the effectiveness of the Silent Way found that it might be most effective for beginning students. This was because a certain amount of plateauing might occur with the limited vocabulary presented in the charts, as well as the lack of teacher input (Gyi, 1994). Varvel (1979) critically reviews some of the features of the Silent Way and its practitioners, noting that those who were fully invested in the method expressed somewhat of a religious devotion to the program. In addition, many students felt extreme frustration because of both a conflict between expectations for L2 instruction and the methods used in the Silent Way, as well as a lack of understanding of what the teacher wanted during different exercises.

An overall description of the Silent Way will in many ways be incomplete because, as Varvel (1979: 484) cited by de Cordoba (1978:

34) indicates, 'The Silent Way cannot be fully presented in writing. The Silent Way must be experienced, seen in the classroom and studied again'. To push Varvel's (1979) religious metaphor further, there is no real way to provide a detailed description. We can only look at the methods undertaken by previous and current practitioners.

Outside of linguistics, advances in multiple converging fields ultimately came to be known as cognitive science and provided alternative explanations that more closely aligned with what was being learned about the biological underpinnings of human cognition. Computer science, artificial intelligence and cognitive psychology all pointed to more complex means of acquiring complex symbolic systems. In his historical, first-person account of the genesis of cognitive science, Miller (2003) recalls the excitement felt by many at the 1956 symposium presented by the 'Special Interest Group in Information Theory' at MIT. In his reflection, Miller (2003) declares the moment of conception of cognitive science as September 11, 1956, the second day of the symposium, which included presentations by Noam Chomsky, Newell Simon and Nat Rochester, among other founding members of cognitive science. Upon the conclusion of the symposium, Miller (2003: 143) remembers leaving 'with a conviction, more intuitive than rational, that experimental psychology, theoretical linguistics, and the computer simulation of cognitive processes were all pieces from a larger whole and that the future would see a progressive elaboration and coordination of their shared concerns'. This interdisciplinary work formed the basis for cognitive science. The interconnected fields are presented in Figure 1.1, from Miller (2003).

Eventually, this interdisciplinarity helped linguistic researchers cross between and into disciplines like computer science and machine learning, and they were able to model linguistic behaviors via computational methods.

In one of the most famous early cases, Rumelhart and McClelland (1985) showed how parallel distributed processes (PDP) and machine learning could reduplicate the English past-tense learning patterns present in child language. While many criticized the program for producing mistakes that did not appear in English L1A, among other reasons (see Fodor & Pylyshyn, 1988; Pinker & Prince, 1988), their model nevertheless opened new ways of thinking about how 'rules' are acquired and how symbols are represented within a biologically plausible, connectionist network. The effect of this research on language pedagogy is undeniable. The budding field of psycholinguistics with its emphasis on biologically feasible representations of language began to challenge formal approaches that did not take into account a biologically plausible representation of language.

Along with the cognitive revolution came the idea of embodied cognition or the idea that the body itself is part of the biological cognitive system. Wilson and Golonka define the concept as follows:

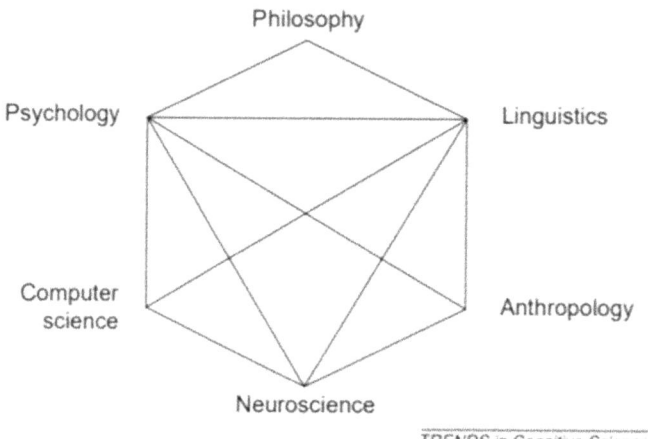

Figure 1.1 Cognitive science in 1978. Each line joining two disciplines represents interdisciplinary inquiry that already existed in 1978

Embodiment is the surprisingly radical hypothesis that the brain is not the sole cognitive resource we have available to us to solve problems. Our bodies and their perceptually guided motions through the world do much of the work required to achieve our goals, replacing the need for complex internal mental representations. This simple fact utterly changes our idea of what 'cognition' involves, and thus embodiment is not simply another factor acting on an otherwise disembodied cognitive process (Wilson & Golonka, 2013). This idea has radical implications for L2 instructions as well. The methodology most closely associated with the concepts integral to seeing the body as part of the human capacity for thought is total physical response (TPR), even though as Ratcliffe and Tokarchuk (2020, n.p.) point out, 'The use of offline embodiment was operationalised by applied linguists for second language acquisition some decades before embodied cognition theorists began to coalesce around the theory, in the form of the Total Physical Response teaching approach'. TPR is a method proposed by James Asher (1969a, 1969b) based on the learning of languages by pre-verbal or beginning-verbal children, where activity and physical responses to language precede linguistic responses. TPR connects motor responses and physical action with L2 learning, specifically that learners conduct certain actions after hearing something in the target language, with an emphasis on listening skills.

Although TPR was not originally connected to theories of embodied cognition, it has since been. Paloma (2017: 101) points to a number of activities associated with TPR that are part of how language learning is embodied, including 'imperative drills, role reversal, skits, dramas, role playing, mini dialogues, and reading and writing'. Kuo *et al.* (2014: 63) even combine the two terms in their study of English vocabulary learning, in which they 'propose an integration of motion-sensing technology and theory of embodied cognition into the total physical response (TPR) approach, called Embodiment-based TPR approach'. As the authors describe in their results section, by 'presenting information with body movements, contextual information in the learning context may produce stronger memory traces for the experimental group than merely presenting information with unitary form of body action for the control group' (Kuo et al., 2014: 68). The reference to stronger memory traces, rather than simply remembering, indicates a significant shift in how we understand memory and recall in an L2.

Other significant SLA paradigms began to emerge in this cognitive arena, including input processing (Benati, 2013; VanPatten, 2004, 2013); input, interaction and negotiation of meaning (Gass, 2017; Gass & Mackey, 2006; Long, 1981; Mackey, 1999); the output hypothesis (Swain, 1993); and processability theory (Pienemann, 1998); along with an array of usage-based models of SLA (N. Ellis, 1999), like the competition model (MacWhinney & Bates, 1987), CDST (Larsen-Freeman, 1997), construction grammar (Goldberg, 1995) and emergentism (MacWhinney, 2006).

All of these different research paradigms, in one way or another, have offered ideas to the emerging and somewhat all-encompassing approach previously described in this chapter as the communicative approach or communicative language teaching. These research areas provided evidence to support teachers who were committed to providing meaningful language teaching to their students. Many of the findings from these research areas provided general information on how to teach and a few laid out specific pedagogical methods to follow. For example, input processing provided a framework for creating meaningful materials that would highlight grammatical forms and meanings. Processability theory provided information about which grammatical features should be introduced by teachers in which order. And interactional approaches played a role in the development of task-based language teaching (TBLT). However, all were interested in how language developed cognitively within the individual.

As with every 'turn' that builds significant momentum, it can have the tendency to take up all the air in the room, so to speak. Even studies on interaction in SLA were focused on the cognitive aspects of learning. All of the journal and conference space taken up by new findings in cognitive approaches to SLA had begun to edge out other perspectives to breaking point.

Language teaching and the social turn

In such an interdisciplinary field, when one theory or research paradigm becomes overly centralized, there is always an inevitable swing of the pendulum in another direction, especially when researchers from different paradigms begin to feel excluded from mainstream discussion. This was the case in SLA when Firth and Wagner (1997) published their seminal reanalysis of data in SLA from a social perspective. This was not so much a replacement of cognitive approaches, but rather provided a more prominent place for the role of interpersonal and social forces in SLA. In their article, Firth and Wagner (1997) argued for a reconceptualization of SLA, wherein learners are not viewed as deficient in comparison to native speakers, but rather in terms of what they can accomplish with their L2 repertoires. In their conclusion to their seminal revisioning of SLA research at the time, the authors directly made a

> call for work within SLA that endeavors to adopt what we have referred to as a holistic approach to and outlook on language and language acquisition, an approach that problematizes and explores the conventional binary distinction between 'social' and 'individual' (or cognitive) approaches to language use and language learning, that attends to the dynamics as well as the summation of language acquisition, that is more emically and interactionally attuned, and that is critically sensitive towards the theoretical status of fundamental concepts (particularly 'learner,' 'native,' 'nonnative,' and 'interlanguage'). (Firth & Wagner, 1997: 296)

Toward this effort, a new 'social turn' within the 'input-interaction-output (IIO) model' (Block, 2003) of SLA sought to forefront social paradigms coming from sociolinguistic, sociohistorical and sociocultural theories. This transition was described by Benson (2019) as a move from an 'era of "learner-centredness"' to an 'era of "person-centredness"'. Case studies and the experiences of individuals gained significant prominence and had some of the biggest impacts on our understanding of how and why language learning happens (or not). One of the most well-known case studies, which was conducted before but aligned with the spirit of the social turn, studied Wes, an L1 Japanese L2 English artist (Schmidt, 1983). The investigation of this individual's language practices and development led to a deeper understanding of the purpose and goals of the individual in relation to their relative language learning outcomes.

As reflected in Firth and Wagner (1997), the social turn helped to reimagine IIO phenomena from another theoretical perspective. One of the most significant reanalyses of a language learning theory came from Swain (2000), who reworked her original output hypothesis (Swain, 1993). She began to view output as more than just a source for additional input for the learner. Rather, in the language produced by her participants, peers were engaged in constructing a dialogue that was mediated via the tool of language. She argued that 'Through saying and reflecting on what was said, new knowledge is constructed' (Swain, 2000: 113). This idea that new knowledge is being constructed through the use of language itself is quite different from the originally formulated understanding within the IIO framework that self-produced language was just another source of input for the language acquisition device (LAD) to process.

Another major social theory to flourish during this turn, which was a primary source for Swain's (2000) reanalysis, was sociocultural theory (SCT). Derived from Vygotskian theories of child development (Vygotsky, 1987), the application of his ideas to SLA (Schinke-Llano, 1993) led to new veins of research, including concept development (Lantolf & Beckett, 2009), dynamic assessment (Lantolf, 2009) and, probably the most well known, the zone of proximal development (ZPD) (Dunn & Lantolf, 1998).

Some frustration about the generalizability of SCT findings was voiced, especially for education. One example is Zuengler and Miller's (2006: 51) assertion that 'the limits of what can be generalized across classroom contexts' does not always allow for specific recommendations. However, in general, sociocultural approaches have 'increased awareness and sensitivity to local contexts that sociocultural perspectives bring us, we have reason to hope that we are closer to understanding and creating the kinds of classroom communities that learners need' (Zuengler & Miller, 2006: 51). In addition, newer applications of dynamic assessment to test-taking procedures (Leung, 2007) and concept-based language instruction (C-BLI) (Negueruela, 2003) have led to generalizable practices that any language teacher can utilize.

In their 10-year retrospective article, Firth and Wagner (2007: 801) declared that 'it is probably fair to say that our article (Firth & Wagner, 1997) touched a proverbial raw nerve within as well as around the periphery of the second language acquisition (SLA) community'. This has led to researchers on both sides trying harder either to defend their position, define and refine their position or find new ways to unify cognitive and social perspectives. Firth and Wagner (2007) laud those efforts that try to reconcile and unify the essential principles of these approaches within an overarching framework:

> If this process is based on sound, creative scholarship, one that leads to advances in knowledge of the many and varied ways in which L2s are learned, acquired, and used (in mutually reinforcing and enlightening ways), then surely SLA will become a more theoretically and methodologically robust and encompassing enterprise. (Firth & Wagner, 2007: 813)

In the years following, the array of perspectives and theories applied to language learning has seen an abundance of growth. This is true for advances in already established theories, new approaches and those that look for connections and understandings in and across theories that work to provide nuanced understandings of the plethora of L2 learning phenomena that now fall under the purview of SLA.

Balancing the cognitive and social

In the wake of the social turn after the cognitive revolution, there was significant cross-talk. While arguments from those in the cognitive camp did not necessarily contradict those in the social camp, and vice versa, there was widespread controversy about and defense of theoretical traditions. The major difference came from the emphasis of each camp. Those focused on the social aspects of L2 learning did not reject the proposals of the cognitivists outright, and likewise those focused on cognitive processes in the individual did not oppose the ideas of the socially minded. While some emphasized that this turn was a result of misunderstanding the 'nature of cognitive science research in general, and SLA research in particular' (Gregg, 2006: 413), other researchers provided more nuanced explanations about the connected role of social and cognitive factors in SLA. However, much of these efforts resulted in researchers talking past one another, rather than with one another.

In a first-person perspective on this controversy and the attempts to rectify the fissures appearing within SLA, Larsen-Freeman (2007) recalls the circumstances and feelings within the field. In her article, she divides researchers at the time into three camps: those who mostly agreed, partially agreed or disagreed with the arguments brought forward by Firth and Wagner (1997), as well as some of the propositions brought forward to remedy the situation. From her perspective, she argued that the adoption of CDST would help alleviate many of the supposed dichotomies present between the cognitive and social camps. As mentioned, while some researchers dug in, others were 'exploring the possibilities of developing a holistic, encompassing SLA—one that seeks to draw together the social and the cognitive' (Firth & Wagner, 2007: 813).

In a similar vein, Atkinson (2002: 525) proposed what he called a sociocognitive approach to SLA, which he defined as 'a view of language and language acquisition as simultaneously occurring and interactively constructed both "in the head" and "in the world"'. This duality, probably better understood as a dialectic between the inside (cognitive) and outside (social) of the individual, is also reflected by Kramsch (2003), where she collected perspectives on language acquisition and socialization from researchers of disparate research traditions. She, like Atkinson (2002: 1), claimed that a broader view of how 'social, cognitive and semiotic frameworks that shape both the acquisition of language, and the constitution of social actors' would be beneficial to a more complete understanding of language learning as both a cognitive and social phenomenon.

In her 2007 article, Larsen-Freeman (2007: 784) made the following prediction: 'I find evidence that a new critical mass is emerging, and in keeping with our history, I anticipate that the field of inquiry will once again broaden and move on'. In the wake of these changes, Ortega (2011) emphasized two major ways in which the field has been improved: (1) unique insights have been brought to the field that would not have been found from previous purely cognitive methods, and (2) there is more epistemological diversity in SLA. Today, there is broad acceptance, even if pockets of resistance do exist, of a unified approach, or at least one that is cognizant of the benefits that the more either socially or cognitively inclined has on the other.

During this period of reorganization, a void existed in the discussion of what was happening in SLA for praxis-focused pedagogues. Individuals who were focused on training teachers, developing curricula and developing pedagogical implications for the classroom were forced to fill the gap with what these differences meant for teachers and students in terms of actual practice. Block (2000) found that one of the major reasons for the disconnect between researchers and teachers was the different discourses in which they engaged, and a highly controversial time in SLA history was likely one of the reasons that SLA moved farther out of focus for language teachers.

The death of the native speaker and the 'new' multilingual norm

The most recent turn in SLA, one immensely relevant to the current state and future of ISLA, is the multilingual turn, an inevitable, but all-too-long-awaited result of the cognitive and social advances in SLA, combined with the dismantlement of the native speaker as a model for learners. This theoretical paradigm frees both the learner and the teacher from the yolk of some mystical, perfectly accurate, culturally omniscient native speaker and opens possibilities for learners to choose and teachers to guide them toward multiple fulfilling, purposeful and enriching multilingual selves.

The idea of the death of the 'native speaker' in SLA and language pedagogy has two substrands. First was the need to dismantle the idea that the native speaker is infallible, or that they do not make mistakes. Multiple studies have shown that not only does the speaker have incomplete knowledge of multiple aspects of their own language, but they often make what one would consider 'errors' in the case of L2 learners in all areas of language comprehension and use (Davies, 2003; Han, 2004; Mahboob, 2005; Paikeday & Chomsky, 1985; Todd, 2006; Trimbur, 2008). Second was the need to remove native speakers as the goal for language learners' ultimate attainment. L2 learners will become bilinguals, not native speakers (Tsuchiya, 2020) of the target language, and the route toward this bi/multilingual state does not necessarily mirror the same stages, pathways or end states that L1 speakers have formed (Ayoun, 2018).

We now ask questions related to what we want our students to be and what they want to become. The answers to these questions are much more nuanced without the comparison of every utterance against some fictitious monolingual encounter. Now we have the tough work to do, which thankfully already has a cornerstone in place from researchers who have studied bilingualism and multilingualism. We must now translate our educational practices into ones that create late-bi/multilinguals, as Ortega (2013) in May's (2014) edited volume on the multilingual turn, calls for. What do we want out students to be able to do? Should they be able to do all the things other bilinguals do? Are there things we expect them to do better or worse than those who were raised bi/multilingual? Maybe a reflection on non-Western practices, like those discussed in Moore *et al.* (2004) from earlier in this chapter, where she compares monolingual versus multilingual African groups, can provide some greater insight into how our students might differ (fewer intuitive language learning strategies, etc.) from bi/multilinguals using multiple languages from birth or early on in life.

With this freedom comes great responsibility on the part of the language teacher. Teaching someone to be bi/multilingual means ensuring they have a choice between languages. This is critical to investigate with regard to learner strategies of avoidance. How do we ensure that we are supporting students to make choices about which languages they want to use and how, and providing models and time for reflection? The focus on learning outcomes for students must support agency via choice, rather than avoidance.

In any case, we might be asking our students to do more now. Specifically, that they learn how to operate in and navigate both monolingual and bi/multilingual spaces. Methods to support such a learning trajectory have yet to be clearly devised, let alone broadly implemented in language learning programs across the country, although frameworks like those proposed by Norton (2013) may act as helpful springboards for researchers and practitioners alike.

While there may not be any widely distributed means to achieve this, these ideas are already being incorporated into research today. In a current study on Korean, Yoon *et al.* (under review) confronted the issue of how to teach honorific verbal morphology. Like other studies on grammatical forms and their pragmatic uses (Van Compernolle, 2011; Van Compernolle *et al.*, 2016), there is no 'right' form, only alignment between form, intended meaning and resulting reactions. In contrast to traditional instructional methods before the multilingual turn, the forms that textbooks consider 'correct' or that 'most' speakers would use in a specific context are not the core of instruction. Rather, when we teach grammar to students who are learning to become bilingual, we want them to be able to match up grammatical form with pragmatic intent and allow them to create the meaning that they want in that scenario, which might take multiple forms and be highly influenced by their identity as multilingual speakers. This all works toward the end goal that language learners need to see themselves as having authentic voices in their L2, explore this new identity through language use and play, and be able to make choices about how they use and mix their languages, through a continuously developing multilingual agency.

As we find ourselves at this current moment focused on multilingualism, L3A and other multi/bilingual learner issues, it is not quite apparent what the next 'turn' in SLA will be. However, the extended focus on the learner may eventually lead to a return to the teacher in SLA, but this time with a broader, richer SLA tradition behind it.

The Future of (I)SLA: A Closer Relationship between Researchers, Theorists and Educators

While there is a wealth of data and abounding theories and models, SLA is, in many ways, a young field, and ISLA even more so. Especially when one contrasts it with L2 learning and teaching practices, which spans millennia. So where do we go from here? There are a number of fruitful directions, but a vital one is a stronger connection between theory and practice, researcher and teacher, and lab and classroom. If the field of SLA is going to fulfill the goal of using what we learn to improve the quality, ease and outcome of language learning, then we need buy-in from the majority of people doing the bulk of the teaching. We need to make our research applicable in the language classroom and easily accessible via the language we use to talk about our work, the materials we produce and the networks of educators we (should be) build(ing).

In that regard, ISLA could have a privileged role in the expansion of SLA from a niche subfield inhabited by linguists, cognitive scientists, educational researchers, psychologists and anthropologists, to one that teachers and students regularly use to inform their own language teaching and learning. There are two important ways in which ISLA can help bring about this advancement. First, ISLA should call for an expansion of classroom-based research and begin testing all of the theories about learning in a real-world setting. From this larger set of studies, meta-analyses with a focus on creating clear guidelines or best practices for teachers and students should be disseminated in a language accessible to people outside of the SLA field. Additionally, ISLA should offer opportunities for researchers to actively reach out to and collaborate with educators. The more that teachers are exposed to the ways in which research is conducted, the more they may be willing to try out new practices in their own classrooms. Reciprocally, researchers in ISLA could gain insight into how language learning plays out in various classroom contexts.

ISLA as a field has many growing pains ahead of it, and for good reason. First, ISLA is focused on providing a theoretically sound and empirically motivated pedagogy, and with it, specific recommendations for everything from whole language curricula to day-to-day activities. How these recommendations are actually brought to life will inevitably vary across contexts with different L1/L2 combinations, diverse student populations and teachers with multiple types of educational background and training. Second, as any one field connected to SLA, and therefore ISLA, shifts, we must accommodate and reconcile practices according to new findings. How much is a wave of new research in social psychology balanced with a full-on revolution in cognitive psychology? Do we have to wait until the dust settles before we make changes to our recommendations? And finally, how do we, as an incredibly interdisciplinary field, ensure that we make an impact on the fields from which we have drawn our origins?

Notes

(1) The term 'foreign' is used here to indicate the instruction of languages which are not (widely) used or seen in the society of those populations. For example, someone learning Spanish in the United States who lives near Spanish-speaking populations and encounters Spanish on a daily basis would be learning Spanish as a 'second' language, while someone who does not encounter Spanish speakers in their daily lives and is learning it to interact with people outside the United States, is considered as learning Spanish as a foreign language.
(2) This paper argues that more students need to be taught in their L1s. I'm using it to say that certain languages have more materials created in them and are a barrier to accessing information if you don't know that language.
(3) Universal grammar is not a new term invented by Chomsky, evident from its long traceable history (e.g. it is the title of part 2 of Beattie's (1788) book *The Theory of Language: In Two Parts. Part I. Of the Origin and General Nature of Speech. Part II. Of Universal Grammar*, although Chomsky's (2017) definition of UG is different from the original in that it is a 'genetically based language faculty'. The original term had to do with universals shared between languages, rather than universals shared by a species that endowed them with the ability to learn and use human languages.

2 The Conscious|Unconscious Divide

At its core, the field of instructed second language acquisition (ISLA) simply asks: What can instruction do, if anything, to influence the acquisition of a second language (L2)? Hopefully, this influence results in greater accuracy, comprehension, fluency and an overall faster pace of acquisition. However, influence is a two-way street, thus the negative effects of interventions should not fall outside the scope of investigations into ISLA. To gain an understanding of how we can influence learning, it is necessary to ask: What is there to influence?

The following sections outline the various psychological mechanisms and cognitive processes that operate during language acquisition, learning, processing and production: in other words, language use. This chapter begins with a discussion of the learning processes that often fall outside of conscious thought and occur automatically for adult L2 learners, and ends with a discussion of the cognitive functions that, in contrast, are more often considered conscious activities.

Behind the Scenes: Automatic Psycholinguistic Processes and Mechanisms of Learning

In ISLA, we are very interested in understanding what our students and participants are focusing on. What are they actively paying attention to? What are they actively thinking about? How does their attention change throughout an activity or throughout a conversation? And what about the psycholinguistic processes that are working in the background to support these conscious activities? Surely they are equally important to ensuring successful communication and learning, even if they do not currently hold the limelight. In this section, we explore the myriad of cognitive processes that are essential basic functions for language use and are always running in the background.

Information processing

As defined by Proctor *et al.* (2012), information processing is

> a cognitive approach that is often equated with contemporary cognitive psychology. The central tenet of the information-processing approach is that the human can be characterized as an information-processing system, which encodes input, operates on that information, stores and retrieves it from memory, and produces output in terms of actions. The architecture and operation of the subsystems can be revealed through use of various behavioral, psychophysiological, and brain-imaging methods. (Proctor *et al.*, 2012: 1458)

Applying this definition to the acquisition of an L2 in a classroom setting, we can define the array of inputs available to an individual; review how learners operate, store and retrieve information from experimental and modelling studies; and observe the language and actions that learners produce within this environment. As to the methods, behavioral ones have taken precedence in the literature because of the difficulties in conducting psychophysiological and brain-imaging studies in the classroom. The future proliferation of wearables may make this possible; however, currently, laboratory experiments are used to validate constructs that influence how ISLA is studied. In the following subsections, the various sources that combine within the human information-processing system to produce and reproduce human linguistic systems across multiple time frames are explored (MacWhinney, 2005b).

Auditory information

Auditory information is foundational to language learning (assuming we are not dealing with a sign language). In Christiansen *et al.*'s (2009) article, the authors outline the importance of the signal in the sound of human language and how patterns of phonetic information reinforce and maintain plausible and important combinations of sounds within a given language. For normally developing children, this process begins before birth. In utero, fetuses encounter speech sounds from the mother and others, as well as every kind of background noise. Even at this stage, fetuses respond differently when presented with various auditory stimuli such as changes in temporal patterns (Groome *et al.*, 2000) and can discriminate between low-pitch musical notes (Lecanuet *et al.*, 2000).

Following birth, children continue to develop processes important to speech perception, although the information, or cues, that the child uses to recognize and process speech changes throughout development. As Bailey and Snowling (2002: 137–138) summarize, 'The prevailing, but not settled, view on the normal development of speech perceptual abilities is that from birth, infants are sensitive to the acoustic cues that signal phonetic contrasts, but that the cues they use will change with age in response to the environmental input'. An important question here for SLA is whether adult L2 learners are able to, or even need to process new language signals in the same developmental stages as first languages (L1s) are perceived, or if adult mechanisms of phonetic processing are able to handle the different acoustic environments that build up the signal of the target language. Even further, for ISLA, can auditory training or other interventions impact L2 learners' ability to process an L2 more effectively?

Visual information

Visual information is another essential element of language representation in the brain, and at multiple levels. Typically, we may look to written language when we think of visual information, but body language, deictic and symbolic gestures and facial expressions are simultaneously interpreted during aural language processing.

Theories of visual information processing overlap with SLA primarily through graphemic processing. In other words, the written form of a language plays a significant role in the way it is interpreted from graphemic to phonetic units, and in the case of logographic and pictographic languages, simultaneous semantic information.

I begin with the largest 'grain size' (Lallier *et al.*, 2013; Schmalz *et al.*, 2017; Ziegler & Goswami, 2005) or kernel of information that closely maps a graphical form to a semantic interpretation. At this level, pictographic languages have a direct link between a given grapheme and its meaning. Unlike other forms of written speech, pictographs do not require a phonetic pairing for interpretation because they are meant to directly represent the meaning expressed by the writer. For the most part, pictographs do not play a role for most L2 learners, except for those engaging with ancient Mayan or pre-alphabetic Egyptian hieroglyphs.

The next largest grain size, logographic languages, or at least languages that use logographs in conjunction with other graphemes, are used by a number of modern languages today, including one of the most commonly written languages in the world, Chinese (not only Mandarin but in all of its dialectical/linguistic variants). Logographic languages have one-to-one mapping from a symbol onto a phonetic and morphological interpretation (Koda, 2005). This means that when a person encounters a logographic symbol, they will know both the meaning of the word or morpheme that is represented and its pronunciation. Logographic languages do not have to represent whole words in and of themselves, as long as each symbol has a singular meaning associated with it. These logographs can be combined to form words through compounding, which can add complexity to their interpretation.

Morphosyllabic languages, of which Chinese is argued to be, are similar in processing requirements to logographic languages, but restrict one morpheme to one syllable (Koda, 2005). In a logographic language, one could technically attach any length of sound to the grapheme, as long as that symbol and sound pairing is unique. In morphosyllabic languages, the unit of meaning is restricted to a syllable length. In an interesting twist for Chinese, though, learners get some extra help with compound characters. While an individual character must be learned for its meaning and sound pairing, Chinese compound characters, which make up over 80% of all characters, consist of two radicals: a semantic and a phonetic (Zhou et al., 1999). The semantic radical, which usually appears on the left field of the character, often provides information about the core meaning. For example, the semantic radical for water can be found in the words 'wash' and 'pour'. The phonetic radical, which usually appears on the right, provides information about how it is pronounced. So, although Chinese characters still require an immense amount of memorization, the nature of the compound characters still allows for some analysis at a smaller grain size, although that is only possible if one realizes that this information is available (Koda, 2005). For example, Figure 2.1 shows smaller and smaller grain sizes available for processing within Chinese characters.

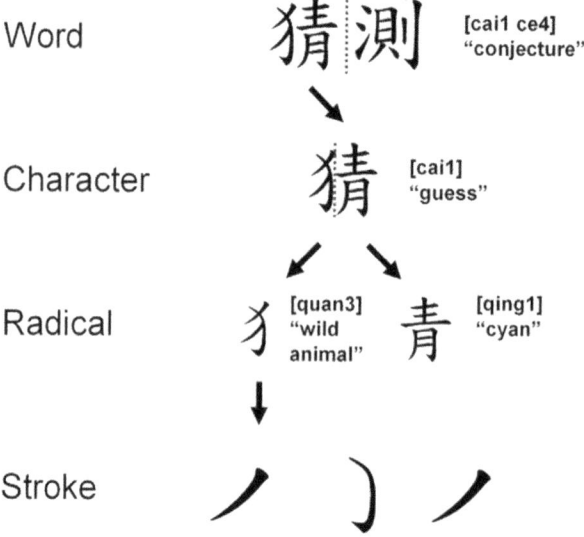

Figure 2.1 Levels of grain size and analysis of Chinese orthography (Source: Yeh et al., 2017)

The next smallest grain size makes quite a large processing leap. In syllabic and alphabetic languages, graphemes themselves are devoid of meaning. Sometimes, single syllables or letters can represent meanings, but they are more like parts that need to be combined to form morphemes and words (Koda, 2005). This means that for syllabic and alphabetic languages, the learner faces a two-step process, rather than one. Since the symbols themselves do not represent meaning, they first need to be interpreted into their sound representations before they can provide semantic information. While this complicates processing to some degree, it decreases the learning time. Instead of memorizing individual characters for each word, the learner only has to memorize the number of syllables or letters necessary to create all of the sounds and sound combinations possible in that language. This is why languages with syllabic and alphabetic scripts have so few symbols compared with those that use logographic and morphosyllabic scripts.

Although this simplification in the overall number of symbols required for learning alphabets and syllabaries can be helpful for learners, transparency, or how reliable graphemes and combinations of graphemes map onto one-to-one phonetic representations of sound–symbol pairings, varies by language (Koda, 2005). In some languages, i.e. Spanish and German, there is a relatively close relationship between a letter and its pronunciation within a word. This transparency enables learners to rely on phonetics to help them sound out new words and identify sounds or morphemes that they recognize from spoken language.

On the other hand, languages with relatively little transparency, i.e. French, make the use of phonetic decoding strategies difficult (Zieger et al., 1996). This is visible in multiple situations. In one instance, the combination of two or more alphabetic graphemes can produce a sound or sounds that do not map onto their independent phonetic pairing. A common example from English is 'gh'. The thought that a tough-to-interpret pairing of two clearly mapped independent letters, 'g' and 'h', respectively, can cause such a ghastly problem for L2 learners is enough to make the bough break. Thus, the grain size that is relevant and usable by an individual varies by proficiency and transparency. For alphabetic and syllabic languages that are more transparent, learners can utilize those close mappings to pronounce words they have never heard before as they become more proficient. For less transparent languages, or morphosyllabic ones, the option to utilize a smaller grain size for new words is either unavailable or not helpful without greater knowledge of how particular clusters of letters are pronounced in various linguistic contexts. For example, when a letter is located at the onset or coda of a syllable, or when letters around another letter influence pronunciation through some phonological process, such as assimilation.

To make matters even more complex for learners, some languages have scripts at multiple grain sizes. Take Japanese as a common example. In addition to utilizing morphosyllabic symbols called kanji, which are largely based on Chinese characters, written Japanese also makes use of two syllabaries (Koda, 2005). The first, hiragana, is used to fill in the gaps left by kanji to express various morphological elements of Japanese that do not exist in Chinese and therefore do not have kanji available for representation. The second syllabary, katakana, is used for foreign and loan words. This means that a person reading Japanese is processing some symbols which encode sound and meaning simultaneously, and some symbols which require a two-step analysis of sound first then meaning. The amount and variability of paralinguistic, contextual and symbolic information provides a clear picture of just how rich the visual landscape of language can be, and that this information requires learners to integrate it in multiple ways.

Contextual information

As we combine aural and visual information, including both linguistic and non-linguistic, we are continually aware of and incorporate that information into our understanding of current contextual information. This combination of contextual information with linguistic processes is essential for pragmatic functioning.

Contextual information comes from many sources, including external, non-linguistic sensory information, such as objects in a field of vision and the current soundscape, as well as touch, smell and taste information. It also includes actions, such as what a person, other people and aspects of the environment are doing at a given moment. One also holds contextual information internally about the nature of the context. For example, what do you associate with where you are? How does that inform how you fill in gaps about what has happened, what is currently happening and what might happen? Also, knowledge about interlocutors and other actors is crucial. Relationships between an individual and others, including what those others know or what an individual thinks they know, provide probable assumptions that fill in gaps in knowledge.

Both the classroom as a context and the expectations that teachers and students bring with them into that context can have a profound impact on the learning process and the ways in which certain behaviors and practices are viewed by different community members (students, teachers, parents, administrators and researchers) (Chaput, 1997; Kozaki & Ross, 2011). What makes contextual information so important is that no language, at least not one useful for human communication, can encode everything one intends to express (Moore, 2019). This results in two interesting outcomes. First, that language, via cultural and historical processes, has come to highlight the most culturally and possibly also evolutionarily important aspects of our context via grammatical forms (Newmeyer, 2017). Much of the contextual data that has been deemed either evolutionary or culturally relevant through historical processes is encoded. For example, many languages formulate tense as a grammatical structure, rather than via stand-alone lexical items (e.g. yesterday and tomorrow). This grammaticalization, while easing production through the elimination of lexical items to indicate time, provides only a general sense of time, which removes exact information of when something is occurring.

Second, humans must be able to fill in contextual information without explicit mention. Human communication often requires an immense amount of work on the part of the listener or reader to fill in gaps with their own knowledge formed by their own world knowledge. For example, if I say, 'I went there', it lies fully on the listener to interpret when the 'going' occurred. If I'm any good at conversing, I hopefully know that the 'when' has already been brought up in the conversation, or that the person(s) I'm conversing with has enough background knowledge of me or the story to at least have a general sense of the time frame of events. But this is not always the case. Maybe a third-party joined the conversation late and didn't want to interrupt. The ball would be fully in their court either to ask for clarity and perform some nuanced conversation management that got them answers without ruining the story or to use the information they receive from then on to estimate a time that made sense to them, based on their experiences, even if it wasn't the exact time the story really occurred. And sometimes it is just as important to know that something has already happened. The time itself might not be necessary for the story to make sense or to be funny or intriguing, just that it has already happened, which is, in a way, quite freeing from a language without tense marking where lexical items tied to specific times must do the heavy lifting. Thus, contextual information not only comes both from the outside world and current dialogue but is also something a person has to frequently fill in from their own experience. They must build their own mental model of what's happening with the limited amount of information conveyed via language (Zwaan & Radvansky, 1998). In sum, an important balance is continually negotiated between what is said explicitly, what is implied or conveyed paralinguistically and what is left assumed in every communicative interaction. In building a curriculum around the psycholinguistic principles of instruction, we cannot leave out the integration of contextual information and its role in the classroom.

Memory activation

Various inputs from our surroundings not only trigger mental models and expectations for particular contexts (Ford, 1985; Lombardi, 2003; MacWhinney, 2008), but also activate various memories (Pressley & Harris, 2009), which in turn invoke patterns of spreading activation (Anderson, 1983). Thus, formerly submerged memories of myriad linguistic experiences flow to the forefront of conscious awareness. These memories can contain both explicit and implicit information that we learned about word order in Japanese or case marking in Russian, which help us monitor and reflect on the language we are trying to comprehend or produce. Memories about grammar topics, idioms, rules of thumb or concepts can all be useful, especially when we are doing less online activities, such as reading and writing, where more time is available for reflection on the language than during oral comprehension or speech production, where time constraints on processing eat up available cognitive capacities.

However, language learning also makes us recall episodic memories (de Masson D'Autume et al., 2019). Distinct stories about how we learned, who we learned from/with and why we learned something. These episodic memories, especially when tied to grammatical or lexical learning, can have a strong influence on the quality of the input, particularly when they intertwine with emotions not only of joy, accomplishment and humor, but also fear, humiliation and frustration.

Therefore, any psycholinguistic approach to language teaching must take into consideration the role that episodic memory and emotion can have on the acquisition of the language. One just needs to keep in mind that these memories and emotions will work out differently for different learners. Whereas one embarrassing moment in class may shut one student down, an embarrassing moment for another student might be a catalyst for them to work harder to not make the same mistake. There is no way to predict which emotions or memories might help students in general, but a great teacher knows their student, and thus, insight, instinct and a strong teacher–student relationship might be just enough to make memory activation a useful tool in their teaching toolbox.

Input integration and comprehension

From the fusion of current inputs and previous memories, which is really an integration of bottom-up and top-down processes, we then begin to comprehend our reality as presented to us through language and our senses. One of the clearest examples of this is the McGurk effect, first discovered by McGurk and MacDonald (1976). This effect is a result of a mismatch between audio and visual information. In a classic example, a person hears an audio clip of someone saying /ga/ while simultaneously seeing that same someone on video mouthing the sound /ba/. The glottal sound information is combined with the visual bilabial information, which causes many people to 'hear' /da/, an alveolar-dental approximately in the middle of the two consonants with which the person was presented. This effect goes away immediately when one closes one's eyes or turns off the audio, now leaving only a singular source of input. While this phenomenon might at first appear as a novelty of cognition, it has serious repercussions for our understanding of how language is processed in the brain.

Two major theories of visual information processing have focused on data-driven, i.e. bottom up, only theories (Gibson, 1966, 1979) versus those top down (Boring, 1946; Epstein, 1973; Gregory, 1993; Rock,

1977, 1983, 1997) reliant on 'contextual stimuli' and 'past experiences'. A major implication is that what we think of as hearing or comprehending at the smallest level is already influenced by other areas of the brain. So, if a small amount of visual mismatching can cause such a disruption of one's ability to perceive something as simple as a consonant, what other processing phenomena can we expect to occur when more complex linguistic, cultural and contextual information is also being simultaneously integrated?

Habits

For better or worse, habits guide an extremely large amount of our daily behaviors (Graybiel, 2008). These behaviors can extend into out conscious view, but, in large part, operate in the background. Despite the back-burner nature of habits, they are critical to human behavior (Bernacer *et al.*, 2015). The reasons habits are of such import to human functioning is that they free up resources while still allowing the body and mind to act. As Bernacer *et al.* describe:

> Habits allow human agents to release cognitive resources in the performance of well-known actions. This is essential for dual-tasking, as many experiments in neuroscience suggest. Furthermore, it is also useful to enhance the cognitive control of actions, as well as to direct habits to achieve a goal and consciously redress them when needed. (Bernacer *et al.*, 2015: n.p.)

What is essential for human activity is the fact that habits are something we can do mostly unconsciously as well as recall for conscious reflection. Many everyday examples can highlight the utility of habits, like getting dressed. If you had to ask yourself every morning which order you should put your clothes on, it would be a much more tedious task, rather than one we do while thinking about what we are planning on doing that day or what we are going to make for breakfast. Language use, just like many other activities, is full of habits (Lado, 1970; Lee, 2011). Each person develops certain ways of speaking that they fall back on when they are deciding what to say and they come in many forms and perform many functions.

We also have the habit of using particular words, which is where our ability to reflect and update our habits is important (Shanon, 1993). A major linguistic controversy that has been playing out in public in the United States and in many other countries across the world is the use of gendered language (Jakiela & Ozier, 2018; Mucchi-Faina, 2005). Typically, male-dominated roles (as well as typically female-dominated roles) are being taken up by an increasingly diverse population of people with all types of gender identities, and reflections and a growing consciousness of this divide in language have caused a significant shift in how many people understand how language can and should or should not change. In languages with highly structured grammatical gender systems, such as German, Greek, Italian, Spanish and French, the debate is even more intense (Vainapel *et al.*, 2015). Not only do you need to change vocabulary, but you also need to think about the morphology that goes along with it. In German, at least, there is a neuter form to which one can begrudgingly switch.

When there is obvious linguistic disparity in terms of gender representation in language, why is there such resistance? It may not be that the person is opposed to saying something that might be less problematic, but rather a subconscious bias against changing their habit, and changing a habit is hard.

Center Stage: Volition and Consciousness

Unlike the aspects of cognition described in the previous section, which operate mostly without our noticing or monitoring, we do have the ability to control (many of) our own actions and guide (to some degree) our thoughts (Fried *et al.*, 2017; Haggard, 2008). The power we can put behind intentional actions and thoughts is vast but limited in scope at any moment in time (Liljenström, 2022). Many psychological studies that have tested how much information a person can handle at one time, like word and number span tasks, show how difficult it is when participants are asked to hold other pieces of information in their head simultaneously (Conway *et al.*, 2005; Gordon *et al.*, 2020; Unsworth *et al.*, 2009). If we imagine consciousness as a spotlight on a stage and volition what we do with and through things in the light, it is easy to see how the elements on the rest of the stage (the world we live in, our current context, our other thoughts, etc.) can melt into the background.

The ideas of volition and consciousness bring together many perspectives and fields, such as psychology, philosophy, neuroscience, cognitive science, biology, physics, chemistry, theology and religion. One thing that is clear is that there is no universally accepted theory that can explain these phenomena in a truly satisfactory way, but insights from multiple theories can help us at least begin to understand what volition and consciousness are and how they are involved in SLA.

Consciousness

It is extremely important that we begin here by recognizing that there is no singularly agreed-upon understanding of what consciousness is (Del Pin *et al.*, 2021). The varied fields that question the nature of consciousness in and of itself come from all aspects of human inquiry, including psychology, theology, philosophy, neuroscience and cognitive science. All of these fields bring different lenses to the study of consciousness and therefore reach different conclusions. This section brings together some of what experts in the field of consciousness agree on, before moving on to specific functions that can and do take place within the realm of conscious thought, including working memory, focus and attention, goal orientation and metacognition.

Beginning with the rift between fields, Dennett (1993) highlights the different levels of consciousness being studied. He notes that, as an 'interloper' between fields that study consciousness, he is often confronted by experts in each field questioning the methods and conclusions from the others. He describes these interchanges in the following way:

> I have grown accustomed to the disrespect expressed by some of the participants for their colleagues in other disciplines. 'Why Dan,' ask the people in Artificial Intelligence, 'do you waste your time conferring with those neuroscientists? They wave their hands about 'information processing' and worry about where it happens, and which neurotransmitters are involved, and all those boring facts but they haven't a clue about the computational requirements of higher cognitive functions.' 'Why,' ask the neuroscientists, 'do you waste your time on the fantasies of Artificial Intelligence? They just invent whatever machinery they want and say unpardonably ignorant things about the brain.' The cognitive psychologists, meanwhile, are accused of concocting models with neither biological plausibility nor proven computational powers; the anthropologists wouldn't know a model if they saw one, and the philosophers, as we all know, just take in each other's laundry, warning about confusions they themselves have created, in an arena bereft of both data and empirically testable theories. (Dennett, 1993: 254–255, original emphasis)

From this starting point, it is a wonder that we have any joint understanding of consciousness at all. And while much more interdisciplinary work has been underway since this statement in 1993, the epistemology and methodology passed down within disciplines to new generations of researchers still pose a steep challenge to building a unified theory of consciousness. In a more recent collection of philosophical and scientific theories, Cavanna and Nani (2014) contrast the perspectives of 15 philosophers with 15 scientists. In their introductory chapter, Cavanna and Nani (2014: ix) confirm this rift similarly when they state, 'The demarcation line between philosophers and scientists is far from straight and univocal; however, it rests upon the observation that philosophers and scientists tend to adopt different perspectives in their approach to the study of consciousness, mind, and brain'. If we cannot agree on a single way to approach consciousness, what subcomponents or aspects of consciousness can we agree exist? For the intentions of this book, we might start with Dennett's (1993: 8) articulation that 'Language... plays an enormous role in the structuring of a human mind'. This sentiment is shared by many, if not all, of the fields that study human consciousness. While underlying neurological features, such as neurons, exist in humans, there is some consensus that the mere existence of a linguistic system in humans changes the organizational structure of the brain. An excellent illustration of the various aspects of language distributed throughout the brain comes from Price (2010). In a review of 100 functional magnetic resonance imaging (fMRI) studies, Price created a 'modern view of some language-related regions in the left hemisphere' (Kemmerer, 2014) (Figure 2.2).

Looking at Figure 2.2, it is clear that specific language-related regions are organized into different physiological areas in the left hemisphere, across multiple lobes and yet interconnected through the joint function of making human language possible.

The role of language in human consciousness and thought is also referenced as crucial in many theories of language (Arbib, 2001; Cattell, 2006; Jackendoff, 2009; Merleau-Ponty, 1973; Schmidt, 1990; Searl & Willis, 2002; Wittgenstein, 2010). In sociocultural theory, the use of language as a tool for mediating tasks and organizing actions is seen as a revolutionary part of a child's developmental process. Specifically, that outer speech turns inwards to act as something that is still language, but distinct from language we direct toward others. This inner language functions in conjunction with our consciousness which increases our ability to mediate our thoughts and actions (Vygotsky, 2012). The use of language as a tool for mediation has direct relevance to higher-order thinking. In her study, Berk (1986) showed that the majority of private speech, i.e. self-directed speech, was used to describe a child's actions.

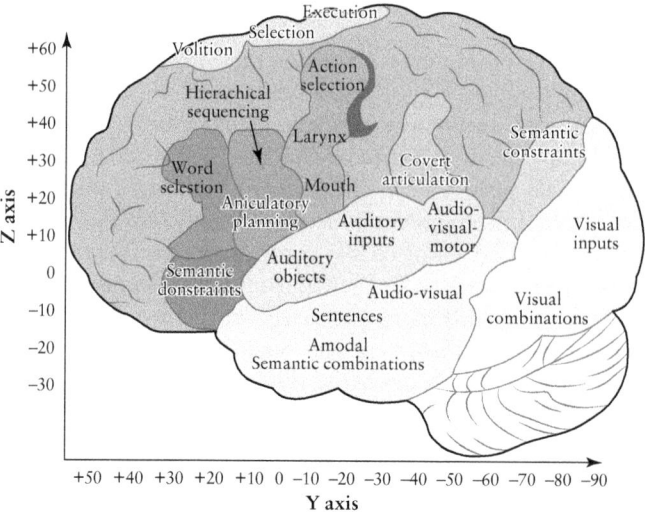

Figure 2.2 A modern view of some language-related regions in the left hemisphere (Adapted from Price, 2010: 76)

The amount of private speech increased with task complexity and when a teacher was not present for support. The use of an inner language that takes on alternate functions beyond interaction is essential to understanding human consciousness. Vygotsky (2012: 271) notes a direct correlation between the development of inner speech and consciousness: 'Thought and speech turn out to be the key to the nature of human consciousness'. Whether looking from a bottom-up or top-down perspective, it is evident that those studying human consciousness must confront the influence of language and its inevitable impacts on the phenomenon of consciousness itself (Hasan, 1992).

Now that we have established that the existence of language is a core element of human consciousness, what other elements of consciousness are established enough across disciplines to rely on as shared functions across all humans?

Working memory

Possibly one of the most studied conscious processes in all of psychology since the cognitive revolution, working memory has earned its place among long-term and short-term memory as a separate psychological phenomenon. In a general sense, working memory is the ability to retain and manipulate a limited amount of data for short periods of time through volition or active thinking. Baddeley (2017) outlined a more detailed description in which he compiled a number of his and his colleagues' studies on working memory since 1966. Over the course of decades, our understanding of working memory as some form of short-term memory was replaced by a multicomponent model including, initially, three key parts: the central executive, the phonological loop and the visuospatial scratch/sketchpad.

According to Baddeley (1998: 527), the central executive 'certainly exists, but as a concept', which 'provides a useful basis for studying the complexities of executive control and identifying subprocesses, which may then be mapped on to their anatomical substrate'. This master control over other subcomponents, such as the phonological loop, acts as a conductor, providing inputs to and receiving outputs from other aspects of cognition.

The two original subcomponents of working memory that function as operational systems[1] (Anderson, 2005) for the central executive are the phonological loop and the visuospatial sketchpad. Of the two, Anderson (2005: 153) notes that 'the phonological loop has received much more extensive investigation than the visuospatial sketchpad'. It consists of multiple parts, including an articulatory loop and a phonological store (Anderson, 2005). The articulatory loop holds information, as the name implies, in a loop produced by an inner voice that is then made available for retrieval by the central executive at the opportune time. The phonological store, as a separate component to the articulatory loop, is then believed to hear and process the stored information in phonological form (Anderson, 2005).

The visuospatial sketchpad, as previously noted, has received less attention, but in general acts in much the same way as the phonological loop. It is a semi-independent subsystem that interfaces with the executive function and serves as a place to store and hold visual and spatial information (Barton *et al.*, 1995; Bruyer & Scailquin, 1998). As with all aspects of working memory, there are computational limitations to how much and how long information can be stored and successfully retrieved (Frick, 1988).

An episodic buffer has also been proposed as part of working memory. According to Baddeley (2000: 417), the episodic buffer 'comprises a limited capacity system that provides temporary storage of information held in a multimodal code, which is capable of binding information from the subsidiary systems, and from long-term memory, into a unitary episodic representation'. In other words, the episodic buffer unifies inputs from the more independent subsystems of working and long-term memory into a cohesive unit. It is also of particular importance to our emphasis on consciousness, because 'Conscious awareness is assumed to be the principal mode of retrieval from the buffer' (Baddeley, 2000: 417). Note in this quote that both the terms consciousness and awareness have been invoked as pivotal to the functioning of the episodic buffer.

An important reminder about all four aspects of Baddeley's working memory model is that they are concepts for understanding and grouping functions. Each of the subsystems can be broken down into further subcomponents and do not need to be, neurologically speaking, located in the same region or area to operate with one another.

To this point, we have explored the importance of consciousness and the capacity of working memory as psychological foundations of human thought. Consciousness, especially as it is instantiated in humans and influenced by the development and existence of language, provides a platform uniquely evolved to support thought. Overlying this foundation is a working memory system that can be used or is the mechanism itself for directing and controlling thought through storing, focusing on and manipulating multiple types of input data simultaneously, with computational limits, of course (e.g. plus/minus 7 rule introduced in Miller [1956]). Now I turn to some of the functions that result from the existence of consciousness and working memory that can be influenced through interventions and instruction.

Awareness, attention, focus and noticing

The terms awareness, attention, focus and noticing are frequently used in SLA to describe learners' engagement with their target language and linguistic forms. Because these terms describe somewhat overlapping phenomenon, they are rather difficult to distinguish from one another and without a clear definition, understanding the subtle, but important differences of each can sometimes muddle understanding of the points a researcher is trying to make. This leads to some confusion regarding which, if any, of these cognitive functions are necessary for learning. This section defines these terms in the following way for language learning.

- Awareness: A general phenomenon of cognizance that there are things in the input that exist to which one can attend or that one could be attending to.
- Attention: An active process of applying some cognitive resources toward a particular linguistic element.
- Focus: A more intense, active process than attention where all or almost all conscious, directable attention is pointed at a singular or small array of linguistic features within a particular moment or over a specific period of time. In a state of focus, inhibitory processes may be induced which block out other linguistic information.
- Noticing: Noticing is a phenomenon that can arise on its own but is more likely to occur through awareness and attention. If awareness is a more general phenomenon of cognizance and attention is an active process applying cognitive resources, noticing occurs at the exact moment when a particular linguistic feature comes to the forefront and is recognized among all of the other linguistic input.

Using these definitions, we can see that these different cognitive phenomena can and do have different impacts on language learning and pedagogy. Awareness can be raised by instructing someone that pieces of information in the input are going to be available and they should keep an eye out for them. This type of information can help learners notice that information, even if they are not actively trying to pay attention or focus attentional resources on that information. Attention, on the other hand, can be asked of a person, but it is up to the individual to recruit the necessary resources and point their conscious mind at a particular linguistic form. Focusing follows a similar, albeit more intense course as attention, and again, is something that must be initiated by the learner, although training with and instruction from another individual may spur on this action. Thus, with regard to instruction, there can be external forces that act on an individual to support them, but the states or actions of awareness, attention, focus and noticing are internal processes.

In relation to the conscious|unconscious divide, attention, focus and noticing all seem to exist primarily in the conscious mind. Even if some of the processes that result in someone noticing something are happening at the sub/unconscious level at the moment of noticing, the information has crossed over to the conscious realm. Awareness, on the other hand, is something I prefer to conceptualize as an ebb and flow between conscious and unconscious thought. One can be told to be aware of something and reflect consciously on the need to be aware of it, but one can still be aware of things without using any conscious resources. This is often the case when noticing happens without attention, which I call 'incidental noticing'. This is a frequent occurrence in language learning and often leads to incidental learning.

Goal orientation

Another common activity in conscious thought is our ability to orient ourselves toward goals, or future achievements, states or gains (Bongers & Dijksterhuis, 2009). We can see from the previous discussion of Vygotsky's work that private and inner speech can guide our actions toward some end (Harris, 1990). As a child, these ends could be as simple as placing a block onto another block. As children grow, their goals change and become more complex as their social and cultural understandings expand. A first grader might be attempting to kick a soccer ball into a (literal) goal. Later in life, they focus on winning a soccer game which requires combining previous skills and goals, including kicking a ball into a goal, with new activities, like passing, playing on a team, listening to coaches, facing opponents and incorporating personal and team strategies. Other goals, like making friends, becoming a professional athlete, participating in the Olympics or using sports as a springboard into college can all integrate into the goal of playing soccer. All these changing goals are not only a result of social development, but also a shift of consciousness that builds on previously conscious activities that have moved to the background, allowing reflection on new social and cultural opportunities that existed within the child's environment, but were outside the purview of the child's understanding.

The L2 learner, especially adult L2 learners, have already learned how to set these and more complex goals. A child does not question whether their L1 will help get them into medical school, but I had plenty of high school friends who took Latin for that exact reason. In sum, goal orientation is a constantly active part of human development. The specific goals themselves change as the individual and their environment change over time, but guide much of our activity, especially when we are actually applying our consciousness toward completion of those goals. In the L2 context, the act of goal setting and reorientation to these goals can have significant impacts on language learning (Hayashi, 2013; Karbakhsh & Ahmadi Safa, 2020).

Metacognition

Thinking about thinking is one of the most complex high-order activities a person can perform to control themselves. Like goal orientation, teaching someone metacognition might look different by age (Palmer *et al.*, 2014). Children might need more guidance or specific language provided by caregivers or teachers that prods them to think in a more adult-like way. For older learners, we can directly ask them, what is your plan? What are you going to do next? Why are you doing that? And then, based on their explanations, we can get some insight into how they are thinking. But it is really not metacognition until the students themselves begin to internalize questions that others have posed and turn them inward on their own ways of doing things. This has important implications for language learning. We talk to our students about how they should prepare for tests, learn new vocabulary, study, practice, work in pairs, work in small groups, work alone, read, write and so on. Every L2 task is an opportunity to think about why you are doing what you are doing, and how you might do it differently/better/more efficiently/more accurately.

Metacognition is especially important for those learning a language 'in the wild' (terminology coined by Clark *et al.* [2011]). And while not the focus of this book per se, our classroom students use the language they have learned, with all its nuances, culture, grammar and history, with other users of that language. In those situations, we hope that learning continues, and not only through a rich, complex variety of linguistically diverse contexts and dialogues, but also through metacognition. The ability to think about and plan ahead, what you might say in this versus that context, in that or another store, with this or the next person.

Metacognition is essential for future learning (Efklides, 2014; Siegesmund, 2017), and so it is essential that it is taught in the L2 classroom with specific emphasis on how students can use metacognition not only to question how and why they comprehend and produce their L2 the way they do, but also to question what they understand about the language itself, or their metalinguistic knowledge.

Conclusion

In summarizing this chapter, I end with a question and an everyday example. My question is, how much on a day-to-day, hour-to-hour, minute-to-minute and even instance-to-instance basis do you balance unconscious and conscious activities, and how do these vary based on your current situation? Let's take an everyday example of unconscious/conscious overlap: driving. Driving, in my opinion, is a great metaphor for language learning, because it is complex and, at the same time, simple relative to language acquisition.

There are two perspectives here to compare: the person learning how to drive and the person who is an experienced driver. The foci of each person are quite different. The learner is confronted with a complex task and their initial intentional awareness focuses on things like starting the engine, identifying where the brake and gas pedals (or also the clutch) are, where the lights and turn signal levers are, etc. The experienced driver, especially in their own car, has the attentional resources available to do other things while the other aspects focused on by the learner happen simultaneously, like adjusting the seat, looking in the rear and side-view mirrors, talking to passengers and changing the radio station.

The real importance of this analogy comes into play when the experienced driver attempts to instruct the learner, because so much about driving has been proceduralized by the experienced driver and is no longer something they consider, even when they are asked to reflect on the process in a much deeper way than normally needed to perform the action. If an experienced driver tells a learner to start the car, the procedural knowledge about which way to turn the key, what warning signs (and sounds/smells) they might need to look out for and that they should be engaging the parking brake before turning the key is often left out. It is no longer part of the conscious process of starting the car for the experienced driver. For the learner, however, it is an essential piece of declarative, explicit knowledge needed to start the car. The conflict between the expert and the novice is all too familiar to parents and grandparents who have taught someone else how to drive. The expert is often frustrated by the novice for not performing the way they expect, and the novice is often frustrated by the expert for not telling them explicitly what they need to do.

So, what does this metaphor, or what one might consider a simplified, parallel process of skill acquisition utilizing the same mechanisms of learning, have to do with L2 learning? Following this analogy, L1 speakers (previously described as, and often still so-called 'native speakers') have a very difficult time providing explicit information about the language features of their L1 to L2 learners. While they are often considered 'experts' from a processing and production standpoint, they frequently cannot explain complex linguistic features to 'novice' L2 learners. Thus, L2 learners are often left with partial, unsystematic explanations about the norms and patterns that exist in the language they are learning and are often left to much trial and error. An important distinction to be made between expert car drivers and expert language users is that the expert car driver was taught to do this complex task at a later point in life. The L1 expert learned how to use language across a broad developmental spectrum, including information processed during the pre-verbal stage, which would lead to an even bigger gap in what they can easily recall explicitly for someone learning their language.

Previously proceduralized processes in the L1 fade from consciousness to make room for higher-order cognitive functions, while simultaneously supporting these higher-order functions through subroutines and proceduralized activities. Thus, attentional awareness previously dedicated to a particular type of input can shift to a new target. This is only possible because the number of resources needed to integrate the previous input type has been reduced to subroutines that free up attentional resources.

Chapter 3 explores how L2 learners experience the same transition, where they move from fundamental skills like parsing and grapheme resolution to more advanced linguistic processes like recognizing and understanding morphology and complex syntactic structures, integrating cultural and contextual information for pragmatic and discourse purposes and eventually using their L2 as a tool to mediate their actions and interactions.

Note

(1) The term 'slave system' is avoided here. It was the original terminology used to describe the subordinate working memory systems that are operated by and contribute to the executive function.

3 Re-envisioning a Conscious–Unconscious Continuum

Chapter 2 outlined a traditional view from second language acquisition (SLA) of conscious, subconscious and unconscious linguistic processes and psychological mechanisms that allow adults to learn and use a second (L2) or additional language. In doing so, it can often seem that these mental activities are, in fact, separate from one another. Rather than starting from a point of conscious versus subconscious division that may, for good reason, have been prematurely laid upon various types of linguistic activity, this chapter presents a re-envisioning of these processes on a continuum of consciousness. Specifically, the idea that seemingly conscious activities like goal orientation or grammar learning cannot become subconscious activities is opposed. Likewise, it is argued that for L2 learners, many tasks thought of as unconscious for fluent language users, like parsing words from a continuous speech stream, or first language (L1) transfer come under the scrutiny and observance of learner consciousness. The spotlight of the conscious mind, the momentarily hidden subconscious and the obscurity of the unconscious operate in conjunction with one another. Enforcing the boundary between conscious and unconscious activities in our overall view of SLA is detrimental to our approach to instructing L2 learners and has led to unnecessary divisions in research paradigms, especially those that focus on internal mechanisms of grammar acquisition.

The following sections outline how mechanisms of learning contradict views in SLA that separate activities into either conscious or unconscious operations. Rather, a dynamic understanding of consciousness that incorporates multiple layers that can change focus in an instant more appropriately models cognitive behaviors both within the short time span of a single activity and across the lifetime of the learner. This chapter takes the findings discussed in Chapter 2 and shows how they are related. These findings have implications for instructed SLA (ISLA) and require both conscious and unconscious mechanisms to function and develop. Here, the previous categorization of conscious and unconscious activity is re-envisioned into a unified psycholinguistic model along a continuum of conscious and unconscious processes.

Dynamic Attention

In many ways, ISLA is obsessed with attention, and for good reason. Every teacher, no matter how many years they have been teaching, can easily recall a time when they told a student to pay attention. It is inherently understood by teachers that attention is something essential to learning, and many modern researchers have proposed models and concepts to describe these processes.

One of the earlier SLA models attempting to describe the importance of attention in L2 learning was proposed by Krashen in his monitor model. Krashen (1978) based this model of L2 development as a split between two systems: one of acquisition and one of learning. The acquisitional system arises from the learner's language use and is the same system for language learning that guides child language acquisition (CLA). The learned system, on the other hand, is a system only available to older learners. It operates as a monitor that can, but does not always, observe output stemming from the acquisitional system and then, depending on the ability of the learner and the amount of metalinguistic knowledge about 'correct' grammar and forms known by the learned system, can alter the output produced by the learner. According to Krashen (1978: 175), 'Learned language consists of conscious mental representations of linguistic rules and is the result of either a formal language learning situation or some kind of self-study program'. In other words, Krashen believed that the 'real' acquisition of language occurs through subconscious processes that are involved when learners interact with and use language, and the conscious, learned system provides a sort of conscious band-aid to cover up blemishes known to be erroneous by the learned system but not yet refined in the acquired system. This lines up quite directly with models of language that assume an innate language instinct and a highly specified human language acquisition device (LAD) as a structure in the brain, often also viewed as a unique module of the brain. In so doing, the supposed modularity of language both shields it from influence and keeps it separate from other cognitive functions. While this model focuses primarily on the role of consciousness on an individual's output and relies heavily on innatist models for its mental hardware, it was one of the first to investigate the role of consciousness in L2 learning. The idea that adult learners were conscious of the divide between what they could produce and what they knew (or thought they knew) to be correct highlights the Chomskian perspective on the difference between proficiency and performance. However, from another theoretical perspective, it could be perceived as a way to signify the existence of multiple, competing types of knowledge available to the learner. What we can glean from this initial model of attention relevant to this discussion is that a learner's own output could be a source for learning.

Another major theory in SLA dealing with a nuanced approach to attention was Schmidt's (1990) noticing hypothesis. According to this theory, noticing and understanding are two forms of awareness. When someone notices something, they are simply detecting that it is a recurring event, whereas understanding brings with it knowledge or growing knowledge of the pattern. Other researchers disagree with Schmidt about the level of consciousness required for noticing (Tomlin & Villa, 1994). Whether the learner is noticing, detecting or aware of a particular linguistic pattern may be, as Loewen (2020: 68) states, 'less helpful for teachers for whom the most noteworthy detail is that not much learning happens subconsciously'. However, the prior focus might just be on the initial stages of learning and not representative of the entire process of learning. The recognition of a pattern and a growing understanding of the function or role of the pattern within the language are not even half the battle. In a fully functional acquired L2, learners should be able to attend to and process these patterns without relying on many or any conscious attentional resources, in both receptive and productive tasks.

Looking at this another way, the real question is, do we want someone who we claim to have achieved a high level of language fluency to have to pay attention to grammatical minutia while they are speaking or listening? We may want them to be able to reflect on different linguistic forms and have a certain level of metalinguistic awareness of their L2, but we would expect that they could apply correct morphology and syntax even when they are required to apply all of their available cognitive resources to higher-order thinking and semantic information. In this regard, studies on task complexity shed light on how attentional resources are pulled between linguistic form and semantic understanding.

Task complexity

The construct of task complexity, especially within the framework of task-based language teaching (TBLT), has been fruitful in helping us to understand how limited cognitive resources are used by learners across a variety of task types. Robinson (2001: 29) defined task complexity as, 'the result of the attentional, memory, reasoning, and other information processing demands imposed by the structure of the task on the language learner'. Unpacking this definition, we can see that task complexity must be understood as a multidimensional construct. Of the three components named, attentional demands seem to be the most conscious. By this, I mean that the conscious mind is focusing on the task demands as well as the tools, in this case the linguistic tools necessary to complete the task. Reasoning is also heavily reliant on consciousness (although mentions and references to 'subconscious reasoning' can be found in various psychological areas such as science education [Gette et al., 2018] and intuition [Hussain & Asad, 2017]). Memory is much more difficult to define as either a conscious or subconscious activity. We can make a conscious effort to remember things, like where verbs go in a sentence or the rules of a game we know how to play. For tasks, this means bringing to the table what you already know about the task, the times you participated in the same or a similar task and what linguistic features you might need to employ (past tense, subjunctive, future tense, etc.). But this cannot explain other memory-related processes like spreading activation (Anderson *et al.*, 1983). Other subconscious processes must affect not only what you remember, but also how and when you remember them. And finally, the term 'other information processing demands' seems to be a catch-all for undefined subconscious processes. Thus, the construct of task complexity itself requires an understanding of how both conscious and subconscious activity affects task performance and success.

Linguistic-level attention

So if, as Loewen (2020: 68) argues, 'Generally, learners prioritize semantic content of an utterance as opposed to its morphosyntactic components' and 'focus on form proposes that noticing linguistic structures is most likely to occur when meaning is relatively clear and learners have the attentional resources to process linguistic form', how can we structure tasks in a way that allows learners to focus on form during task completion without overloading their ability to see linguistic patterns in the input? And how do we support continued attention to linguistic forms as we ask students to perform increasingly complex tasks as they progress through a curriculum?

VanPatten's (2004, 2020; VanPatten & Cadierno, 1993) input processing (IP) paradigm saw this as one of the major goals of material development along with types of instruction, like the addition of explicit instruction (Henry *et al.*, 2009; VanPatten & Borst, 2012; VanPatten *et al.*, 2013). The goal of IP is to either alter, highlight or select the input that students are receiving to force noticing and processing of grammatical information in order to appropriately comprehend and interpret the target language. This is especially important to make students notice grammatical information that contradicts with L1 processes that they might transfer, or general language learning strategies, like the 'noun-first' principal discussed in VanPatten *et al.* (2013), where L2 learners tend to assign the subject role to the first noun that they encounter in a sentence. For languages with object-verb-subject (OVS) or object-subject-verb (OSV) word order that have a subject-first syntax in their L1, IP calls for learners to encounter input that forces them to see that the first noun is either unlikely or impossible to act as the subject of the sentence.

IP is not the only theoretical approach that calls for a closer link between grammatical features and functions. Systemic functional linguistics (SFL) also emphasizes, as the name implies, the function of grammar, but has a larger focus on how learners can use grammar as a tool to help them create meaning through the semiotic–symbolic system of language. As Llinares and McCabe (2020) describe, paraphrasing Ortega and Byrnes (2009):

> SFL provides an approach to language through linguistic analysis which links language use to its sociocultural contexts, sees language as a meaning-making system, provides tools for linguistic analysis of written and spoken texts, embodies a functional approach to grammar in context, and recognizes the effect of educational practices on language use and literacy development. (Llinares & McCabe, 2020: 294)

Within this framework, attention is paid to form with a heavy focus on the ways in which these forms operate. Students and teachers alike learn to perform linguistic analysis while developing metalanguage to talk about forms, functions and their implications for meaning making (Carpenter *et al.*, 2015).

Finally, from a general psycholinguistic approach, awareness-raising tasks (ARTs) allow for a broad range of student engagement with forms (Crivos & Luchini, 2012; Ellis, 2014). They can see, become aware of, notice, pay attention to, understand and even critically analyze grammatical features within the context of a particular text, interaction or activity (McNicoll & Lee, 2011). ARTs are usually designed ahead of work with a text aligned with the content focus of the course or within a course unit that contains grammatical forms that a teacher wants to highlight, although ARTs can be employed on the fly if a teacher notices a grammatical form that has relevance to the meanings created within a text. ARTs are highly effective at tying linguistic forms to contextual usage, as well as genres, and grounds them within a text. ARTs can simply be used to draw attention to where and how different grammatical aspects appear in a text, but they are more effective when teachers utilize the opportunity to query students about the functions these features are playing or why the author(s) decided to use one form over another. In doing so, teachers can check student understanding and provide explicit instruction about how forms are selected (consciously or unconsciously) by authors to achieve certain textual effects.

Language learners are continually moving the focus of their consciousness as they develop, and there is a need to guide learners' attention to linguistic forms and their functions. The questions that separate many of these approaches, e.g. altered versus authentic texts, when and how attention is drawn, the need for explicit instruction and what that explicit instruction looks like, are never about whether attention to linguistic forms is necessary.

At some point, we want those forms that were at first the focus of attention to be automatically processed. There are, of course, times when linguistic forms can and should be revisited, but after a certain amount of time, we stop bringing up forms that we (rightly or not) assume are being processed without the need for us to ask students to direct their attention toward them. If we did, we would never be able to ask them about other new grammatical features that allow learners to make new meanings through new linguistic forms and functions. Attentional resources cannot be pointed everywhere at once. They must be relieved by sub- and unconscious processing, with the former attention-requiring activities being either proceduralized or fully automatized, if attention is to be applied to something new.

While the former is true, it is also true that entire processes that are controlled by the conscious mind do not always transfer as a whole into proceduralized and ultimately automatized processes, especially when used for new tasks (Speelman & Kirsner, 1997). And there always seems to be some type of complexity order that is followed by instructors and materials that ignore some aspects of relevant grammar. Some grammatical features are always meant for 'later', or for an advanced grammar course, or only come up when a student notices them (when we don't intend to talk about them). There is a common assumption that certain linguistic features are too complicated or that they require a foothold provided by some 'easier' grammatical feature (McLaughlin, 1992). A prominent example of this in SLA research is the instruction of case marking in many languages. For example, German textbooks often introduce the nominative forms of the definite article for each grammatical gender (masculine, feminine, neuter) with the plural (der, die, das, die, respectively) introduced first, but they don't mention the other three case forms (accusative, dative, genitive) at the same time, even though students are encountering these other cases in almost every sentence they read.[1] Therefore, what we intentionally call into focus seems to be an assumption about what learners can understand and process regarding new grammatical features.

In ISLA, whether we realize it or not, we work with, around and through an established practice of an ideal(ized) sequence of grammatical features and that the order in which we introduce these features is as important as the order in which we either stop spending time discussing and pointing to them or ignore them all together. This *modus operandi* has serious implications for ISLA and brings with it often unspoken theoretical frameworks that guide, consciously or unconsciously on the part of the instructor, what grammar students are intentionally introduced to and when (Byrnes, 2019). These assumptions need critiquing, as they suppose three things:

(1) Language learning occurs in a linear, predictable fashion.
(2) When students notice something out of order, something has gone wrong.

(3) Language teachers and researchers can always predict when learners 'know' enough about a particular grammatical feature and are ready to move on to a new one.

From multiple studies from the perspectives of both complex dynamic systems theory (CDST) (Larsen-Freeman, 1997) and emergentism (MacWhinney, 2006), we know that this is not the case. CDST research has clearly shown that an individual's performance is non-linear (De Bot *et al.*, 2007; Larsen-Freeman, 2015; Rosmawati, 2014). Emergentist work on language acquisition (Eskildsen, 2009) has likewise shown that a linguistic form or feature does not suddenly appear as a fully integrated part of a learner's linguistic repertoire, but rather emerges in a particular instance and then grows in use and function across time and contexts.

From a psycholinguistic point of view, it seems more important to know where and when learners are either becoming aware of or guiding their consciousness to particular grammatical forms. In saying this, I am by no means indicating that teachers do not serve an essential function as experts through training and experience in guiding students toward, drawing attention to and clearly explaining how various linguistic forms create meaning and how learners can use these forms to create meaning and express themselves. Rather, I am advocating here for space to allow students to express what they encounter through their experiences with language and texts, a la incidental language learning, because it may have a more significant impact on acquisition, as the learners themselves have expressed awareness of and possibly readiness for an explanation of a pattern they have noticed. If grammatical forms are only introduced as a pre-planned, assumed order, there could be mismatches between when students are ready to either begin to understand how a particular linguistic form is used and for what purposes, or gain a deeper understanding of a linguistic form that was already introduced and assumed to have been acquired.

Meta-level: Beliefs, goals and motivation

For ISLA, the beliefs, goals and motivations of students have gained import in understanding the language learning outcomes of students (Mohebi & Khodaday, 2011). Beliefs about languages and the language learning processes affect not only what languages students, along with input and guidance from their families, decide to learn, but also what they expect to achieve from the language learning class, what types of activities they expect to do and how they think they will develop their language abilities over time (Kormos & Kiddle, 2011; Papalia, 1978).

Various learning community members, such as teachers and administrators (Pufahl & Rhodes, 2011), set goals, but students can also bring their own goals into their learning experience. Rather than proficiency outcomes or tasks that people on the educational side might be interested in, students who opt for a particular language can have very concrete goals in mind.

Motivation, understood as the will to continue to learn and achieve the goals set by oneself and others, is somewhat more dynamic than beliefs and goals, as it usually changes more frequently or more rapidly over time. It is also describable in terms of positive and negative aspects (in contrast to goals, which, one would assume, a person would not set or be subjected to negative goals, e.g. we hope you can't do X, or you won't be able to X) (MacIntyre & Vincze, 2017). Most studies on these factors have used interviews and surveys which usually involve students recounting what they can remember and telling researchers about what they believe is important to them. Some studies have gone farther and looked at how these factors impact learning outcomes over time (e.g. Moeller *et al.*, 2012).

It is easy to see how one's own life experiences can affect beliefs, goals and motivations, but it is significant that these experiences can also affect language acquisition. They are mitigated by both experiences with and reflections on language and language users (Anya, 2011; Davidson & Lekic, 2010; Gordon, 2011). They can change over time and, in some cases, in an instant. A person can be motivated to learn Spanish because it is the second most used language in the United States until a friend tells them that their Spanish is terrible, and they lose all interest in the language. One can have no reason to have learning Cantonese as a goal until they receive the job offer of a lifetime in Hong Kong. One can believe that German is an ugly language until they hear their future spouse speaking it.

While research has outlined how and why beliefs, goals and motivation can change, the field lacks clear accounting of how these factors are mentally represented and processed during language learning in real time. When they are not being brought in for reflection, what impact do they have on the process? It must be true that a person has beliefs, goals and motivation that are always a part of their mental state, without the simultaneous need to be continually thinking about them (Bargh, 2014; Forgas *et al.*, 2005; Glaser & Kihlstrom, 2005). If reflecting on beliefs, setting and changing goals and recalling the experiences relevant to one's motivation are all higher-order mental operations, then they would consume the majority of one's conscious resources. If a complex task is currently operating in the center of consciousness, this does not mean that one's motivation is completely out of mind. On the contrary, one must have some type of reason motivating them to attempt this complex task. Studies in SLA are still needed that can link asking participants to reflect on their beliefs, goals and motivation before they begin a task to see whether there is an immediate effect for increased task performance. Such studies would provide even more evidence for the idea that these factors are being processed or considered even when conscious attention is being focused elsewhere. As attention transitions between why someone is doing what they are doing and the actual task at hand, it reveals the dynamic nature of attention, both across longer time spans, such as years of education and/or experiences, as well as in the moment, like remembering what your goals are or what is (or not) motivating you right now. All of these play a role in the conscious to subconscious fluctuation of mental processes related to beliefs, goals and motivation, which impact language learning.

Conscious–Subconscious Fluctuation and Interaction

As outlined with both linguistic forms and language (learning)-related concepts, the spotlight of consciousness can only shine on a limited space of mental processes at one time (Whitney & Levi, 2011). However, numerous processes are happening away from the spotlight (Kihlstrom, 2018; Wexler, 1992). The spotlight can shine on many of these processes, but it can't really get much bigger or smaller.[2] Rather, the spotlight of consciousness moves between and among processes.[3] As it does, previous processes that held the spotlight may fade in and out of consciousness, but they do not stop processing information completely; they are just not supported by additional attentional resources and do not take up space in conscious working memory via the central executive. Ample research has shown that cognitive processes that drift or fall out of conscious consideration do not halt or pause until they re-enter consciousness (Kihlstrom, 2018). Even if one holds a modular rather than an interconnected view of language processing, the evidence for continued unconscious or subconscious processing would still include the domain of language.

Research into unconscious or subconscious cognition, which is reviewed here in brief with a focus on its relation to ISLA, has followed two major strands. First, there is work on the processing of subliminal or primed stimuli, which participants do not recall seeing, hearing or experiencing prior to, during or after the study. Greenwald (1992) noted two key developments in understanding conscious and subconscious processing. The first is the concept of the 'subjective threshold', or the lower limit of stimuli exposure below which conscious attention does not catch stimuli and cannot call it into focus or memory. The subjective threshold, as used in psychological research, might not be particularly relevant to ISLA at first, but there are many aspects of the classroom as a physical space, as well as a place of shared activity, which may not be consciously called into focus by a student but their presence in the space and the activity of the student would still impact their behavior and thought processes. The second development that Greenwald (1992: 773) points to is the 'great extent to which memory operates independently of verbal ability to report past experience'. Memory, as previously discussed, includes explicit, implicit and episodic forms, and these can all affect conscious processes (LeDoux & Lau, 2020; Rubin, 2022).

The second area of research into unconscious cognition is more contentious. Questions abound about the limit of unconscious cognition to carry out higher-order cognitive functions like 'causal reasoning, decision making, conflict management, metaphor comprehension, understanding and reasoning by analogies, problem solving, self-control, inferences of various kinds, executive functions, working memory, abstract thinking, and planning' (Hassin, 2013: 196), which Hassin categorizes into three general functions: cognitive control, pursuing goals and managing goal conflicts, and information broadcasting. Looking at event-related potential (ERP) effects, Silverstein *et al.* (2015: 224) acknowledge that 'standard cognitive theory argues that unconscious processes are relatively impoverished and dissipate rapidly'. However, their 'findings contradict these proposals. Rather, they demonstrate functionally active, remarkably complex and sustained unconscious processing' (Silverstein *et al.*, 2015: 224). Increasing data and evidence have led to a spectrum of theories. The strongest of these can be described by Hassin's (2013: 195) 'Yes It Can' principle, in which the author posits that 'unconscious processes can carry out every fundamental high-level function that conscious processes can perform'. Other researchers are less certain of this principle. For example, in a response directly to Hassin (2013), Hesselmann and Moors (2015: 4) counter, 'While we agree with Hassin that progress in science requires new ideas and defaults, we would argue that rather than "yes it can" a more skeptical "definitely maybe" is in much better accordance with the current state of affairs'.

While there are varying degrees of skepticism and optimism, there seems to be a growing acceptance that sophisticated cognitive processes could operate sub- or unconsciously. Based on a review of their own and other experiments, Wokke *et al.* (2011) argue that:

> Although these (and more) studies have revealed that unconscious information processing is relatively sophisticated, critics might still argue that the evidence for (high-level) unconscious cognition is often obtained in situations in which the unconscious stimulus is consistently and frequently paired with task performance on the same conscious stimulus. Then, after substantial practice, unconscious stimuli are able to trigger behavioral and neural effects. (Wokke *et al.*, 2011: n.p.)

Here, the discussion has turned from whether higher-order cognition is possible subconsciously, to how it might be in order to account for new results.

The way in which subconscious and conscious activity interact is another increasingly contested area where the previously assumed split between consciousness and unconsciousness is questioned. For example,

Kiefer (2012: 6) point to the 'accumulating evidence [which] demonstrates that various forms of unconscious processing are susceptible to executive control similar to conscious processing'. This leads to the important question about what is included as part of the unconscious that is available for cognition. Kihlstrom (1999: 194) outlines the content of 'the psychological unconscious' as 'including, in addition to strictly unconscious knowledge structures that compose the architecture of cognition, mental states corresponding to percepts, memories, and thoughts that influence experience, thought, and action outside of phenomenal awareness and voluntary control'. These remnants of experience, one could easily assume, include both attended to and non-attended emotional, sense-related, social, logical and contextual top-down and bottom-up information. Therefore, the unconscious and subconscious have rich pools of information from which to operate. As Kihlstrom (1999: 196) argues 'empirical evidence of preconscious and subconscious percepts, memories, and thoughts remind us that we are not always aware of why we do what we do and that the difference that makes for consciousness is not merely a matter of activation or attentional effort'. In another formulation, Silverstein *et al.* (2015) claim that the unconscious has 'some form of global access'. This has meaningful implications for understanding both student behavior and their goals.

Multiple researchers point to the function of this subconscious processing as a helpful feature in working toward a particular goal. Within the context of viewing information processed by the unconscious and adaptive, Wokke *et al.* (2011) describe the processing of unconscious information as both 'relatively flexible and goal-directed'. Thus, the goals and intentions of the conscious mind can be supported by unconscious processes that are nevertheless pointed toward an objective by conscious attention. This finding is corroborated by Kiefer (2012: 6), who describes this as 'optimizing ongoing processing toward the pursuit of an intended goal', where 'attentional sensitization of unconscious information processing contributes to an effective goal-related adaptation of our cognitive system'. Whatever the exact interaction may be, the implications of unconscious cognition and a reimagined relationship between conscious and unconscious cognition are immense for ISLA and how we theorize what is happening during L2 learning in the classroom. Beliefs do not disappear once one stops reflecting upon them. Processing past-tense marking does not stop (assuming a certain amount of automated processing capacity) when one is concentrating on understanding a complex narrative. Strategies for vocabulary learning or reading comprehension continue to operate in spite of a focus on the semantics of a particular word or passage. Memories that one can later recall did not fade out of existence while attention was elsewhere.

This is all to say that a strict conscious/unconscious divide doesn't seem to fit with the evidence we have about how information is processed, or what is happening when learners engage with and use their L2. Automated linguistic processing of grammatical features can be brought up for reflective discussion. Motivations need not be front and center in one's mind to impact one's learning. Therefore, understanding various behaviors as either conscious or unconscious activities seems contradictory to how behaviors take, retreat from and re-enter conscious thought. This allows us to understand how language learning plays out over multiple timelines. In the short term, dancing between conscious and unconscious processes may allow someone to accomplish a task that requires multiple types of knowledge to be brought together and processed, but which, combined, represent an amount of information that is well above a person's conscious processing and manipulation capacity in a single instant. This is essential to supporting learners during the completion of extremely difficult tasks.

Questions related to how we teach and enable students to do this type of conscious juggling are covered in Chapter 6, which focuses on classroom instruction and pedagogical implications. Equally, how attentional resources pull aspects of the language learning process into and out of consciousness over longer time spans reveals significant aspects of development (both linguistic and non-linguistic). Chapters 4 and 6 cover longer time spans like course units, academic years and even the course of an entire curriculum.

Conclusion: A Continuum of Activity

Chapter 4 focuses more on how this fluctuation between conscious, subconscious and unconscious processing of various linguistic and non-linguistic processes plays out over the course of an individual learner's development, both over the course of a curriculum and within a single class. However, before moving on, it is important to restate the significance of what this re-envisioning means for ISLA, if one accepts my argument that there is a continuous fluctuation between processes, where in one instance a particular cognitive activity enjoying the spotlight of consciousness (or possibly a limited number of activities sharing the limited space available for conscious attention) inevitably slips out of consciousness in favor of something else that either came or was called into focus. In this moment, it is not necessarily true that processes related to that previous activity discontinue. In contrast, those processes continue to operate and support learning, and affect how and what is going on in the conscious mind.

For ISLA, this has significant implications. First, anything that is being instructed will always, at some point, be interrupted, and the ability for an individual learner to focus on any given grammar topic, concept or other learning object is limited. Second, the end of any activity in which we ask learners to focus on particular aspects of language and communication will ultimately impact performance afterward. This is easily observable in the frequent use of warm-up activities. By asking students to perform simple, already learned activities, we assume some activation effect of language that will have a lasting effect as we move to more cognitively demanding activities. Third, as learners shift their conscious focus from one aspect of an activity to another, we would expect dynamic effects on performance.

As more and more of these activities that require conscious attention are functioning in a subconscious space or via unconscious processes, the more complex and variable the tasks we can ask them to complete. But we should still assume that even so-called acquired linguistic features will increase in accuracy or change in form when they are called into conscious focus. This is true for the most advanced L2 users, and even L1 speakers.

For those teaching an L2, there is one important question left that is answered in Chapter 6 covering pedagogical implications for the language learning curriculum, and that is: how does a teacher guide learners' conscious attention while allowing learners' their own agency to guide their consciousness to linguistic forms and language learning-related concepts? These findings can improve our understanding of how to build in various types of tasks, learning opportunities and reflective practices and support learner agency as an anchor for overall curricular design and day-to-day planning and execution.

Notes

(1) If a sentence contains more than one noun, or two in the case of the verbs 'to be' and 'to be called', then there must be a noun in another case.
(2) Although it may get brighter (e.g. being 'in the zone' [Marr, 2001], working within one's expertise [Montero, 2015] or using breathing techniques to increase cognitive performance [Khng, 2017]) or dimmer (e.g. alcohol use [Weiland *et al.*, 2014], hypoxia [Ochi *et al.*, 2018] and toxicity [Hung *et al.*, 2008]).
(3) Although it might be able to capture a few things at one time or flip quickly enough between foci (Lisman & Sternberg, 2013; Manhart, 2004).

4 The Conscious Continuum in Individual Development

Chapter 3 proposed a re-envisioning of conscious and unconscious division and elucidated a conscious–unconscious continuum that allows for the rehashing of, reflection on and dynamic application of proceduralized and automatized information (implicit knowledge) and second language (L2) metalinguistic and linguistic knowledge learned through instruction, incidental learning or deduction on the part of the individual themself (explicit knowledge). In this chapter, this new conceptualization is utilized to imagine an individual's L2 development.

In this chapter, it is essential to keep in mind that this book is written mostly for the purposes of US (and generally Western) classroom experiences and instructed second language acquisition (ISLA), where certain assumptions about the learning environment, student expectations and teacher practices have been made. Therefore, in this section on language learning development, the focus is on the trajectory of an individual within this context. Language learning in the wild, full immersion programs, study abroad and other alternatives to what is typically offered to US students are all important to consider, but outside of the language learning experience of the student whose almost sole access to language education happens within the walls of a school or university. While the trajectory outlined below for language development should still hold true for all learners, other outside experiences and culturally diverse or purposed ways of teaching an L2 could alter the order or pace of learning, the type and amount of various linguistic aspects learned, proceduralized and automatized, as well as the ultimate attainment of learners.

If we continue with the idea that consciousness is dynamic and that it is not only capable of shifting between attentional foci based on the needs of the individual, but that it is also essential that it does so in order to fully envelop the scope of information necessary to learn a complex system like language, then we allow a system to develop that can help explain non-linearity in L2 development. Typically, non-linearity in development is presented through the production of specific grammatical forms over time, but this does not exclude the reality that other aspects of language and language-related knowledge also develop non-linearly (De Bot *et al.*,

2007; Evans, 2019; Larsen-Freeman, 1997). One well-observed pattern is U-shaped learning (Ellis & Wullf, 2014; Williams, 2019; Williams *et al.*, 2022). This learning pattern is of particular interest, as it provides a nice contrast between first language acquisition (L1A) and second language acquisition (SLA). In L1A, it is unclear whether U-shaped patterns of learning are affected by the interventions of caregivers, teachers or the like. It is well documented that children not only over-ride previously learned irregular words when they acquire regular patterns that apply to certain word categories (like past tense -ed marking in English, despite having knowledge of irregular verbs like went), but they also often ignore corrective feedback, even when they have previously shown that they knew how to produce those forms. The following example from Gleason (1967) shows this type of aversion to correction in action:

> She said, 'My teacher holded the baby rabbits and we patted them'.
> I asked, 'Did you say your teacher held the baby rabbits?'
> She answered, 'Yes'. I then asked, 'What did you say she did?'
> She answered again, 'She holded the baby rabbits and we patted them'.
> 'Did you say she held them tightly?' I asked.
> 'No', she answered, 'she holded them looslely'.

Once the regular -ed pattern has been acquired, it is overgeneralized to irregular and regular verbs alike. Through increased input, children eventually overcome this hurdle and return to producing the regular and irregular forms in a target-like fashion.

L2 learners also exhibit U-shaped learning behaviors (Ellis & Wulff, 2014; Williams *et al.*, 2022). Despite multiple explanations, and even with the ability to verbalize the correct form, they still overgeneralize and apply rules they learned to irregular words. This is especially true when they have sufficiently learned a pattern to the point where they can apply it implicitly, and either have no time to reflect on their L2 knowledge (e.g. in speaking or speed-writing activities) or simply do not remember that this particular vocabulary item is an exception. If teachers do not realize that U-shaped learning is a normal and necessary part of language acquisition for first language (L1) and L2 learners alike, they may become frustrated with what they perceive as a lack of understanding and development.

Despite the U-shaped behavior exhibited by L2 learners, they also exhibit a greater ability to correct themselves when presented with previously learned grammar. Adults can be brought to notice errors in their speech and can consciously apply attentional resources to previously learned structures when the acquisitional process of overgeneralization begins, especially when another individual, such as a teacher, guides their attention to the structure in question.

This chapter provides an outline of how consciousness shifts from between these top-down and bottom-up processes. In the beginning, when consciousness shifts to a focus on linguistic awareness and knowledge, consciousness is primarily concerned with bottom-up, small grain-sized, fundamental language features such as sounds and word meanings, as well as low-level processes in need of automatization before other processes can be applied, like conversation maintenance. As more and more of the lower-level language features become established through language use, the learner's consciousness, and therefore attentional resources, become available to notice more complex linguistic features and their related communicative functions.

The Initial State

The initial state of an individual learning an L2 (or additional language) is one of the hardest to define. This term is usually found in the context of generative approaches, likely because of the importance of the accessibility of universal grammar (UG) to the individual. A general definition of the initial state from VanPatten and Benati (2011) is 'the starting point for L2 learners; namely, what they bring to the task of acquiring another language'. For researchers who approach SLA from a minimalist/Chomskian perspective, it entails what can transfer from L1s, L2s and third languages (L3s). What can and can't be learned based on the L1 or L1s of the individual. What features do and do not exist across languages.

From a psycholinguistic perspective, the initial state is an equally important, albeit more nebulous concept, and one that is rooted in the individual's experiences and linguistic knowledge, rather than the general application of an either accessible or inaccessible universal underlying system and the transfer of the L1. Rather than a discussion of parameter (re)setting, psycholinguists describe the initial state as entrenched linguistic patterns and culturally specific conceptual representations realized in mental models for understanding the world (Wilson, 2018). This does not mean that cross-linguistic differences between L1 and L2 (or L3s) are irrelevant. On the contrary, the differences in linguistic structures between languages can help, to some extent, predict where learners of other languages may encounter the biggest problems in terms of understanding and uptake (Lenzing *et al.*, 2013). Knowing that L2 learners are operating from an L1 without grammatical gender, tonal minimal pairs, topicalization, multiple second-person forms based on formality or number of interlocutors, or syntactic scrambling and are starting to learn a language that has one of these features is helpful for anticipating L2 learning issues.

Contextual cues and prior language(s) supremacy

While it is important to decentralize the monolingual speaker as the norm from which we view L2 learners, it is important to analyze the contextual and linguistic environment that many monolingual learners bring to the task of L2 learning. For most monolingual students, the starting point of learning an L2 has already been tainted, for better or worse, by societal beliefs and possibly some limited vocabulary. It would be difficult to imagine a monolingual student who hadn't heard at least some foreign language phrases or words in their life experiences, be it in film or through everyday interactions. But these minor sojourns into foreign means of expression have more to do with the beliefs and values of those languages than any type of acquisitional process.

The nature of L1 speakers' processing has entrenched a particular way or ways of processing language (Hernandez et al., 2005). The more visible aspects of language such as verbs and nouns are likely stable structures in the broad sense, between their L1 and the likely L2s being offered in the US (and world) educational systems. These easily identifiable, fairly concrete vocabulary items serve as gateways into a murky path forward. From this point on, the over-reliance on L1 pathways leads to predictable hurdles, especially when complex morphological and syntactic structures between the L1 and L2 have contrastive forms.

Multilingual students learning another language in an L2 or foreign language classroom bring an even more complex linguistic (if not also diverse cultural) background. Not only do they have experience understanding how two or more linguistic systems can express the same or similar ideas through different lexical and grammatical means (e.g. Byon, 2005), but they also have experience switching between languages, employing bilingual and multilingual skills like translation, code-switching and cross-cultural interpretation. Students who come to the task of L2 learning having grown up around and using multiple languages already know what it means to be bi/multilingual and may be more aware of what they will be able to do and what their identity will be beyond some imaginary native speaker. Learners who have prior experience learning an L2, either as a child or later in life, will bring similar experiences, but they may also have more refined strategies that support their learning than students who learned all of their languages as L1s. All of these complexities both enhance and challenge their experience in the classroom and is something that would hopefully be beneficial to other monolingual peers who are learning the same language with them as part of a learning community.

Developmental steps within the construct of the four skills

Listening, reading, writing and speaking have held privileged places in our understanding of language instruction, and for good reason. Each houses a Cartesian outline of productive versus receptive skills along a timeline of online, in the moment processes versus chances for reflection.

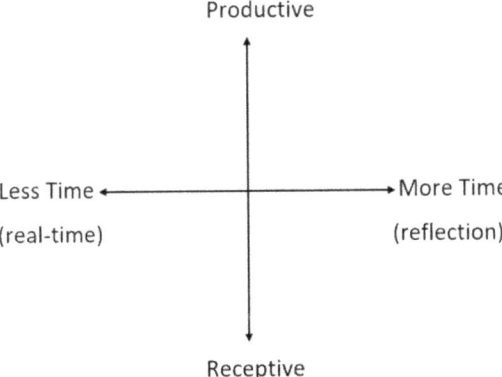

While many activities comprise a mix of these skills, such as writing a speech or reading aloud, beginning with the necessities for each of the four skills provides a solid basis to explore the resources required for learners to be successful when they encounter more complex, combined skill activities.

Listening

Every sentence that contains a new word is a sentence in which a learner must dedicate resources to parsing, analyzing, questioning and then either guessing based on available knowledge, skipping and allowing for whatever lack of comprehension results from not understanding or saving it for later when more contextual information makes its deduction feasible or a trip to the dictionary resolves it. Simultaneously, a speaker of a new language will recognize both words and phrases. It is clear that language learners encounter spoken language which they try to both decipher into individual words as well as hear full chunks that are associated with whole meanings rather than any linguistic connections beyond the sound of the phrase. When an L2 learner encounters the sounds of a new language, they are confronted with a few monumental tasks. First, they need to distinguish between sounds that are the same or at least similar enough between their language or languages and the new language to transfer, those that are very different and, hardest of all, those sounds that are different from but close enough to sounds the learner already knows but from which they need to be distinguished. L2 learners, unlike child L1 learners, and especially pre-verbal babies, already have specific sounds that they have been trained through usage to recognize. Sounds around and near those established sounds, depending on relative closeness, might not even be distinguishable for L2 learners. For example, it has been shown that children can hear differences in phonemes from other languages up to a certain age, but afterward lose the ability to discriminate between them (Narayan, 2019).

The second major challenge that learners face is learning the consonant and vowel combinations that are and are not allowed. For example, L1 Arabic speakers learning English encounter a consonant onset /p/; L1 Japanese speakers encounter multiple CCC clusters (where C = consonant, V = vowel, e.g. CVC = consonant-vowel-consonant cluster like /bob/) as in the words *strong* and *risks*; and L1 English learners of Japanese would be surprised to hear only vowels or /n/ in syllable codas. These patterns of allowable consonant and vowel clusters aid L1 speakers in a number of ways. First, it allows them to better predict vocabulary based on knowledge of allowable upcoming sounds (Nixon, 2020). Second, and toward the third hurdle, it can also help them determine the beginning and end of words, especially when sound groupings form different morphological markers (e.g. *-ness*, *-able* or *pre-*) (Schmidt-Renfree, 2020). L2 learners encounter a speech stream, from a teacher in the classroom, a speaker in 'the wild' or via some form of media, as a mostly unbroken chain of sound (Figure 4.1).

Therefore, one of the most important aspects of early SLA, one that learners not only do automatically in their L1, but cannot stop doing, is parsing sound into separate words and, hopefully, also parsing words into composite morphological pieces where possible. In the first encounters with these sound symbols, there is little to help the beginning learner beyond prior knowledge, language transfer from L1s and other L2s and cognates. Visual aids and contexts can go a long way in supporting word segmentation, especially if students are provided with written language (Karimi, 2013) and even more so if there are spaces between words in the writing system of that language (Huettig & Pickering, 2019).

At the same time that learners are encountering a speech stream made up of smaller sound symbols, they are also experiencing larger chunks of language that, as a whole, they can typically assign some sort of meaning to, especially if that comprehension is aided by outside resources like a teacher's hand gesture or facial expression (Sueyoshi & Hardison, 2005), a visual aid or the context in which they find themselves in the real world. The classroom itself, as will be discussed in Chapters 5 and 6, brings with it its own context that students can leverage to understand larger chunks. Here, suffice to say that there is a heavy dose of top-down processing at play to compensate for the severe lack of bottom-up capabilities. Processing whole chunks for meaning can bootstrap listening comprehension (McCauley & Christiansen, 2017) and students are often surprised at how much they 'understand' on the first day, assuming they have some aptitude for combining contextual cues with the instructor's visual aids, gestures and modelling.

However, scaffolding can only go so far before learners need to identify words and their boundaries to comprehend more complex oral communication. Especially if students want to be successful at tasks that do not allow for visual aids, like talking over the phone (Iwashita *et al.*,

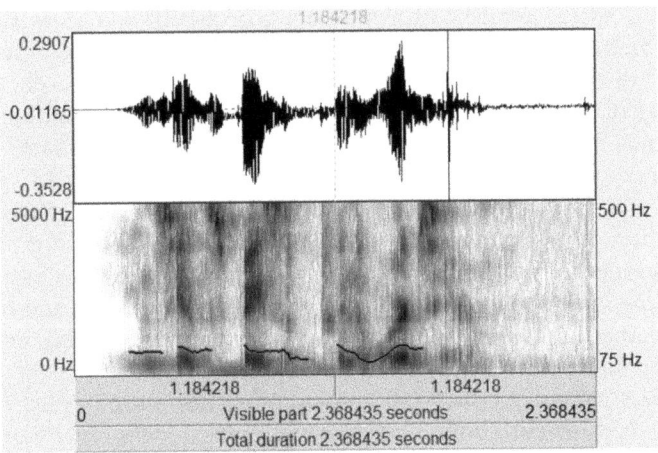

Figure 4.1 'I don't think you can see the spaces between the words here'

2001). This is probably why phone conversations are perpetually listed as one of the least favorite tasks of L2 speakers; they have no visual aids to support comprehension, and things that might have been picked up by non-verbal or contextual cues that aren't always automatically processed are solely available as oral input. The identification of word boundaries and the anticipation of allowable, or at least the inhibition of non-allowable sound clusters, hopefully lead to at least two advanced listening behaviors. The first is the identification of morphological aspects of individual words. Repetitions of clusters in various word-internal positions which appear with other words of a similar type (e.g. nouns versus verbs) should become more apparent as less conscious effort is needed to hear the boundaries between words and more processing space is available to the learner to analyze word-internal composition.

The second behavior is the growing automatization of predictive abilities. There are at least two types of prediction. The first type is predicting the meaning or intended meaning of what someone is trying to convey orally. Oftentimes, we know what someone is going to say before they say it, but that is assuming we know what they have been talking about. As L2 listening competency grows, so too should the learner's ability to predict to a certain degree where the conversation is going. A lot of this skill might have the opportunity to transfer from L1 listening skills and strategies, now that L2 proficiency is not acting as a barrier.

The other type is more linguistic in nature. It is the ability to predict syntactic structures as they are being built in real time by the speaker. Initially, when learners are listening to oral input in the L2, they do not know enough of the L2 syntactic possibilities to predict what should come next and any confusion arises from L1 or other previously learned language expectations about the order of constituents and their component parts.

However, as L2 learners gain increasing proficiency in their L2, they learn which syntactic structures are possible and build them in real time along with the speaker. This has been evidenced through event-related potential (ERP) studies. They show that after a certain amount of L2 proficiency has been achieved, L2 learners can develop the same neurological reactions to ungrammatical and illogical language as L1 speakers (for examples, see Bowden et al., 2013; Caffarra et al., 2015; Rossi et al., 2006). Interestingly enough, it should be seen as a sign of major progress for L2 learners if they do fall into garden path sentences. This means that they know what the most common syntactic structures are and fall into the same predictive predicaments that L1 speakers do. This might, in fact, be a way to test advanced L2 aural proficiency.

As less cognitive effort and conscious attention are needed for and directed at connecting sound–meaning mappings, identifying words and morphemes and processing syntactic structures in real time, learners can shift that focus on planning what they want to say while they successfully comprehend and predict what someone is going to say.

Speaking

While listening could best be described as the disentanglement of symbolic code into meaning in real time, speaking could be described as the opposite process, with an additional step. First, the meaning a person wants to express needs to be translated into the appropriate symbolic system involving both conscious and unconscious processes. That is, a person knows what they want to say, but the way in which lexical items are selected for particular meanings, how morphology is applied and the syntactic structure selected occur without necessary conscious thought. This does not mean that one cannot apply a conscious filter to what one is saying and how one formulates it, but that requires monitoring that is not necessary in the generation of the utterance. The second step is translating that symbolic code into sound symbols via the articulatory system. Here, we are involving the motor cortex and the oral articulators like the jaw and tongue, and also combining these with body language-like gestures (be they meaning-bearing or self-serving) and facial expressions.

The amazing phenomenon of human speech capacity exemplifies the connected parallel processing of which the human mind is capable. We build sentences and discourse in time while we are articulating the already formulated meanings we have translated into symbols. We do not wait until we have completely constructed the symbolic code in our minds before we hand it over to the motor cortex for articulatory coordination. As Hopper (1987) explains:

> in natural discourse we compose and speak simultaneously (Smith, 1975: 60). There is no room — no need — for mediation by mental structures. It

is in this sense that, as Bolinger has pointed out (Bolinger, 1976), speaking is more similar to remembering procedures and things than it is to following rules. It is a question of possessing a repertoire of strategies for building discourses and reaching into memory in order to improvise and assemble them. Grammar is now not to be seen as the only, or even the major, source of regularity, but instead grammar is what results when formulas are re-arranged, or dismantled and re-assembled, in different ways. (Hopper, 1987: 145)

This quote needs some unpacking, as it was originally formulated around L1 speech but is also highly relevant to the L2 speaker. First, we may want to think of 'remembering procedures' as using implicit knowledge that is automatically fired, as compared to 'following the rules', which, in an L1 context might be seen as calculating and applying morphology. Within an L2 context, it is even more important to describe the 'rule' mentioned above because, unlike L1 learners, many L2 learners are taught and know, explicitly, rules for computing morphology and word orders.

Here, we return to chunking, or the repertoire of pre-assembled phrases available to a learner for which they do not need to apply rules in the sense that we teach them (Carey, 2013). If they are to be successful and deemed both 'fluent' and 'accurate' by their interlocutor, they cannot stop every time they encounter a noun-verb agreement conjugation or take time to think about inversion when asking yes-no questions. They simply need to grab a functional, appropriate chunk and spit out the whole thing. Later, we will talk about the proceduralization of applied morphology, and to what extent chunks versus patterns are utilized, but for the beginning stages of speech, the early L2 speaker is wholly reliant on chunks of language to do the dirty work of containing all the necessary morphosyntactic operations that express the meaning they intend to convey.

For L2 learners, language planning ahead of time can aid in fluency for beginners who are starting to produce language that goes beyond memorized chunks and requires some degree of computation or pattern application (De Jong & Perfetti, 2011). This includes both anticipating what you would like to say along with actual repetition, be it mentally, subvocally or out loud. For beginning learners and throughout a large part of their learning experience, balancing fluency and accuracy will remain arduous because spoken language necessarily requires the cooperation of multiple language-related areas simultaneously, especially since listening comprehension may not be fully automated and takes up some of the conscious and working memory capacity of the individual for new or unfamiliar vocabulary, difficult morphological and syntactic constructions and longer utterance lengths or extended discourse. This means that consciousness, and in relation to computations and the application of patterns, working memory, can only pay attention to so many non-proceduralized functions at the same time. For many learners, the trade-off comes at the cost of either the accurate application of patterns or learned rules, or a reduction in fluency, or even a decrease in target-like pronunciation. Only once a significant portion of language production has been automated does speaking become more manageable and something that consciousness can reflect on even partly in real time.

As the learner advances in proficiency, two sources of fluency should increase in capacity. First, the application of various grammatical aspects and the construction of increasingly complex syntactic constructions should become proceduralized and remove the need for conscious effort. Second, the learner's repertoire of both functional and whole chunks should be expanding both in terms of breadth, i.e. total number of expressions known, as well as depth, i.e. the complexity of the types of chunks as well as the variability of their functionality and the number of items they can apply in slot-filler constructions. These two advances allow the conscious mind to focus more on other important aspects of conversing, like paying attention to emotional and other interpersonal states being expressed by the interlocutor, choosing appropriate registers, making observations and interpretations of what is being said, and managing the conversation. These higher-order interpersonal skills require extensive training and consciousness to manifest effectively, so some learners may act very differently when conversing in their L1(s) than in the target language.

Reading

One of the first issues that learners have to deal with when learning to read a foreign language is identifying sound–symbol mappings. Recall the description of writing systems from Chapter 2, and the way that linguistic information is represented through graphemes varies greatly. When learning a logographic or morphosyllabic language, a learner is confronted with three pieces of knowledge simultaneously: a symbol, a corresponding sound and a corresponding meaning. However, for a person learning a syllabic or alphabetic language, there are two steps. The grapheme(s) only has two pieces of knowledge: the symbol(s) and the corresponding sound. The corresponding meaning is only revealed once the learner has translated the graphemes into a phonetic expression.

Multiple factors go into L2 reading. Koda (2005) states that there are three distinct constructs that affect successful L2 reading comprehension: L1 reading, L2 proficiency and L2 decoding. L1 reading refers to the general reading skills and proficiency that the learner brings with them and transfers to reading in an L2. L2 proficiency, which is gone into in more detail later in this chapter, can be safely described here as L2 knowledge, both explicit and implicit, or in other words, what the learner knows about and what the learner can do in the L2. L2 decoding is probably most relevant when we talk about the first hurdle that an L2 learner will encounter when they are presented with their L2 in writing for the first time.

The encoding of both sound and meaning in one symbol reduces the number of processing steps, at least computationally, in contrast to languages that use graphemes to encode sounds only, like syllabic and alphabetic languages, which then must be processed for meaning after the sound has been recognized. However, the one-to-one mapping of symbol, sound and meaning results in a very large set of symbols needed to represent each word or meaning that can be expressed in that language, which makes learning the requisite number of symbols necessary to be able to read a daunting task. In fact, Taylor and Taylor (2014) estimate that 3500 characters are needed for everyday use, and that 6000 are needed for academic purposes.

Syllabic writing systems, or syllabaries, like Cherokee, and katakana and hiragana in Japanese, require far fewer symbols to be learned because only the sound is mapped onto the symbol, so the combination of multiple sounds results in the appropriate word or meaning (and, of course, some meanings are just one syllable) (Koda, 2005). There are a number of other syllabary-like writing systems, such as Thai and Telugu, but the use of diacritics or other markings, or the combination of alphabetic-like symbols into a syllable make them slightly different to process, in that grapheme internal markings allow for the identification of individual sounds found within the syllable. For example, the individual diacritic on a grapheme in Telugu might tell you that the consonant-vowel pair has an /a/ sound, and you wouldn't need to remember the entire symbol to make the appropriate translation.

Alphabets, falling at the opposite end of the spectrum from logographic languages, map a grapheme onto a single consonant or vowel (Koda, 2005). This creates the smallest number of symbols necessary to represent spoken language. Those sounds are then combined to form words. Or at least that is how they are supposed to work. Unfortunately, alphabetic languages present their own set of problems for learners based on their transparency.

More transparent writing systems have fewer overlapping letter clusters that make the same sounds and fewer overlapping sounds formed by different letter clusters (Koda, 2005). Here are two clear examples of each case from English, respectively:

- multiple letter clusters making the same sound: '*a*', '*bay*', '*sleigh*';
- single letter clusters making different sounds: '*though*' '*tough*' '*thought*' '*thou*'.

There are also sounds in a language that do not map to any individual letter, like /ʃ/ in English, represented by 'sh'.

The second problem with sound–symbol mapping is the fact that sounds that do not exist in another language can and are represented with the same or similar symbols, assuming the two languages share an alphabet, such as /x/ in German, represented by the letter combination 'ch'.

In addition to the challenges a learner faces when they learn a language with a single writing style, some languages, like Japanese, make use of more than one orthography. Japanese uses both logographic/morphosyllabic Chinese characters, called kanji, and two syllabaries, hiragana, for Japanese morphology that cannot be represented by kanji, and katakana, which is used for foreign words. This means that readers of Japanese need to process graphemes that have both sound and meaning encoded, as well as graphemes that only encode sound and require phonological processing to access meaning (Koda, 2005; Tamaoka, 1991).

The written script of each target language presents its own challenges to learners, who have the difficult task of memorizing grapheme–sound (and possibly grapheme meaning) combinations and processing them in order to extract meaning from texts in the target language. The ease of reading in another language is strongly related to the amount of transfer possible (Holm & Dodd, 1996). And here I mean transfer both in terms of linguistic and cultural knowledge, as well as processing routines. The more similarly structured a writing system is to another, the more easily learners can transfer their knowledge about how the writing system operates and their ability to process it (Koda, 2005). However, similarly designed orthographies can still cause issues for learners, especially when top-down L1 information overlays differing L2 processing requirements. Thus, if too much L1 knowledge or processing is assumed, learners might miss differences that are needed to properly interpret graphemes. Another issue that learners encounter are languages with a shared alphabet or script but with additional letters or diacritics. Here also, the similarity in form between a grapheme in the L2 writing system poses a larger problem than letters that are easily distinguished from graphemes in previously learned languages' writing systems.

Some of these reading errors continue long after they have been explicitly corrected because the L1 activation pattern for that letter combination has been protected by other fully appropriate transfers of grapheme processing. In a language using a different alphabet, it is less likely that these types of errors occur because either there is no way, or the learner assumes there is no way to transfer grapheme processes from the L1 to the L2.

Whatever the language and whatever the writing system used, decoding is an important skill that is highly beneficial for L2 learning. This is true if one views reading as a way to build vocabulary or reading as a place where learners can reflect on grammatical usage, text structure and author choices, or even just as a means of input. L2 reading is a skill of translating complex sound–grapheme relationships into their corresponding sounds. As Koda (2005: 33) argues, 'the benefits of decoding competence are not restricted to (...) alphabetic languages in general. Crosslinguistic studies repeatedly suggests that phonological decoding also is important in nonalphabetic languages'. Thus, the benefits of decoding skills are numerous, including speeding up reading, assisting in text comprehension and improving L2 morphological awareness. Before moving on from decoding, it seems appropriate to use Koda's (2005: 34) own formulation to emphasize the importance of gaining procedural knowledge of L2 decoding ability: 'All in all, it seems reasonable to conclude that phonological decoding is perhaps the most indispensable competence for reading acquisition in all languages'.

Once a learner has begun the process of learning and hopefully automatizing grapheme recognition and phonological decoding, the next step is similar to the first phase of listening, that being parsing. For English speakers, and those of many other languages, this might seem like a trivial step, but written languages, like ancient Greek and modern Chinese, do complicate the parsing of written words. And there are other difficulties with word recognition in written language that go beyond identifying the edges of words. For instance, written standard Arabic has two different versions: pointed and non-pointed. In pointed Arabic script, short vowels are indicated by diacritic markings. However, in non-pointed Arabic, these diacritics are left out and the reader needs to have significant knowledge of the word to automatically fill in the missing sounds (Abu-Rabia, 2001). Hebrew, another Semitic language, functions similarly. No vowels are listed in the Hebrew alphabet. Ancient Hebrew used diacritics to indicate all vowel sounds, but these are not typically included in modern Hebrew (Schiff & Ravid, 2004). Another processing problem for English learners that arises from learning a foreign language like Arabic or Hebrew is the direction of visual display. That is, if your L1 is English, or Swedish, or Hungarian, you are used to moving your eyes left to right when moving from one word to the next. However, if you are learning Arabic, you need to process right to left, both at the grapheme and word level (see e.g. Zhang & Roberts, 2021).

As the learner progresses in their L2 reading abilities, they begin to identify words faster and faster. They no longer need to break down every word into its constituent pieces, assuming that the language they are learning uses a syllabary or alphabet, through a growing list of sight words. At this stage, learners are still learning how to read, although the process is a bit different from children at a similar stage in their reading development. For children, learning to read is mostly the application of known words to a new visual representation of those words (Fox & Alexander, 2011). Once they are comfortable with words they already know, they move on to a phase called reading to learn,[1] where they encounter new words and ideas not already present as part of their spoken vocabulary. L2 learners are usually learning to read and reading to learn at the same time. They have world, contextual and L1 linguistic knowledge to help them interpret new L2 words, as well as skills to find out words they do not know, including guessing from contextual and linguistic cues and using tools such as dictionaries. The simultaneous learning of the language and learning with the language is one of the most pervasive aspects of the language classroom that divides L1 and L2 reading acquisition. While this idea of simultaneous language learning and use will be covered in more detail, suffice it to say that it is a challenge for both learners and teachers.

Through continued practice with reading, the language learner begins to automatically process graphemic information at a more rapid pace. In doing so, computational resources that were once dedicated to interpreting symbols, sounding out words, guessing the meaning of unknown words and recognizing known words, are now free to direct their attention elsewhere. Two important areas are text comprehension and grammatical knowledge. First, text comprehension requires the integration of the text, known information and new information. Second, now that words are automatically recognized, there is time for reflection on the language itself, including morphology, syntax, idiomatic expressions and pragmatics, which may have previously been possible in smaller segments of texts, but can now be seen throughout larger or more complex pieces of writing (Kroll *et al.*, 2002).

Writing

Unlike fluid speech, the production of a written text is a slower, more deliberate process (Williams, 2012). Where habits and implicit processes play a major role in speech, the fact that writing is drawn out over a longer period of time allows learners to rely more heavily on their explicit and metalinguistic knowledge about the L2, the task's genre expectations and production and planning strategies. In other words, the task of writing allows access to strategies and reflection in the moment and as part of the editing process (Daive, 1997). The slowed-down and reiterative nature of writing, which Vanderburg (2006) describes as interactive flexibility, or recursion, between the writing stages of planning, translating and reviewing (Hayes & Flowers, 2016), theoretically allows for more time to access linguistic and metalinguistic knowledge, or explicit information useful for text comprehension.

This added time for reflection holds true for both before and during the writing process. Before writing begins, what some might call pre-writing or the planning phase, assuming that it isn't some type of free write or stream of consciousness activity, writers have time to think about things like genre, purpose, audience, text structure, as well as rhetorical concepts like stakes, evidence and claims, where to find sources to support their arguments and other rhetorical practices that make for effective writing. Although it must be stated that writers do not necessarily do all or any of these things, as it takes years of instruction and practice to master as much in the L1 as in the L2. Along with these larger concepts should come the linguistic resources to begin and hopefully accomplish the writing task ahead of the individual. The tenses are needed to tell a story. The subjunctive forms are needed to discuss hypothetical situations. Different word orders are needed to build topical cohesion. For L1 speakers, some of these forms might automatically apply, but L1 linguistic knowledge, especially knowledge learned for the specific purpose of writing and to form different registers, is also available for L1 speakers to reflect on. All of these thoughts are also available during the writing process since writing is not nearly as linear a process as speech (Hayes & Flower, 1981). Writers have the opportunity to reflect on their work in the middle of its creation, making changes and edits on the fly before anyone else has the chance to read it; therefore, the language produced by L2 writers is often much more complex and well-structured because they are able to rely on resources that they cannot recall in real-time language production, like speech.

For L2 writers, this is one of their first challenges. They might know what they want to say and have ample L1 writing skills and knowledge at their disposal, but they do not know the form–function mappings in the L2 to get across their intended message, with the intended tone and form, to their readers. For beginning and even more advanced writers, they might not know what the appropriate L2 form is to express their intended meaning. There are also many linguistic decisions that might only be relevant in the L1 or the L2 that do not apply in the other language.

In addition to issues of inadequate L2 knowledge, transfer of what L2 writers know about the writing process from their L1 may be beneficial in terms of giving them insight into how to build a text, genre expectations and writing strategies, but it can also cause problems for L2 writers (Karim & Nassaji, 2013); different cultural expectations within and between writing communities are frequent sources of error or negative transfer.

Citation practices are a prime example of negative transfer effects. For many international students in the United States, citing sources is either not part of or not important to the writing process in the culture from which they come, and doing so is not only a foreign concept, but one that takes a significant amount of time for them to understand the differences between what can and cannot be cited (Fazilatfar *et al.*, 2018). With this mismatch recognition, many L2 English speakers focus very intensely on making sure that they cite everything, to the point that there are citations for things that are so obviously common knowledge that the papers are almost unreadable due to citations and references in every line.

Conscious attention to this issue is important, but it is also critical that teachers understand that these students' conceptual development of what does and does not need to be cited is not solved by lectures or descriptions of expectations, but rather continued writing, with the opportunity to reflect and ask questions about the citations within a meaningful context, over multiple iterations and a long period of time. The appropriation of cultural norms is not something that is done overnight. A writer might explicitly know that they need to cite information, but the answers to when, how and why take time to accumulate and condense through situated learning.

Another common problem that L2 writers must overcome is formulating their texts in their L1 or some other language and attempting to translate directly from the L1 to the L2. In the beginning stages of language development, this often causes students to attempt L2 structures that they either don't understand or maybe don't even know, with the aid of outside resources.[2] Writing a first draft or large amounts of text in an L1 or another language in which the learner is more proficient is a strategy that can last well into advanced stages of development.

Beyond the Four Skills: A Proposed Trajectory of Individual Language Learning

To provide clearly defined developmental processes and milestones for each of the four skills, I began with a division between those skills and their actual application to activities in which learners are engaged that require coordination of these skills, as well as other sources of knowledge. In this section, an interconnected perspective is taken on the stages of individual language development, through which a learner goes over the course of their language learning trajectory, specifically from some initial stage to some advanced stage,[3] understanding that many, if not most learners, at least those who learn an L2 in a US context, do not reach an advanced stage of language development in actuality.[4]

Parsing

As laid out in the previous sections on the receptive tasks of listening and reading, parsing is one of the first challenges that language learners must overcome. Parsing is a skill that comes in time, with repeated exposure to meaningful elements of languages. Some aspects of parsing have been learned in isolation, like individual words or chunks embedded within utterances. Others have been learned by hearing and seeing larger segments of language in use, like phonological patterns of word beginnings and endings. And most likely, exposure to written language has supported parsing, assuming the language has a writing system, and that the writing system allows learners to see spaces between words and clauses through spacing or punctuation.

Parsing is not a skill that comes to a learner all at once. Repeated use and work with the L2 gradually allow learners to distinguish between words more easily. It often comes as a result of the intersection of reading and listening. It requires at least some recognition of words (parts or whole), what words come where, morphological affixes and other patterns of phonetic, syllabic, morphological and syntactic features present in the L2 (Hopp, 2016).

Parsing words in real time, let alone recognizing words and assigning them meaning, takes an enormous amount of concentration and conscious attention for L2 learners to have any success. As the learner's vocabulary and L2 knowledge grow, parsing known words should become easier, allowing the learner to at least recognize what parts of the utterance they weren't able to parse yet. As learners begin to automatically recognize known words, they can then apply more conscious attention to other parts of the language they are not able to parse. As L2 knowledge grows and the practice of parsing and producing language increases, learners should be able to parse and 'hear' words that they do not know so that they can look them up later. In addition, learners also have a growing sense of word-internal boundaries, such as the differences between lexemes, like roots and stems, and morphological affixes. This does not mean that word recognition must precede morphology-level boundaries. Especially if learners are being introduced to various agreement patterns, they should notice that word roots are accompanied by morphology, and this does not need to wait until learners have been able to successfully distinguish between all or even most words in an utterance.

Parsing is often seen as an unconscious activity, but for L2 learners, it takes a lot of conscious effort before anything remotely automated occurs, even if unconscious processes are recruited (Marcel, 1983).

Automating sound/grapheme mapping

Specific to reading and writing, the most important process that a beginning learner can automate is the mapping of graphemes (and for many types of writing systems like alphabets, combinations of graphemes) onto their corresponding sounds. In some respects, learners at this stage (assuming they are already literate in another language) are returning from a state of 'reading to learn' to 'learning to read', although not quite the same. When child learners begin to learn how to read, they bring a solid linguistic repertoire and vocabulary with them when they learn to read for the first time. They know what words sound like, and it is their job to figure out how these sounds map onto the graphemes presented to them in their respective languages. L2 learners face a similar problem but bring different resources to it. L2 learners know they can use texts to learn new things. L1 learners, on the other hand, initially encounter texts containing words and concepts with which they are familiar or already know about. Thus, their learning to read precedes much of reading to learn. L2 learners are presented with the challenge of learning to read while simultaneously attuned to the fact that they are also reading to learn. In other words, they are looking for information in texts that they don't already know.

The problem that L2 learners face here is that they have an extremely limited amount of L2 linguistic knowledge, including everything from vocabulary and grammar, to syntax, text structure and cultural knowledge. Thus, when they encounter even elementary texts, a large part of their time is learning meanings of words as they are mapping the language's phonetics to its graphemes. This double duty makes reading an especially trying task for beginning learners.

However, adult L2 learners bring other, mature cognitive resources to the table that child learners do not, including learning and reading strategies, an immense amount of prior knowledge about the world, an understanding of classroom practices and teacher expectations and L1 (and maybe other L2) metalinguistic knowledge. This plays out in different ways as learners gain more and more L2 knowledge, but some of the primary concepts they bring with them in their first attempts at reading include the idea that written language can reflect spoken language, but that written language often differs from spoken language in terms of vocabulary, structure, length, grammatical complexity, style and purpose. They also know that texts serve different functions. For example, if an L2 student is told that they are reading an email, they will probably expect the first word or words to be some type of greeting and the end to include some type of sign off, whereas child L1 learners are not aware of many text and genre expectations, be it explicitly or implicitly.

As learners grapple with the challenge of learning to read and reading to learn at the same time (Koda, 2005), they will encounter one of two hurdles (or a combination of the two). For languages with an alphabet, they will see words that have combinations of letters that they have not previously encountered, or they will encounter combinations of letters that they have seen before but that are mapped onto different sounds (think back to the example in Chapter 2 on *ough* in English). If the language they are learning is transparent enough, they will be able to sound out the words. However, the less transparent the relationship between letters and sounds, the less successful this strategy will become, and they will need to rely on outside resources to decipher the correct sound/symbol(s) mapping. If they are learning a language with a syllabary, which tends to be more transparent, as the creation of syllables and sound combinations is not reliant on a combination of individual letters, there should be fewer problems for learners to use a sound-it-out method, assuming they have had the time to memorize the entire syllabary.

The most challenging languages for beginning learners are those that employ morphosyllabic or logographic languages.[5] This is because there is almost no transparency between grapheme and sound.[6] Even if a learner is coming from another morphosyllabic or logographic language, and assuming they don't share some base or historic character system, even that learner will have to memorize all the new character–sound pairings (even if they might have the advantage of memorizing characters from their prior experience).

In sum, a learner at this early stage of reading and writing development is highly reliant on any and all L1 or previously learned L2 strategies, with only a small amount of L2 knowledge available to them. Continued reading (and assuming correct phonological mapping onto the writing system) will lead to proceduralization and eventual automatization of this process, although highly homophonic or homographic patterns, or ones that contrast with entrenched L1 phoneme–grapheme mappings might prove troublesome for quite a while.

Chunked language and grammar

For both oral and written production at the beginning stage, the ability to apply grammatical features falls into a few categories. A grammatical form:

(1) is produced correctly as an uninterpreted part of a memorized chunk;
(2) has been identified and to some extent analyzed, assuming it is easily identified in the input or has been specifically pointed out by another individual and is simple enough in form to be correctly produced in writing and maybe even speaking, assuming enough time for the learner to consciously apply it;
(3) has been identified and to some extent analyzed, assuming it is easily identified in the input or has been specifically pointed out by another individual, but is not simple enough in form to be correctly produced in speaking, and maybe not even in writing;
(4) has been identified but has not been analyzed to the point of comprehension or ability to apply accurately and is either randomly correct or incorrect.

Of the possibilities, the first and last are the most common for very beginning learners, which makes the most effective method of communication for the processing and production of chunks of language which the learner can rely on for a complete meaning. By this, I mean a chunk of language that expresses the entire meaning the learner wishes to communicate without the need to think about vocabulary choice or grammar. These chunks can be used within the classroom environment fairly reliably, as both the teacher and the students have used them together in this context, the intended meaning of the phrase was learned as a class and so there is shared knowledge, and the context itself doesn't change drastically from day to day, making it a fairly reliable resource from which to make assumptions. In the real world, these chunks, especially if used as predictors of what someone is going to say to the learner, are not as useful, because a number of contextual, social and pragmatic factors have been assumed within the context of the classroom and the learner is usually not aware of how they could alter this chunk to make it more appropriate based on a change of interlocutor, tone or register. All this is to say that while chunked grammar might not be the most effective tool outside the classroom, it can be extremely useful in ISLA as the context in which the learner produces these chunks is relatively stable.

Two of the reasons that chunks are learned so well are that they are meaningful within the classroom context and they are frequently used throughout the class not only by the teacher, but also by all of the other students who are reliant on these chunks to navigate the L2 classroom with a limited amount of L2 proficiency. These chunks can often be remembered long after individuals have stopped learning their L2.

In addition to the automatization of word boundaries, learners also begin to gain some anticipatory and predictive expectations for what words or word types will follow others. This could be very simple in the beginning. For example, in subject-verb-object (SVO) languages, a learner will probably become very familiar with a pronoun beginning an utterance with a verb following it. On the other hand, someone learning an object-verb-subject (OVS) language should begin to anticipate the position of the pronoun after the verb. Whether they do this from the start is highly dependent on the syntactic structures allowed in their previously acquired/learned languages, so this might end up being easier or more challenging depending on the L1/L2 language pairings of an individual learner. If we reflect for a second on the role of consciousness in the L2 learning process, these top-down expectations from the L1 are initially unconsciously transferred, and would likely stay this way until the learner finds that this entrenched L1 expectation of subject-verb sequence conflicts with the sequence found in the L2. Then, assuming the learner is aware that this is possible and notices this difference, they will then likely focus more of their conscious attention on this order. Saliency first comes to learners as obvious overlaps or contradictions between the L1s and other previously learned languages and the L2. Then, as more L2 knowledge is gained, other less obvious patterns become visible to the learner.

Early Active Learning: The Search for Systematicity

Another early L2 learner behavior is the search for patterns. Humans are excellent at seeing patterns (Mattson, 2014), which probably stems from our primal need to categorize the objects in our world to make sense of them. When applied to languages, learners recognize salient and reliable patterns in the input (MacWhinney, 2005a). However this does not apply to all linguistic patterns available in the input, especially complex ones like declensional morphology in some case marking systems.

So, why do learners not notice or acquire patterns that are ever present in the input, like the third-person /s/ in English verbal morphology? This issue arises from the fact that the learner does not see or associate a meaning with the pattern (Guo & Ellis, 2021; MacWhinney, 2022; Murakami & Ellis, 2022). Taking the English third-person /s/ example, none of the other subject-verb agreements in English apply any morphology, and it is not like English is a pro-drop language in the sense of Spanish where the processing of the verbal morphology is necessary to correctly interpret the omitted subject pronoun. For very complex patterns, this might also be the case. Either the number of forms, or some confusion from the forms related to homophony/-graphy, prevent the learner from actually using the information to process the form for meaning. If there is a difference between the L1 and L2, where the form in the L2 isn't even something that the learner would normally process in their own language, like grammatical gender, for instance, then it makes it even more difficult because there are no L1 processes that could transfer which would be usable to decode such information. So, while early L2 learners may be looking for patterns, some patterns may be hidden or incomprehensible to early learners until greater L2 proficiency and knowledge are attained.

Early Acquisition

As learners encounter more of the target language and receive more instruction on what to look for, they begin to recognize learned vocabulary and start proceduralizing some early processes like grapheme–phoneme mapping, word boundary recognition, some morphological identification and even knowledge of possible simple syntactic structures (Kachinske, 2021). The following sections outline how these early automated processes are formed and open up room for the learner to apply working memory and consciousness to the analysis of both smaller and larger aspects of the L2.

Smaller, productive chunks

While the language learner is heavily reliant on the use of entire chunks for early communication, over time and use they gain the ability to use chunks in a different capacity; namely, the chunks become frameworks that serve as slot-and-filler constructions which allow for substitution (for a fuller explanation of construction grammar, see Croft [2007], and especially usage-based construction grammar, see Bybee [2013] and Diessel [2015]). Let us use an example starting with a typical chunk that one might encounter early on in an L2 class and how that phrase might develop from a single chunk into a more productive chunk that allows for the replacement of particular elements within itself, creating a frame of language with a slot that can be filled with similar types of words and phrases to the one that was removed.

From very early on, most language learners are taught to both ask and say how old they are:

'How old are you?'
'I am twenty years old'

For much of the initial use of these chunks, language learners are using them in this very same way to ask the same question, so these phrases are memorized as wholes. However, the learner will soon come to recognize that the word 'old' shares many of the same properties (position in a sentence, possible morphological attachments, functions) as other 'adjectives'. Once this connection has been made, the learner can utilize the learned chunk in the question to ask other questions that use adjectives:

The frame = 'How X are you?' X = any number of adjectives, such as tall, short, etc.

The learner can now use this frame and X, defined as such, to produce new questions:

'How tall are you?'
'How short are you?'

The statement 'I am twenty years old' can also change over time, and it is not only single words, but whole phrases that can be replaced. For example, once the learner realizes that 'twenty years old' is the same type of constituent as other descriptive phrases or even single words, the learner now has another productive chunk:

The frame = 'I am X', where X = some description, from a single adjective to other longer chunks.

The learner can again use this frame and X to produce new statements:

'I am tall'.
'I am very tired'.

As more and more chunks are learned, they provide more frames that the learner can use to produce more language (Ellis, 2013). These productive chunks act somewhat differently from computing single grammatical forms, since they consist of chunks that already contain obligatory morphology (Bybee, 2008). Thus, the production of slot-filler constructions in early acquisition can aide significantly in learner accuracy during production; much more so than explicit knowledge of L2 grammatical information for oral production, and especially since learners have not yet proceduralized any of this explicit information into the implicit application of grammatical patterns.

Grist for the mill

The growing number of chunks a learner knows not only helps them in production, but also acts as language segments that can be both unconsciously and consciously analyzed. Because these chunks contain accurate grammatical information that learners use in appropriate contexts, the meaning of the grammatical elements can take shape. This is even more so the case when larger chunks are disassembled into more productive frames where morphology is even more visible. MacWhinney *et al.* (1989) reflecting on his own (MacWhinney, 1978: 272) observance of the role of rote memorization in the acquisition of morphology 'placed heavy emphasis on the importance of rote-memorized forms as the basis of morphological learning. His account viewed the first words as unanalyzed associations between sounds and meanings. When a child learned the word "dogs," it was learned as a unit, not as a combination of "dog" and the plural'. L2 learners have an advantage on children, because they not only know that there are 'rules' and patterns in a language that need to be learned, as well as transfer from positions of entrenched L1 morphological processing, but they also have the added capacity as cognitively mature individuals to direct their conscious thought at identifying patterns and mapping those patterns to meanings, which young children do not (Robinson, 1997; Schmidt, 1990). MacWhinney (1978) 'viewed these rote forms or "amalgams" as *grist for the mill* of morphemic segmentation and subsequent rule extraction' (MacWhinney, 1989: 272) (my emphasis). For L2 learners, the more chunks they know, the more 'grist' they are providing themselves to 'mill'. For this reason, learning chunks within appropriate contexts and motivating attention to the analyses of these chunks at the beginning of L2 instruction is very important to support both syntactic and morphological acquisition.

Attention available for task completion

As soon as some language processes are proceduralized, the consciousness previously required for continuous language processing allows room for other cognitive processes to use those resources (Kester *et al.*, 2004). One way that learners can direct attention now is to monitor and assess their work toward completion of tasks. Here, learners have the conscious attention to attend to what is being asked of them, with the ability to keep in mind certain linguistic structures needed to accomplish the task. This is one of the first times the learner really has to work to shift attention between cognitive processes: between language-specific to task-specific needs and back again. And, since they do not have the L2 proficiency or knowledge to manage task needs in the L2, the L1 invariably comes into play, even if only internally directed. The learner cannot be conscious, aware of and attending to everything they need to do to successfully complete the task at hand because they do not yet have the necessary L2 proficiency and knowledge to automatically process all the linguistic information they need to without attention, and they cannot use the L2 to complete the task because much of their intentionality is still being controlled by their L1 (Mallikarjun *et al.*, 2017).

Therefore, all of the things one can eventually do, i.e. process most of the linguistic input automatically and focus fully on the task at hand, the learner is forced to move the spotlight of consciousness to the various aspects they need to accomplish the task.[7] The learner has the capacity to focus on language or the task, but not both simultaneously, and therefore executive control over rapid movement between objects of thought and attention is employed by the learner. As the learner collects pieces of knowledge from different mental areas (e.g. what verb form do I need to express past tense? what order do I want to tell this story in?), they can then integrate them in order to accomplish the task at hand.

Growing Proficiency

Only after a certain amount of acquisition or learning has taken place does the concept of proficiency make sense to discuss. Up until that point, it is really a patchwork of a few incompletely proceduralized processes, like parsing, lexical access, sound–symbol and grapheme–sound mapping and chunked production, with a defined and relatively small set of vocabulary and morphology. These basic, and still very incomplete proceduralized processes are supplemented by additional L2 knowledge that has not been established as implicit knowledge, as well as usable or repurposed L1 processes and language-related strategies, like formulating and practicing utterances before they are produced.

However, even with this miscellany of explicit and implicit knowledge, combined with other language-supporting processes, learners can do much. Before we turn to specific psycholinguistic processes that are developing, along with how we can support these developments and help students successfully partake in a number of language-related activities, it is important to go over a few definitions of what proficiency means.

Defining proficiency

The definition of proficiency varies significantly based on the theoretical perspective one takes, and the goals of the agenda associated with the person, people and organizations involved. Academics and researchers in SLA, for example, define proficiency much differently from educators and educational organizations. Let's look at two definitions of proficiency: one from an SLA researcher primarily targeting other researchers, and one from an organization primarily targeting an audience of language teachers.

For the SLA researcher definition, Hulstijn (2011) provides a detailed construct of proficiency:

> Language proficiency (LP) is the extent to which an individual possesses the linguistic cognition necessary to function in a given communicative situation, in a given modality (listening, speaking, reading, or writing). Linguistic cognition is the combination of the representation of linguistic information (knowledge of form-meaning mappings) and the ease with which linguistic information can be processed (skill). Form-meaning mappings pertain to both the literal and pragmatic meanings of forms (in decontextualized and socially-situated language use, respectively). Linguistic cognition in the phonetic-phonological, morphonological, morphosyntactic, and lexical domains forms the center of LP (core components). LP may comprise peripheral components of a less-linguistic or non-linguistic nature, such as strategic or metacognitive abilities related to performing listening, speaking, reading or writing tasks. (Hulstijn, 2011: 242)

This definition highlights, as I did in the beginning of this chapter, the need for distinction between the four skills, as doing so allows us to ask what competencies and behaviors are necessary components of each one. It is important to recognize that this definition of proficiency also includes 'core' aspects as well as leaving the door open for 'peripheral components'.

Other definitions of proficiency with a mind toward what educators, students and parents might be interested in, focus on what an individual can do, rather than focusing on linguistic subcomponents. One such definition comes from the American Council on the Teaching of Foreign Languages (ACTFL). In their preface to their guidelines for assessing proficiency, the ACTFL (2012: 3) states:

> The ACTFL Proficiency Guidelines are a description of what individuals can do with language in terms of speaking, writing, listening, and reading in real-world situations in a spontaneous and non-rehearsed context. For each skill, these guidelines identify five major levels of proficiency: Distinguished, Superior, Advanced, Intermediate, and Novice. The major levels Advanced, Intermediate, and Novice are subdivided into High, Mid, and Low sublevels. The levels of the ACTFL Guidelines describe the continuum of proficiency from that of the highly articulate, well-educated language user to a level of little or no functional ability.

These Guidelines present the levels of proficiency as ranges and describe what an individual can and cannot do with language at each level, regardless of where, when, or how the language was acquired. Together these levels form a hierarchy in which each level subsumes all lower levels. The Guidelines are not based on any particular theory, pedagogical method, or educational curriculum. They neither describe how an individual learns a language nor prescribe how an individual should learn a language, and they should not be used for such purposes. They are an instrument for the evaluation of functional language ability.

Again, we see references to the four skills, but there are no references to psycholinguistic subcomponents that aid students in the completion of the various functions outlined by the ACTFL. This chapter focuses more on the psycholinguistic aspects highlighted in Hulstijn's (2011) definition, as it outlines the psycholinguistic development of the individual; however, on turning to classroom and pedagogical considerations, links are drawn between these psycholinguistic processes and the functional usage of language highlighted by the ACTFL proficiency guidelines.

Fluency versus accuracy

In writing this and the following subsections, I was unsure what I should put first, fluency or accuracy. The early focus of language instruction even well into the 20th century seems to have been on accuracy. From the formation of SLA through to today, there has been greater emphasis on fluency. These two concepts, accuracy and fluency, are not only in a theoretical and pedagogical skirmish with one another, but they also collide within the mind of the learner themself. When the learner focuses too heavily on accuracy, their fluency is pitted with awkward pauses. When the learner focuses too heavily on fluency, their accuracy[8] suffers, which could lead to them not being understood. There has always been a balance between a need for students to gain fluency and accuracy in language, and for language teachers, the pendulum always seems to be swaying in favor of one, only to return back to the other (Eskey, 1983).

Fluency

According to De Jong and Perfetti (2011: 534), 'fluency is often understood to refer to the flow and smoothness of delivery'. For the learner who has achieved some proficiency in their target language, they should have the ability to achieve, to a certain extent, a level of 'flow and smoothness of delivery', but what does that look like? The answer seems to be, it depends on the situation, context, familiarity and L2 requirements (Ishikawa, 2006; Kuiken *et al.*, 2005; Michel, 2011). Students can achieve fluency, if only briefly, if they are operating within normalized classroom communicative frameworks like partner work or answering questions, participating in activities for which they have already established communicative protocols, their interlocutor also knows what the expectations are and if they have a significant number of complete or productive chunks. For new activities, or known ones using new vocabulary or grammar, the learner will likely struggle to produce fluent speech.

For better or worse, fluency has been promoted to some extent above accuracy for students to achieve, which I link to the promulgation of the communicative approach to language teaching. Hammerly (1991) comes to a similar conclusion, where he criticizes 'the "communicative classroom" approach (…) for its lax attitudes' (in abstract) toward linguistic forms. No matter how much of an emphasis we place on fluency, accuracy is always being weighed against it, and there are consequences for an overemphasis on fluency over grammatical accuracy. As Eskey (1983: 319) warns, 'rewarding a learner's fluency may, in some cases, actually impede his or her achievement of accuracy'.

Accuracy

As reviewed earlier, grammatical or linguistic accuracy in productive skills was the major focus for much of the history of language pedagogy. Like fluency, accuracy must be viewed both in terms of L2 proficiency and task requirements. Factors like the complexity of the language needed to complete the task, the modality or modalities of the language used and other contextual affordances and constraints. For example, one could hardly expect the same level of complexity, accuracy and fluency (CAF) (Housen *et al.*, 2012) from a student who is cold-called in the middle of class when they are not paying attention, to talk about an unfamiliar topic, as one could from a student who is asked to write a short, autobiographical story as a homework assignment. Besides the availability of outside resources, like dictionaries, verb-conjugation tools and automatic translators, accuracy is also dependent on the amount of knowledge, resources and time. As Larsen-Freeman (2009: 587) argues, 'no longer can we expect CAF to operate independently from each other, let alone independently of particular individuals or independently from particular contexts. Neither can we expect that any one of the three is a unitary and unchanging dimension'. For this reason, it is more appropriate to discuss accuracy for an individual as dynamic along a spectrum governed by multiple personal and contextual factors (Polat & Kim, 2014; Spoelman & Verspoor, 2010).

On one side are tasks that require complex linguistic forms, unfamiliar grammar, vocabulary or content in a modality that doesn't allow much if any time for reflecting on correct forms (usually speaking, but activities like quick-writes also fall on this side of the spectrum). On this side, we would expect learners who have become moderately proficient in their language to still have significant errors in production. On the other side of the spectrum are tasks that can be accomplished with simpler grammatical constructions, cover well-known topics and require only familiar vocabulary. In these tasks, learners can employ a number of learned chunks, whole or productive, and produce them in a modality that allows ample time for reflection (mostly writing, but activities like memorizing a speech would also provide similar affordances). On this side of the spectrum, we would expect almost no errors, at least not any systematic ones. For example, Polio and Fleck's (1998) study found that simply providing learners with extra time on writing assignments for editing without any feedback from the instructor improved their accuracy. All tasks fall somewhere on this spectrum. The more on one side or the other, the more or fewer mistakes we should expect. Implications for the balance of tasks along this spectrum will be discuss in Chapters 5 and 6.

Other factors that play a role in grammatical accuracy come from the beliefs of the student and teacher. If the teacher has emphasized fluency over accuracy, this could have a negative impact on the student's own motivation to produce accurate language. The student also has their own ideas about the importance of grammar. One way to think about these affects is through the lens of (over/under)monitoring (Krashen, 1978). While psycholinguistics has, to some degree, left this model behind, the importance of awareness of and attention to grammatical form is still an integral part of our understanding of L2 development (e.g. Wallace, 2022). These individual differences in preferences for fluency over accuracy or vice versa can create very different learning paths to fluency from one individual to the next.

For many, initial thoughts about accuracy go to grammatical (morphological/syntactic) accuracy. However, accuracy can also be related to pronunciation. The factors affecting pronunciation accuracy overlap with many of the factors described for grammatical accuracy, such as familiarity with vocabulary and content, time for reflection and L1 transfer. Suter (1976) also identified the speaker's own concern for their pronunciation accuracy and the amount of time they spent speaking the language. Pronunciation accuracy is highly dependent on the input the learner receives from their instructor, classmates and other classroom-external resources, like media and L1 speakers of the target language who they interact with from their community. Pronunciation accuracy, like grammatical accuracy, is a bit easier to define within a classroom setting than if the individual was learning the language 'in the wild', because much of the material, maybe unfortunately, is focused on the 'standard' language, however that is defined within the context of that language, in their curriculum and by their teacher(s).

Chapters 5 and 6 discuss the importance of dialectical and between-speaker variability on listening comprehension as well as the formation of a multilingual identity; however, for now, suffice to say that learners' pronunciation accuracy should be viewed as a match between how they want to sound, what they think they sound like and how they actually sound. Chapter 6 discusses pedagogical methods to enhance L2 pronunciation accuracy, as defined by this overlap between the learners' intentions and their actual production.

Interactional competencies

L2 learners are not just acquiring knowledge they need to interact, they are also acquiring the means with which to interact in another language, which we call interactional competencies. Doehler (2019: 29) describes the development of interactional competence as follows: 'Changing patterns of participation are conceptualized in terms of increasing interactional skills as regards turn-taking management and the sequential organization of the activity by the target learner'. As learners continue to engage in various language activities with others, they begin to develop interactional competencies in their L2. In doing so, Doehler (2013: 154) argues that 'L2 speakers not only augment their linguistic repertoire (syntactic complexity, hedges, etc.), but also diversify their interactional techniques'. Of importance is that L2 interactional competencies emerge in context from usage over time. Developing interactional competencies is not something that happens all at once. In other words, 'people's ways of carrying out social actions are the driving force for the learning of the inventory of semiotic resources' (Eskildsen, 2018: 73), and it is the changing ways in which they carry out these social actions that force learners to employ different semiotic resources to accomplish the goals of their interactions. It is not only the semiotic and linguistic resources that are needed to develop interactional competencies, but also, as Doehler (2013: 154) argues, 'in the process of L2 learning, L2 speakers recalibrate their "methods" (i.e. systematic procedures) for accomplishing social interaction and related resources (including language)'. Thus, the way in which learners approach interaction changes as well as the resources they need and can use to manage and negotiate interactions.

The ability to include contextual information in the decision-making about which semiotic resources to employ requires ample knowledge and, at first, time to recall and reflect on more appropriate and possibly more complex linguistic forms. Doehler (2013: 135) also argues for this intertwining of contextual information with linguistic resources, saying 'this diversification (...) indicates that the development of interactional competence can be usefully understood as involving the deployment of increasingly context-sensitive (i.e., situationally, interactionally appropriate) conduct in which linguistic resources and the sequential organization of actions are inextricably intertwined'. These forms may be necessary to fully accomplish the participants' interactional goals. This requires a certain amount of availability in terms of cognitive, social and situational resources that allow for a greater variety of choices for the speaker.

Hall (2018: 34) has made an interesting proposal to change the way we think about L2 learners' growing interactional competence, which is 'the term repertoire (Hall, 2016; Hall et al., 2006)', where they define interactional repertoire 'as dynamic and malleable "conventionalized constellations of semiotic resources" (Hall et al., 2006: 232) for taking action'. Hall (2018) argues for this change in terminology for several reasons, especially when one reflects on the non-linear trajectory of L2 development:

> First, it counteracts the implications of solidity and inflexibility that have become affiliated with the term competence and resonates more with present-day understandings of language. Second, it suggests a more empirically valid understanding of learning, not as a linear, homogeneous, stable one-path-fits-all process, but rather as biographical and malleable trajectories occurring over L2 learners' lifespans. As the paths that L2 learners' life experiences take are not linear, neither do their repertoires develop along a straight path of ever-increasing size and complexity. Rather, they grow dramatically in some stages of life, such as when learning a new career or becoming a member of a new community, and gradually in others, with the varied conditions of learning contexts, leading to fuller and more enduring L2 repertoires of meaning-making resources for some contexts and more temporary, fleeting repertoires for others. (Hall, 2018: 34)

This definition fits quite well with what we see in learners with growing proficiency. They may not have a statically well-developed competence for interactions, but they do have a variety of repertoires to employ based on the various learning paths they have taken. This emphasizes that the types of interactions they have engaged in have shaped the emergence and development of their interactional repertoires, so they may be more or less successful depending on how their experiences have prepared them for a particular situation, with particular interlocutors and context-specific expectations.

From declarative knowledge and conscious manipulation to proceduralized knowledge to automated processing

As an individual gains more declarative information about their L2, and the more they pay attention to and try to use this knowledge in production, they gradually proceduralize this knowledge and continue on to fully automate these new procedures. Ellis (2011: 36) describes the process as follows: 'With this controlled use of declarative knowledge guiding the proceduralization and eventual automatization of language processing, as it does in the acquisition of other cognitive skills'.

The first step, from declarative to procedural knowledge, is not well understood and up for significant debate in the field of SLA.[9] Ullman

(2014: 135) defines procedural knowledge as a system 'composed of a network of interconnected brain structures rooted in frontal/basal ganglia circuits. The basal ganglia, and especially the caudate nucleus, play a critical role in the learning and consolidation of new motor and cognitive skills'. From a functional perspective, and importantly for the purposes of this book, procedural knowledge can be thought of as knowledge that has been organized to trigger multiple steps in order without the need to reflect consciously on ordering, connecting and implementing each step. From there, the next step would be automatization. In their description of how learners develop advanced language processing, Suzuki *et al.* (2020: 4) argue that '[p]rocedural knowledge still needs to be fine-tuned or automatized for even faster and stable linguistic processing'.

For learners, how one moves from declarative knowledge to procedural knowledge to automated linguistic processing is probably not as important as the fact that they can and do move toward automation. This happens for different linguistic forms and features over time, rather than a blanket transition by the learner from one type of knowledge to another. For the teacher, however, Chapter 6 attempts to unpack how this debate can impact how they approach their classroom and curriculum.

Overgeneralization and the other side of the 'U'

One frustrating and likely necessary stage in L2 development is when learners start to make errors in areas that both they and their teacher thought they had mastered. What is ironic is that students and teachers should see this as an amazing leap forward in their L2 development. One of the sources for this error is overgeneralization, which occurs when 'learners approach the task of learning complex linguistic structures by creating prototype categories' (Zyzik, 2006: 122). The formation of these categories allows learners to quickly apply regular (as opposed to irregular) patterns to the categories. This means that memorized irregular forms may be overwritten in the moment as automated L2 processes take over for declarative knowledge. Assuming they had a stable understanding of the irregular form, the learner might still know what the correct form is, but automated processing occurs faster than the application of declarative knowledge, especially if the learner doesn't have the resources necessary to monitor their speech in real time to correct the error produced through automation. These errors of overgeneralization can persist for quite a while. As Ghilza (2020: 753) notes, 'it may be difficult for learners to unlearn over-generalized errors because for that L2 learners need to rely on "negative evidence" to restrict their interlanguage grammars'. This means that until they are presented with negative evidence from a teacher or peer, they might not recognize that a word takes an irregular form.

During this stage, learners will continue to overgeneralize until they have gained enough working knowledge of the appropriate irregular form through usage. This results in U-shaped behavior, where some, but maybe not all, L2 features go from reliably correct usage to reliably incorrect usage, and back to reliably correct usage. Some researchers argue that this U-shaped trajectory is essential to L2 learning. Williams (2019: 230) goes so far as to say that 'the existence of U-shaped behaviour in the L2 suggests universality as opposed to simply L1 transfer, and that this learning process is an integral part of acquiring and establishing knowledge in the mental lexicon related to regular and irregular morphology'. I hedge here with the term 'reliably' because learners almost never present perfect U-shaped behavior (from 100% correct to 0% correct back to 100% correct). Oshita (2014: 166) promotes this idea, because 'the notion of a relative U is highly compatible with the progressive nature of language acquisition because it does not call for near-perfect performance, either at the beginning or at the end of its pattern'.

Newly available resources from decreased cognitive demand

At this stage in learner development, the proceduralization of processes that previously required conscious attention and access to explicit knowledge has reached a point where cognitive resources are available to the learner (Lyster et al., 2013). They can do other things while still processing and producing enough language to interact with others. In terms of receptive processes, this means that they no longer have to pay conscious attention to forms to interpret them for meaning (e.g. past tense versus present tense) and can therefore think about other task- or communication-related things while understanding what they are reading or hearing. For productive tasks, they can now spend more time focusing on what they want to say rather than figuring out how to say it. And the cross-over effects between receptive and productive tasks enable them to have real conversations for the first time. By this, I mean they can process, to a large extent, what someone is saying to them and simultaneously think about what they would like to say back without losing track of what is being said to them, and they have the necessary resources available to plan what they want to say while the other person is speaking. This new availability of resources freed from strictly linguistic processing allows learners to do more than just pay more attention to accomplishing tasks. It also liberates learners to be more aware of new linguistic structures and supports the awareness and integration of contextual information which helps learners develop L2 pragmatic competence.

Awareness of and attention to new structures

The cognitive resources available to the language learner allow them not only to pay attention to context and task requirements, but also to pay more attention to linguistic resources and the language they are hearing and seeing around them. From this input, learners can glean new information about new linguistic forms and the structure of the language itself. As Yalçın *et al.* (2016: 154) found, 'Language aptitude and [working memory] capacity is two [independent] variables that can play key roles in L2 learning under various conditions'. Therefore, if working memory is available to focus on other things besides known forms, there is a greater likelihood of noticing new forms. This is often referred to as 'incidental learning' (Hulstijn, 2013), a term that does little justice to the amount of effort it can take on the part of the learner. Incidental learning occurs when the learner is noticing something that the teacher did not intend for them to notice. This does not mean that incidental learning cannot come from a learner's active searching for meaning within the L2. There is ample evidence that 'learners can acquire some knowledge of L2 inflectional morphology under incidental learning conditions following a minimal amount of exposure' (Rogers, 2017: 127). Incidental learning empowers the learner to take control of their own learning process. Tools for how to encourage these behaviors and support incidental (or maybe independent is a better term?) learning in students are an important part of building a language curriculum that promotes learning beyond and after the classroom.

Contextual, social and linguistic integration (or the beginnings of an L2 pragmatic system)

Although SLA research itself has mostly focused on speech acts with regard to L2 pragmatics (Bardovi-Harlig, 2012), in an overarching sense, pragmatics can be generally seen as 'the study of language from the point of view of users, especially of the choices they make, the constraints they encounter in using language in social interaction and the effects their use of language has on other participants in the act of communication' (Crystal, 1997: 301; as cited in Bardovi-Harlig, 2012: 234). From this broader definition, it requires the individual to integrate a number of contextual and linguistically tangential sources of information, such as the status of the person or people whom they are interacting with or the imagined audience of a written text, their own status, their relationship to others, as well as historical, cultural and social factors situated in broad, global down to narrow, local contexts. With more resources available to consider all of these factors, learners can try to use this information to inform the language that they are producing, or the way they are interpreting what they are hearing or reading. Some of the pragmatic aspects we hope to see developing with learners at this stage are interactional competencies, terms of address and formality, implicatures and maybe even a little humor (Taguchi & Roever, 2017).

Budding Multilingualism

What I term here 'budding multilingualism' is probably the most diverse state on the way to advanced L2 proficiency and multilingualism.

As each learner follows their own non-linear trajectory, which complex dynamic systems theory (CDST) has clearly demonstrated, various aspects of the L2 learner's development, from pronunciation, L2 knowledge, proceduralized knowledge, automated processes, L2 pragmatic knowledge, vocabulary breadth and depth, cultural understanding and many other cognitive and social aspects make up the gamut of what it means to learn an L2. Individual experiences highlight certain linguistic forms and contexts for one individual and other forms and contexts for another individual, in which different learners are sometimes more and sometimes less proficient. They develop different strengths in terms of the four skills as well as other skills, such as intercultural communication, conversation management and reasoning. One aspect of budding multilingualism that might play an important part in developing toward advanced multilingualism includes dreaming and thinking in the L2 in short spurts.

One of the many problems that learners face at this stage is the feeling that they are not learning anything 'new'. There is a constant struggle for small gains. In contrast to the early stages of L2 development, where learners encounter new things like vocabulary, grammar and L2 cultural information on a near if not actual daily basis, this is no longer the case for the 'budding multilingual'. They don't realize how far they have come nor the next steps to achieve advanced proficiency. There are serious implications for continued language study in making sure that learners are able to track their development and take time to see their advances, especially as they grow increasingly less visible.

It is at this stage that learners have also hopefully started to take seriously the idea of developing an L2 identity. They need to build connections to L2 communities which will encourage growth in new areas and challenge them to put in the hard work and continue to develop their language abilities to levels needed for everyday and professional purposes (e.g. see Anya, 2011).

Native-Like Proficiency or Advanced Multilingualism?

While Chapter 1 discussed and emphasized the idea that the native speaker is really a myth against which a learner should not be measured, the term 'native-like' persists in many descriptions of L2 proficiency. Therefore, it is at least important to compare what advanced language behaviors advanced bi/multilinguals share with speakers who learned their L2 as an L1 (i.e. as a native speaker), and contrast other behaviors of advanced multilinguals in addition to or differently from monolingual speakers of the L2 (if any such individuals even exist).

(Near-)subconscious linguistic processing and production

By the time a learner reaches an advanced stage of L2 development, the majority of bottom-up and even many top-down processes should happen automatically, having been proceduralized and then automated through sufficient use and application in a wide variety of language contexts and for a number of communicative functions. This means that conscious attention does not have to be applied for the requisite processes to continue subconsciously, or 'in the background'. Conscious attention could be applied, especially if certain contextual factors make some of these automated processes more difficult, like talking on the phone, where contextual and visual information may be unavailable. These automated processes can also be affected by context. For example, if you are listening to a book on tape about organic chemistry, you might need to pay a bit more attention if you lack a working knowledge of the field ahead of time, since a number of new and unfamiliar terms will be introduced. However, in many situations, learners who have reached a fairly advanced L2 developmental state have gained the freedom to apply their consciousness to tasks that require automated processing and comprehension of the L2 in order to do something with it simultaneously, like oral translation, telling a timely joke or just carrying on a conversation in real time.

We know that L2 learners can reach this processing capacity because they have been shown to exhibit cognitive sensitivities to illogical and ungrammatical constructions just like L1 speakers (Tokowicz & MacWhinney, 2005). Knowing that this L1-type processing is occurring provides the information not only that it is possible, but also the types of knowledge being processed. L2 learners exhibit these sensitivities to all four ERP-relevant measurements: early left anterior negativity (eLAN), left anterior negativity (LAN), negative 400 (N400) and positive 600 (P600) (Caffarra *et al*., 2015). From earliest occurring (eLAN) to latest occurring (P600), these violations involve 'violations of obligatory phrase structure', 'morphosyntactic violations within a sentential context', problems integrating or predicting a word within a given context and, finally, multiple (morpho)syntactic errors, as well as 'thematic-rule structure violations, temporary ambiguities, semantic anomalies, and long-distance dependencies' (Caffarra *et al*., 2015: 33). So, having reached a certain level of proficiency, L2 learners are either processing the L2 in the same way as L1 speakers, or are at the very least reacting to violations in a similar way. This means that the L2 learner should have reached a sufficient state where the processing of the L2 has reached a stage close enough to L1 processing to allow for the conscious mind to move its attentional resources elsewhere.

Full attention to tasks

One of the biggest advantages near-native or very advanced L2 proficiency creates is the ability to focus most if not all attentional resources on whatever task the individual is doing. Part of the task may ask them to reflect on their language use, but that is different from monitoring and attending to the language they are processing, comprehending and producing in real time. A high level of automation allows individuals to successfully accomplish complex tasks, like writing in a particular genre for a particular audience, speaking about an unfamiliar, highly technical topic with uncommon vocabulary or competing in a team-based sport that requires both physical and social coordination (Canan, 2022; Suzuki, 2021).

Prior to this advanced stage, a balance had to be kept by the individual. Consciousness had to switch between a focus on language use needed to coordinate and accomplish the task, as well as the task itself. One of the best-known correlations for non-advanced learners when trying to accomplish a task in an L2 is that accuracy, fluency or some other measurement of language proficiency declines with task complexity, and that a greater focus on language comes with increasing task complexity as well (Awwad & Tavakoli, 2019; Robinson & Gilabert, 2007).

This is true for L1 speakers to a certain extent, as task demands eat up more and more attentional resources with increasing complexity (Lee, 2019). For L1 speakers and very advanced L2 learners, this decrease in language proficiency, if one were coming from an L2 perspective, or perhaps eloquence, coming from an L1 perspective, does not have nearly as drastic an effect on language comprehension, processing and production as it does on L2 learners who have not reached a state of near-subconscious language processing.

Self-directed L2 speech for mediating thinking

The internalization of language from a social tool of communication to a cognitive tool for organizing and guiding thought is a key tenet of Vygotskian sociocultural theory (Sebastián *et al.*, 2021). For L1 learners, internalization takes place alongside other cognitive, social and physical developmental milestones (Smolucha & Smolucha, 2021). For the L2 learner, the process can look different, as the internalization of the L2 does not rely on a time sequence dependent on other developmental achievements. The L2 learner already knows what it means to use language as a mediator of thought, even if they do not consciously realize that is what language is doing for them. Even for child L2 learners, there is usually at least the beginnings of an inward facing and self-directing voice (Yaghoubi & Farrokh, 2022). The L2 learner has two tasks ahead of them if they want to internalize the L2 as a tool for thinking. First, they need to gain enough L2 knowledge and proficiency to allow the L2 to play that role (Cook, 1998). If they are limited by their L2 proficiency to the extent that they cannot use it as a mediating tool, then there really is not much utility in it. Second, the L2 learner has to choose to use the L2 to guide their speech (De Guerrero, 2006). This does not mean that the L2 usurps the position of the L1 or other languages as tools, but it becomes another tool in the individual's proverbial toolkit; that is, thinking becomes a multilingual process rather than a monolingual one (Pavlenko, 2011). This is an extremely difficult habit to build and the use of the L1 for this purpose is an extremely difficult habit to break.

One of the most interesting questions for SLA, and a phenomenon that most advanced language learners eventually experience, is the use of their L2 in their dreams. Maybe as a primary purpose, sleep and dreaming consolidate information (Wamsley, 2014), but for the development of the L2 as a tool for thinking, I leave you with this question: could dreaming in an L2 reflect the internalization of the L2 from a social tool used to mediate interpersonal communication to a cognitive tool capable of mediating thought?

Code-switching

Code-switching is a very common behavior for bilingual and multilingual individuals (Tomić & Kroff, 2021). However, it is rarely, if ever, taught or even discussed in L2 classrooms. Chapter 6 returns to how bilingual practices are both part of and could be taught in the L2 classroom and curriculum; however, this chapter first outlines the development of code-switching within the individual, the differences between code-switching, avoidance and L1 gap-filling, and the different ways in which advanced bilinguals use code-switching for various functional and social purposes.

Especially for monolingual speakers learning an L2, it is important to first talk about the difference between the use of the L1 as a gap-filler or as avoidance strategies and authentic code-switching between two or more languages. Gap-filling, which I define as the use of the L1 to fill in the gaps in L2 linguistic knowledge to support language production, fluency and communication, is an unavoidable and probably not too disturbing part of the language learning process, even if some pedagogues with an extreme commitment to immersion and an L2-only learning environment might disagree. Even if the L2 is the only audible language spoken in the classroom, the L1 is the monologue running the show behind the scenes. As discussed in the previous section, the L2 may not yet be available as a tool for thinking, reasoning and planning, and thus the L1 is used by students for inner/self-directed speech.

Learners who are asked to only use the L2 in the classroom have significantly stifled speech, supported with ample deictic and symbolic gestures that act as a way to convey meaning. For learners who are not asked to speak in the L2 from day 1, the beginning stages of language learning involve a large amount of translation, joint L1/L2 question and sentence formation and the integration of what students know within an L1 structure. For L2 learners, there really is no getting around this initial, L1 heavy transitional phase until the amount of L2 knowledge is sufficient to support the types of activities they are being asked to do, and eventually work its way, hopefully, into a tool for thought. The transition from the L1 as a tool for thought and communication can be seen as one of the main goals of SLA in general, so as long as learners are constantly transitioning to the L2, they are developing toward a fully functional L2 linguistic state.

In contrast with gap-filling, avoidance (Kleinmann, 1977; Schachter, 1974) has two forms. First, avoidance can be a learner behavior in which the L1 is used, despite the fact that the learner has knowledge of the appropriate L2 form. The other form, more relevant to L2 linguistic choices, has to do with the choice of one L2 form over another due to a higher level of comfortability, which may arise from a number of different sources, including better conceptual understanding, similarity between the L1 and L2 or some other prior language forms, facilitation from transfer or simply a high level of complexity of one form versus another in the L2. This section on code-switching focuses on the prior form, where the L1 is used in place of the L2, despite having the required knowledge to use, or at least attempting to use the L2. Learners prefer using the L1 in a number of situations.

Before describing each of these scenarios, it is important to contrast L1 use with L2 development. The development of the L2 can be underway, making huge advances that the individual can see, and yet the use of the L1 can still persist, even though the individual and the teacher know that the student could be using the L2. So, the use of the L1, while somewhat detrimental if we think in terms of time-on-task and the limited amount of time we have with our students in the classroom, may not have as much of a direct effect on L2 development as we think. It is driven somewhat separately by the way learners view the purpose and uses of the L2. Here, we return to the idea in Chapter 2 of habit. Initially, students have a habit of using the L1 for communication. It often takes a significant number of reminders from teachers that students should be using the L2 first, before they resort to the L1 to make themselves understood. It takes a lot of work building up vocabulary, memorizing functional chunks to ask questions and reply to answers and reminding themselves that they are supposed to try out the L2 first. Hopefully, students eventually get the idea and this, especially when interacting with the teacher, becomes the new habit. The L2 is used in this space for this purpose. Hopefully, learners also have enough self-control to try to use the L2 with one another throughout casual conversations with each other as well and use it first when trying to complete tasks without the teacher needing to supervise students' interactions.

For the most part, students come to know that they are expected to use the L2 to *do* tasks in the L2 classroom. However, they are not always aware that they can use the L2 to manage tasks, conversations and future plans. There seems to be a distinction for learners, one that persists across the curriculum and is not necessarily appropriately addressed in the L2 classroom; conversation and task management are outside of the task, and thus the L1 is permissible. In short, the L2 serves to complete the task, while the L1 serves to manage the task (Walter, 2019). Getting students to a place where the L2 is used to manage tasks and conversations is a skill that is just as in need of development as the language necessary to complete the tasks we put in front of them, if not even more important in a real-world situation. This type of avoidance is not even necessarily a conscious choice of learners, and so, it is essential for learners to become conscious of the choice they can make to use the L2 for this purpose.

L1 gap-filling and avoidance are useful observations for teachers because they provide insight into areas in need of further development by the learner or whole class. If learners are using L1 vocabulary when an L2 word is either just as or even more suitable, it can show gaps in vocabulary knowledge that the teacher may have thought were already known. The use of one grammatical form when another is more appropriate might show that a student either has not grasped the use of that form or is uncomfortable using it. In any of these cases, the individual is simply attempting to communicate in the mode in which they feel will result in the clearest understanding of their message, while diminishing their risk of producing errors. One can distinguish gap-filling and avoidance from authentic code-switching by the opportunity for real choice. For gap-filling and avoidance strategies, the knowledge of the most appropriate L2 form is either incomplete or non-existent, so that the learner is forced to use the L1 to complete their utterance or thought. Code-switching, in terms of mixing and matching the L1(s) and L2(s) in grammatically congruent and creative ways, is a skill that is learned by bi/multilingual speakers over time and through context to form language that fulfills a purpose that a single language on its own either cannot do or cannot do as well as the combination of those languages.

Signs of proficient code-switchers can be found in the use of context-specific vocabulary, the integration of L1/L2 syntax and the creation of meanings that take on significant cultural relevance (Toribio, 2001). Advanced multilinguals know, sometimes consciously, but often unconsciously, where appropriate breaks are in their languages' syntactic and morphosyntactic structures, and how they can merge and mesh the two languages to enhance or change the meaning. Opportunities for advancing uniquely multilingual behaviors like code-switching will be covered in Chapter 6 on pedagogical considerations.

Understanding one's multilingual identity

The development of one's multilingual identity is a process that takes place over the entirety of language learning development. In the initial stages of language learning, at least from an ISLA classroom perspective in a North American context, students do not normally have a clearly developed individual purpose for learning the L2. Many students report that they learn an L2 because they are required to, because they need it to get into college or because they want to communicate with family members who speak it (Nolan, 2022). Unlike heritage language (HL) learners, or children who grew up bilingual, many students in the United States do not see a clear relationship between learning an L2 and their future personal and professional lives. However, at a more advanced stage of language development, learners might be better positioned to consider how their identity is different now that they are bilingual, in a sense that they could be using this language in their everyday life. For advanced learners, they might now consider experiences that include the chance to interact with other speakers of the L2 who use it as part of their everyday life, such as study abroad or international internships. From a purely ISLA perspective, the L2 classroom may not be the place where authentic multilingual identities are developed; however, imagined identities may develop. Interactions with speakers of the L2 that engage the learner in ways that challenge their conceptions that they are monolingual go much farther than just telling students that they are bilingual and they can perform specific speech acts in the L2. That being said, ISLA can at least equip students with the skills they need to be self-reflective, critical and interpretive of their cross-cultural experiences, and provide resources like texts that connect students to communities of interest and information about opportunities for personal and professional development in a context that requires use of the L2, among other possibilities.

Reflections on the L1(s)

With the growing space for the conscious mind to move away from using attentional resources to focus on L2 forms to higher-order and meta-level thoughts about the L2, the learner will be capable of drawing on their own cross-linguistic comparisons. Advanced L2 speakers not only question why the L2 has certain forms or acts in certain ways, but also reflect on why their own language or languages operate the way they do.

While the literature is scarce on how and when advanced knowledge of an L2 can provide insights into one's L1 or other previously learned languages, there is ample anecdotal evidence to surmise at least a few things. First, L2 knowledge probably plays a role in increased L1 language awareness and linguistic knowledge. We know that L2 learners gain a significant amount of L2 metalinguistic knowledge over the course of their L2 learning experience (Roehr-Brackin, 2018). L1 speakers are notorious for having an excellent feel for language but lack explicit knowledge to talk about why particular language structures are allowed or not allowed. L2 learners, on the other hand, often gain significant metalinguistic knowledge and vocabulary to talk about the grammar of their L2. From this different basis, L2 learners can apply what they know about their L2 grammar to talk about their L1. Second, we know that the markedness of various L2 features can lead to incidental learning (Pérez-Serrano *et al.*, 2021). Therefore, these features may play an important role for learners as a tool for analyzing other marked structures in their L1 or using these marked L2 structures as a basis for comparing their non-marked L1 counterparts.

The use of multiple languages within the classroom and other spaces has been a topic of much debate recently, especially regarding translanguaging or 'the planned and systematic use of two languages for teaching and learning inside the same lesson' (Lewis *et al.*, 2012: 3). The use of translanguaging is complex and connects with issues related to the multilingual turn, bilingualism and bilingual education, and foreign language pedagogy (Conteh, 2018), not to mention the psycholinguistic aspects of language use and language learning involved in the use, and sometimes avoidance, of various languages within the classroom space.

Much of the current literature focuses on translanguaging as a teaching phenomenon in English as an L2 courses (e.g. Conteh, 2018; Cenoz & Gorter, 2020; Leung & Valdés, 2019), where the instructor decides on the use of one language or another for a particular purpose, like teaching grammar in the students' L1, while conducting communicative activities in the L2. There are many reasons why a teacher might decide to use the students' L1 in the classroom.

From a communicative approach, this might be seen as unnecessary, or even detrimental. For example, Doiz and Lasagabaster (2017) reviewed a number of studies that indicated feelings of guilt from code-switching, and assessments that the person using both languages was lazy. In their study on teacher perceptions, the majority of teachers indicated that they saw the English (as an L2) only approach to be ideal. However, when asked about their own practices, teachers indicated that they did use the students' L1s to conduct some aspects of the course, such as interacting one-on-one during office hours, making announcements, helping students understand context, dealing with disciplinary issues and overall class organization. So, despite the clear preference for L1-only use, the behaviors of teachers are often complex and pressures of time, curricular coverage, classroom management and importance of comprehension can all influence the switch to students' L1s.

Other approaches to teaching do not always see the use of the L1 in a negative light. For example, from a multilingual approach to SLA, learners are not becoming 'native' speakers of the target language. They are becoming bi- or multilinguals. To this end, it is important to introduce them to behaviors that are common among bi-/multilingual speakers, which include code-switching or translanguaging. Other types of multilingual behaviors that are important for careers that involve multiple language use, such as translation and interpretation, would also see a role for understanding the relationship between L1(s) and L2(s).

In addition, some teaching methodologies see the L1 as a tool for meaning making and advancing L2 development. For example, in sociocultural theory, the L1 is important as a mediator. In sociocultural theory, the internalization of language is essential for the development of human thought which helps guide our actions and supports our cultural and cognitive development. In the L2 classroom, especially in the beginning stages of learning the L2, the L1 is still serving important internal functions, even if it is not being produced, because the L2 is not developed to the point of functional use for the purpose of thought. And within classroom discourse, the L1 can serve the function of supporting L2 understanding through 'languaging' (Swain, 2000). In classroom discourse where learners are able to use the L1 to talk about the L2, significant gains in understanding can be made, whereas strict accordance to an L2-only policy may leave students lacking.

Translanguaging can have broader impacts on teachers, learners and society than just supporting L2 development. A study by Carstens (2016) on L2 English speakers of multiple African languages not only identified cognitive and affective gains perceived by students through the use of their L1s, but they also saw how translanguaging could play a role in the scientification of African languages. Therefore, translanguaging should be seen not only as a tool that may help development within an individual, but also as a mechanism for broad-scale change in society. Translanguaging, then, should be seen as a practice with much potential for reflective pedagogies within the L2 classroom and beyond.

How and whether it is the role of the L2 teacher to provide space to reflect on these cross-linguistic differences beyond incidental learning are important to consider for curricula in which students can exit before they achieve functional proficiency in the L2, such as after a two-semester language requirement.

Individual Development and the Conscious–Unconscious Continuum

Throughout the chapter, the concept of the continuum of consciousness and its implications have been discussed as this new framework influences SLA and learning within an individual. Consciousness, when applied to L2-relevant concepts and knowledge, covers a wide scope. However, the productivity and length of conscious attention have different outcomes at different stages, and these are all affected by the amount of L2 linguistic and metalinguistic knowledge, L1 linguistic and metalinguistic knowledge, cultural knowledge, amount of automated linguistic and paralinguistic processes and transfer from the L1 and other previously learned languages. In the beginning, a student can be pointed to a complex grammatical aspect, but without sufficient L2 knowledge of vocabulary, relevant grammatical forms and the ability to map sound–symbol relationships and recognize words, there can't really be an expectation that a learner will be able to use or even really comprehend how the L2 forms map to meaning. This idea has been laid out in theories of learner readiness (Chorrojprasert, 2020), learnability (Pienemann, 1985) and the zone of proximal development (ZPD) (Kinginger, 2002). In each of these theories, the learner is not at a place where they can acquire or use the structure being taught on its own. From a consciousness–unconsciousness continuum analysis, one could view this as the learner not having the requisite resources to recognize, analyze and integrate the new structure into the learner's L2 system. As more base functions of language processing are automated, consciousness directed at more complex linguistic and cultural aspects of the L2 will be available to a larger number of cognitive resources for understanding. This is both in terms of working memory capacity and as a more refined, interconnected L2 network with clear connections available to integrate new grammatical information, even if this entails restructuring the current network.

In the most advanced stages of L2 development, the continuum of consciousness allows for automatic processing of all aspects of language, which frees consciousness to meaningfully delve into any aspect of the L2 that the learner wishes to evaluate. This includes advanced linguistic behaviors we might hope our learners can engage in that require complex grammar, cultural comparisons, reflections on one's own experiences and other high-level processes that involve the simultaneous processing and use of a combination of complex grammatical forms, deep (cross-/inter-)cultural understanding, intertextual connections and other higher-order thinking. But consciousness can also be pointed at or directed to things that have been proceduralized for a long time, like reflecting on spelling, or sound–symbol mappings, allowable phonetic sequences and morphosyntax. With a wide base of automated processes and ample working memory, the advanced learner can direct their consciousness to deepen their understanding of any aspect of the L2.[10]

Notes

(1) Although some challenge this transition and believe that to some extent, learning to read and reading to learn overlap and can/do occur simultaneously (Hall, 2018).
(2) The use of resources by L2 writers is also an important issue for discussion and something that causes much controversy among teachers and confusion for students. Although outside the scope of this book, it is important to note briefly that students also need to be taught how to use these different resources, which resources we as educators see as appropriate and how to appropriately use those resources and strategies that will help students either use them in a beneficial way or avoid the need for them. Tools like online or paper dictionaries, contextual phrasal search engines (Linguee.com), corpora and full text translators (Google Translate) all have

(3) I refrain from using 'end' state for a number of reasons, most importantly may be the fact that we never stop learning any of our languages and that even those languages we see as our L1s continue to change over our lifetimes.
(4) According to Friedman (2015), 'Less than 1 percent of American adults today are proficient in a foreign language that they studied in a U.S. classroom'.
(5) We'll exclude pictographic languages here since there is not necessarily sound mapping.
(6) Although, for example, if you recall the discussion of Chinese (and Japanese kanji) from Chapter 2, you will remember that for compound characters there is a phonetic radical that provides information about how to pronounce the character.
(7) This could be the origins of the processing advantages we see in the bilingual mind, if there is one (Fenoll & Kuehn, 2021).
(8) In my view, accuracy is important because it allows speakers to be nuanced and removes much of the burden of assumption and interpretation from the interlocutor.
(9) Some researchers are proponents of a direct link between declarative knowledge and procedural/automated/implicit processing (e.g. DeKeyser, 2017). Others call for a 'weak' interface or indirect impact of declarative knowledge on proceduralization (e.g. Ellis, 2011). Still others argue for no effect of declarative knowledge on proceduralization or what they might define from their perspective as the core of SLA (e.g. Paradis, 2009; Slabakova, 2015; Ullman, 2014). From my own perspective, an indirect effect of declarative knowledge on implicit knowledge makes the most sense from the available data.
(10) Although not often specifically stated, this may intuitively be why many language programs at the university level have often taught an advanced grammar course after students return from abroad, even though they had already been introduced to all of these grammar points in the first two years (the 'language' part, as has been termed by many, of a program). How this could be better integrated across the curriculum via a continuum of consciousness perspective will be discussed in Chapters 5 and 6.

5 Psycholinguistic Processes in the Classroom

Chapter 4 outlined the developmental trajectory that an individual learner navigates through their own experiences. However, many learners experience second/foreign language learning in a highly formalized classroom environment that prefers and reproduces certain experiences, while downplaying, ignoring or, even worse, discrediting others.

For the most part, our understanding of second language acquisition (SLA) has been relatively narrow, especially historically. Many of our subjects in SLA studies come from white educated industrialized rich democratic (WEIRD) populations (Henrich *et al.*, 2010). These assumptions about who we are connecting with can leave behind other students in the aggregate. This is a result of the system for tenure and promotion, as well as the funding available to researchers in our field. These unfortunate circumstances do, however, have a severe after effect on what we learn from and can say about our studies, especially when we observe learners outside our classrooms in the real world. A more representative picture of instructed second language acquisition (ISLA) in North America and around the world would provide us with a better understanding of language learning processes that play out in the second language (L2) classroom, and how those spaces, places, artifacts and people affect the psycholinguistic processes responsible for L2 learning and acquisition.

In order to create a more detailed picture of the context of instruction, experiences are differentiated from:

(1) monolingual majority language speakers (e.g. first language [L1] English speakers in the United States) who are learning an additional/second language;
(2) bi/multilingual speakers who consider themselves L1 speakers of English and an additional language;
(3) learners who consider English as an L2, as all of these populations are involved in ISLA, but whose contexts of learning are significantly disparate to justify independent analyses.

The Second/Foreign Language Classroom as a Complex Social Environment

The L2 classroom is usually located inside some type of educational institution. That institution is set within a social and governmental framework of institutions, which both inform and are informed by changes to that network, like public opinion about language education and languages more broadly, about cultural histories and laws. Within the classroom, people with various backgrounds, roles and motivations interact toward a joint, albeit sometimes nebulous goal of language proficiency and mastery, as this unique group comes to define it. Each of these positionalities contribute, to varying degrees, their beliefs about what should be taught, including which language to teach, how it should be taught and why it should be taught. Parents, teachers, students and administrators, forming a complex dynamic system, are constantly changing personally and through personnel changes. From year to year, teachers and administrators are faced with the challenge of framing their instructional goals with continually changing populations of parents and students. And while, hopefully, the teacher and informed educational professionals are the ones making the pedagogical decisions about the overarching curriculum, what works day to day is something that is always negotiated anew as a language learning class and cross-curriculum community.

These curricular decisions are made by teachers and individuals in the local educational community, and they are impacted by large national and multinational organizations, such as the American Council of Teachers of Foreign Languages (ACTFL) and the Modern Language Association (MLA), that are meant to support, but also influence, teachers, as well as educational language coordinators. These larger organizations are also visible to teachers at a more local level, such as through chapters of teaching organizations like the American Association of Teachers of (fill in your language), that provide training and materials. These larger organizations also act as a link between SLA (and other language pedagogy) research and teachers, who are introduced to new methods and strategies via conferences, professional development and continuing education opportunities. While much of this is still true at the university level, students may be interacting with researchers who study SLA and receiving instruction based on cutting-edge research. They are often also part of the sample of our studies and interact with us as research participants as well as students.

The extreme range of places, people and things that come together in a single language class makes each of these spaces unique, which is why language teaching is both an art and a science. There is no single route to successful language teaching, just as there is no single route to L2 proficiency. The following sections outline how the factors within this complex dynamic system contribute to ISLA, as well as the role of consciousness in the L2 classroom.

Classroom Place and Space

This section analyzes the overlapping places and spaces that encompass many of the contexts that ISLA investigates. The section begins with the smallest unit of spatial analysis, the classroom itself, and then expands to the classroom as situated within a larger structure, like a school or other institution of learning, and finally external spaces, such as a country or landscape. All of these layers influence the classroom, whether learners (and teachers) are aware of this or not, as they reflect geopolitical, educational and institutional power structures in which beliefs are embedded about the nature, purpose and process of learning.

The language learning classroom

Information about how a classroom is laid out, what kind of technology is available for students and teachers and the resources that were put into the design of the class are integral to providing a space that promotes and supports L2 learning and instruction. Has it been selected and enhanced with appropriate resources and technology? Was the same amount of thought put into its design as classrooms designed for science, technology, engineering and mathematics (STEM) education? This, in and of itself, cues students about the importance placed on language learning by school administrators and the community. Some of the other aspects related to dedicated resources, like student aids, funding for materials and teacher support are discussed in the following sections. Here, the focus is on what the physical classroom space itself says about language learning.

The physical space of the classroom can be thought of in terms of the amount of space available, and the type and positioning of classroom furniture and technology. The various combinations of space, furniture and layout within the language classroom are surprisingly important to a number of pedagogical approaches (Garrote, 2014). Many teachers ask their students to engage in activities that require them to get up and walk around the room, perform physical tasks (e.g. total physical response [TPR]) and meet with different partners and groups (the communicative method).

The relative space available can play an important role in learners' expectations of what types of activities they will undertake in their language course (Wright, 2012). If one walks into a classroom that could fit somewhere between 20 and 30 students, they might assume that they will be engaging in many of the communicative activities that they expect from a language course (in the United States). If, however, they were to walk into a stadium seating-style hall, their expectations of what they will be doing in the language class may shift. They might expect the course to be mostly lectures. Even if the class size is still relatively small in a large space, students tend to sit farther apart from one another, rather than right next to each other, as they would be forced to do in a smaller classroom. This physical space may also carry over to feelings of social distance between students, as well as between students and instructors. This space can affect language teachers as well. Many language teachers walk around the classroom in order to listen in on partner work, to provide help to students who are having difficulties and to make sure that students are using the L2 in instances when they should be able to. In a small classroom, one is able to hear an L1 being used from across the classroom. In an overly large space, whether there are 100 or 15 students, there is no way for teachers to monitor L1 use. This may alleviate some stress on students, but in many cases, that pressure of knowing that their teacher is listening can keep them on task and doing the hard work of trying to communicate in a new language. This amplifies the amount of language produced in the L2.

In addition to the amount of space, the type of furniture and technology in the room impacts pedagogical options. If, like in our giant lecture hall example, the seating is stadium style, this means the chairs and table-lets are fixed. There is no way to rearrange desks to form pods. And even if students do move around, they can't turn their chairs around to face one another. In a smaller, more typical language classroom, fixed furniture can have the same effect. If students and teachers are not able to manipulate their learning environment into a more optimal physical arrangement that can change from looking forward, to forming peer dyads, to pods or even into a circle for a seminar-style discussion, the effectiveness of those methods is, if not blocked, severely hindered by extra effort and physical or social discomfort.

Finally, the position of furniture and technology is a strong indicator for students about the power relations between teacher and student, as well as the expected social dynamics within the class. Imagine the different class expectations a student has in the following two scenarios. The first classroom has desks facing forward toward the board and projector. The teacher's desk and computer are also at the front, facing back toward the students. The second classroom comprises desks formed into a circle, including the teacher's, all facing one another. The educational style of the teacher, or at least as it is perceived by the students, is manifested in the arrangement of the classroom itself.

To end, it requires agency on behalf of the language teacher to both advocate for a space that affords them the space and layout necessary to accomplish their instructional goals, as well as rearrange that space to best fit their goals. That being said, not every institution will or can accommodate every request, that optimal spaces might be limited or non-existent and other disciplines are also vying for coveted teaching spaces.

What may be important here for language teachers is the idea that they should be thinking about space/place as part of their pedagogical planning (see the Language Commons created at the University of Virginia, described in Giering & Fitzgerald, 2019). And for administrators, they should be in the habit of asking teachers in disciplines beyond the sciences how the creation of new learning spaces could best support their pedagogy.

The online classroom

Even before the COVID-19 pandemic forced many language teachers online for the first time, there had already been a heavy shift over the previous 10 years to online modes of instruction. Many volumes have been dedicated to understanding the needs of students and instructors in this environment (e.g. Lamy & Hampel, 2007; Russell & Murphy-Judy, 2020). Therefore, the commentary here is limited to how space and cyberspace interact and their impact on L2 pedagogy.

So, how do we conceptualize *space* in a virtual class? There is obviously the virtual space, like the learning management system (LMS), conferencing technology (e.g. Zoom), email, messaging apps and other possible technologies. Many of our students today are digital natives (Prensky, 2009), but this does not mean that all students come with the same technological background and experiences to automatically understand how to navigate these academic digital spaces. Many studies have shown that variable access to hardware and software, as well as experience using these tools leads to different learning opportunities and outcomes in online language teaching (Alhumaid *et al.*, 2020; Ezra *et al.*, 2021; Shin & Hickey, 2021).

However, one also needs to think about the physical space that the students and instructors are inhabiting while they engage in both synchronous and asynchronous courses. While the course itself may be online, people still need to have reliable access to the internet and a place in which they can focus on learning. A number of factors influence the diverse ways in which classroom participants access the class, such as socioeconomic status, availability of high speed internet, shared space with family members/roommates and proficiency with academic technology (Ezra *et al.*, 2021; Sublett, 2020; Tate & Warschauer, 2022). While instructors should not assume that their students are all on the same footing when they walk into their classroom, they need to take this into consideration even more when working with students in an online format.

Online instruction also has a significant impact on pedagogical considerations. Even if you are teaching a synchronous course on a platform that can handle putting students in pairs or small groups, putting someone in a Zoom breakout room is not the same as assigning someone to work in a pair. Transitioning from one breakout room to the next for the teacher is much more intrusive than walking around the room. This also means that teachers cannot observe the rest of the class at the same time. And teaching to a bunch of blacked out, muted zoom screens is more than disheartening.

In sum, instructors must be conscious of these spatial and virtual environments and carefully consider them while putting together a curriculum.

Institutional environment

The institutional environment dictates a number of ISLA-relevant features of the L2 classroom; from the available space and the number of students per class, to the freedom allotted to teachers to make their own pedagogical decisions. The following sections outline a few of the important distinctions between schools, universities and public and private language learning institutions like the Goethe, Confucius and Cervantes institutes.

K-12 schools

There is a significant amount of administrative oversight within and of US public schools. To the extent that private schools also fall under these provisions is state dependent. But for most students in the United States, public schools are the place where they are first introduced to a new language (American Councils for International Education, 2017). Schools in the United States are funded primarily through state and local budgets, with some money for special programming or for schools with exceptional need coming from the federal government. This makes language learning highly variable from one state to the next, and even within the same state (American Councils for International Education, 2017). It is up to school boards to decide how much they value L2 education, how they structure language within the overall curriculum and what languages are offered. Within this system, teachers are often limited in what they can teach. In addition, many high school teachers are provided with a curriculum from the state and are required to follow it. While some freedom in terms of how they get the material across is still left up to them, it often pales in comparison to the freedom that professors are given to design their curriculum, courses and context.

One of the possible advantages that schools as institutions have in L2 education is that they can theoretically start teaching children an L2 as young as 5 or 6 years old. Some school systems do take this opportunity to begin early L2 educational programs, which require a significant amount of funding and resources to get started. In the United States, immersion and dual-language programs have been expanding over the last 20 years (Gross, 2016). This is encouraging to see, as it hopefully marks a trend in US opinion on the importance of learning other languages and will transfer to more motivation for students in the L2 classroom, in spite of the current troubling trend not only in decreasing enrollments but also in the number of language programs in K-12 and post-secondary institutions (American Councils for International Education, 2017).

Institutions of higher education

At the university level in the United States, instructors have significantly more freedom in designing their courses and curricula than their K-12 counterparts. Most often, even in public universities, the curriculum is designed by the department faculty itself, rather than mandates coming from some larger governing body, like a school board or state education department. Therefore, the courses offered, in addition to how those courses are taught, are often a reflection of the expertise of the professors and their own teaching experiences. One of the drawbacks for instruction, though, is that many language professors, unlike high school teachers, do not have as much formal training in education. As Trautmann (2008: 42) points out, 'Doctoral students who intend to become teacher-scholars typically have little opportunity for systematic professional development as teachers; many complete their doctoral studies without ever having taught a class, taken an education course, or had any sort of organized opportunity to develop their teaching skills'. This results in teaching methods that arise from an unsystematic amalgamation of what they were taught, learned best and/or may have experienced as part of a professional development opportunity.

For the curriculum, there is also an unfortunate distinction made in institutions of higher education that is not as prevalent in primary through secondary schools: the language/content course divide. In this curricular model, elementary and intermediate courses focus on language learning, and from then on courses remove the focus from language and frame courses around content, like literary or cultural themes. In addition to the divide in the curriculum, there is also often a divide in rank and status (Maxim, 2006). Tenured and tenure-track faculty are often the ones teaching the 'content' courses, while lecturers, visiting assistant professors, adjuncts and graduate students often make up the majority of the people who teach the 'language' courses, many times with a dedicated lecturer or professor specializing in applied linguistics acting as the coordinator for these (often 100 and 200 level) programs. So, for students, they not only feel a divide in the importance of language instruction as the focus of the course content shifts from language to culture, but they also see this divide in the labor distribution of courses by rank. Maxim (2014: 93) sees this bifurcation as a systematically reinforced product within US higher education language programs, as he argues that, '[Foreign language] graduate student teacher education typically perpetuates the bifurcation found in undergraduate FL programs by separating graduate students' pedagogical development from their coursework in literary and cultural areas'. These divisions can have a serious impact not only on students' perceptions of the importance of language learning, but also on their continued language development, as features which have been taught but probably not acquired are no longer the focus of instruction, nor are they being systematically cycled through to reinforce and maintain previous gains.

While this unfortunate divide persists in many US institutes of higher education, it is not true for all. Many programs have attempted to reduce or remove this distinction in a number of ways, including having all faculty members teach across the curriculum and integrating the teaching of culture and grammar in all courses (see Maxim *et al.* [2013] for an example of a restructured language department). These approaches to the curriculum tear down the bifurcation that negatively affects both instructors and students and supports L2 development over their entire university experience.

Public and private language institutions

Language institutes boast a wide variety of structures. Some are funded by governmental organizations, others by non-governmental organizations (NGOs), non-profits, private individuals, small businesses and for-profit schools, all with the common goal of promoting the target language and creating more speakers of that language (e.g. Goethe Institute for German, Confucius Institute for Chinese and Cervantes Institute for Spanish). How they get there, the curriculum they develop and the teaching styles they adopt vary widely based on the cultural teaching norms of the host countries mashed together with US student expectations for L2 classes and the training their teachers bring to the classroom.

There is much to be said about the good that these programs do in offering L2 learning opportunities to those who are out of school, whether they are people in the workforce or immigrants trying to learn the language of their new country. There are also problematic issues with the way in which languages are taught and the types of cultural messages that are brought through these programs. For example, many scholars have criticized international government-backed institutes for continuing colonialist messaging and processes in the way they portray the culture and history of the country or countries that speak the L2. This has often been an accusation against English as a second/foreign language teaching practice (Majhanovich, 2013; Pennycook, 2007), and can also be applied to foreign institutes within the United States (Kluver, 2014).

Class-external environment: Foreign or second language learning?

While the physical space and the institution in which the L2 classroom is located are vitally important, so too is the external environment in which learning occurs. Here, three L2 classroom-external contexts are highlighted and a description is provided of how each affects the opportunities to learn outside of the classroom, the role it plays in classroom internal motivations and resources, and curricular decision-making.

The foreign language classroom-external environment

The foreign language classroom is a place where the L2 that is being learned is either not in use in the local, regional or even national context, or is very rarely in use to the point that it is little more than a novelty for the student. For these students, introductions to language and culture come from the information presented in the classroom by the teacher and through materials designed for educational purposes for an L2 audience, with hopefully, the addition of whatever authentic materials the teacher finds appropriate. For the L2 learner, this means that this broad class-external environment offers them little that would prime them to think about their L2.

From a psycholinguistic perspective, this is detrimental, because spaced repetition, incidental learning and conscious attention to L2 forms are usually presented in a short amount of time held only on certain days of the week at specific times of the day within a specific context. This has a limiting effect on what a learner could become aware of and think about if they only had more L2 experiences to connect with outside the classroom.

The 'second' language classroom-external environment

The 'second' language classroom is a place in which the L2 being learned is a dominant, major or highly present language in the class-external environment.[1] In the United States, this is usually the case for immigrants, refugees, exchange students and other visitors from non-English-speaking countries. When they engage in an English as a second language (ESL) class, they do not stop seeing English when they leave. On the contrary, they see English everywhere, especially in the United States where so many of us are monolingual to the point that even hearing someone speak another language makes some US residents shiver or, in the worst of cases, violently react. These learners are not only faced with English in a passive way, but they are also often forced to use English to accomplish what they want (from low-stakes activities like ordering food to high-stakes activities like applying for asylum). This continual exposure to and use of their L2 has a very important impact on the second-language classroom: they have very specific goals for what they want to be able to say in order to live and thrive in this new environment (Lu & Berg, 2008). For foreign language classes, as a comparison, there is no immediate need to gain proficiency that drives learners' goals. They are not confronted with the L2 when they leave the classroom and can ease back into using a language that they have mastered to navigate their life. The second-language classroom learner, however, faces much more pressing needs and brings those needs to bear on the dynamics of the second-language class.

Study abroad and language learning 'in the wild'

While the student in the foreign language classroom often receives little to no class-external input in the L2, the student in the second-language classroom receives maybe too much class-external input in the L2. Thus, the study abroad student in the second-language classroom might be in a perfect position to leverage the opportunities afforded by a majority target L2 classroom-external environment (Freed, 1995). For the L2 classroom within a study abroad context, there are a few differences between it and the second-language classroom. First, all of the students in the study abroad context want to be there, which may not be the case for certain learners in an second-language classroom context, who might be forced to take English classes. Second, these students are usually there either in part or whole to learn the L2. They often do not share the same concerns that students in an second-language classroom do, especially immigrant populations who need to have a functional understanding of the L2 in order to find work or communicate with immigration or government officials, police officers or others who have significant influence over their legal status in their new country of residence. For the students in a study abroad context, when they leave the classroom, they have the opportunity to investigate, pick up, appropriate and try out new language structures 'in the wild' (Clark et al., 2011). This opportunity to focus on the L2 without the high stakes that learners in an second-language classroom might face once they leave the classroom, should theoretically allow the learner to use their consciousness to focus on linguistic and cultural aspects of their host country and its peoples. In sum, the L2-rich context combined with the lower-stakes experience of study abroad compared to extended or forced existence in a country whose language you do not speak may be the optimal environment for students to unite classroom learning and real-world experiences in the L2.

Artifacts We Learn By

The language classroom is also a place that contains and creates cultural and educational artifacts. On the one hand, materials are curated and brought into the classroom for the students, like reference materials, media, literature, photos, wall-art, posters and grammar charts. On the other hand, the L2 classroom is also a place where artifacts are constructed by and with students that are snapshots of their cultural understanding, L2 proficiency and their own personal connections to the L2. The following sections outline some of the major artifacts that can be found in the L2 classroom, what and how they are used, and what they represent for the different members of the L2 classroom community.

Reference materials

In almost any language classroom, certain reference materials and textbooks play a part in establishing what is 'correct'. These artifacts often define what language in the L2 counts as accurate, and what does not through the representation of a classroom-external, linguistically omniscient authority. While the establishment of a standard language is usually comforting for both the students and the teacher, these books are only a snapshot of the language in a particular moment of time, and not even of any particular language spoken by any actual speaker of that language, in addition to frequently missing context relevant for particular language use (Nunan, 1998). No one follows all of the rules of the standard language, especially when speaking. Even in writing, people have their own variations.

The unfortunate nature of these texts and their impact on learners and many teachers are that they come to assume that language is fixed, which all linguists know is a fallacy. These references can also be detrimental in curbing language-play and creativity, which is often seen as an essential step in language development (Bell, 2012). Instructors should take great care, especially for child L2 language learners, to talk about the role that dictionaries should play in learning, and for more mature students, discussions about who writes these books, where their authority comes from and how they view accuracy and correctness in an L2 should be part of the curriculum.

Textbooks

Textbooks are a special kind of reference material, in that they not only represent correct language, but they also espouse approaches to language learning and an overall curriculum (Passey *et al.*, 2004). The layout of grammar, the integration of authentic materials, the activities and supplemental materials, dialogues and the interpretations of the authors make each textbook unique in the way it presents and promotes L2 development. The ordering of grammar topics by chapter can represent which grammatical forms are most appropriate for which content, or they can represent a supposed optimal order for introducing various grammar forms. Again, it is essential that instructors are critical of any textbook that they are either given or they select for their courses, as these textbooks inherently bring with them beliefs about the L2 culture, the L2 itself and the way in which students should be instructed (Gurney & Díaz, 2020; Passey *et al.*, 2004). Students should be made aware that whatever textbook they are using is only one among many, and that the way in which topics are presented in this book may look totally different in another book, which again brings with it ideas about authority, who decides what is correct and who decides what should be included or excluded.

Digital tools and language learning apps

Today, digital tools have become more integrated into the L2 classroom. Whether these are online dictionaries and reference tools, textbook-affiliated supplemental materials, authentic websites, course management tools or language learning apps, they all play a part in creating the virtual space that students interact with as part of the L2 classroom. Many of these tools have been around for years, but newer outreach like Duolingo's 'Duolingo for schools' program (https://schools-v2.duolingo.com/) are trying to move from a general language learning app to one that teachers can utilize as part of their curriculum.

The major hurdles for the integration of these tools into the L2 classroom are funding for technology that would give students and teachers access, teacher training on how to use these resources and also student familiarity and comfort with digital tools (Bailey & Lee, 2020). Not all students have the same opportunities to interact with technology outside the classroom, so it should be recognized that just having the tools available within the classroom is not enough for some students who might need support to make use of these tools.

Locally created classroom artifacts

The language classroom also contains artifacts created by the teachers and students. These materials, in contrast to those imported into the L2 classroom from other authorities and sources, are unique to their L2 classroom context, including the participants within that context. The following sections outline how these artifacts reflect more of the teacher's own beliefs of the SLA process, as well as students' contributions to the classroom.

Instructor-developed handouts, reference guides, videos and other artifacts

Unlike textbooks, reference materials, language learning apps and other materials that are brought into the L2 classroom, artifacts created by the instructor for their students play a significant role in enhancing language learning outcomes because they are developed within or for a specific L2 classroom. I make this conclusion based on the fact that these artifacts are representations of the instructor's understanding of the L2, rather than the instructor's interpretations of what imported materials are intended to convey. These classroom-specific artifacts enhance the instructor's approach by giving them a physical form and a place in the classroom.

Artifacts can take various forms, including grammar explanations, handouts and activity sheets. With the addition of multimedia space, instructors can also create videos, slides and other digital content for their students. I find recordings of grammar explanations by teachers, which allow for screen capturing or recording of their thought processes, for example, to be much more digestible for students than written explanations, be they from the instructor or a textbook.

These teacher-created artifacts are manifestations of the expectations and plans for peer–peer and student–teacher interactions. They can provide learners with chunks and phrases that enhance classroom interaction, as well as lay out the expectations for L2 usage in the classroom.

Student learning artifacts

Students also contribute to the creation of artifacts that are present in the L2 classroom. Every assignment, presentation and essay they create is a manifestation of their language proficiency at that particular moment in time, development and context. These artifacts can be powerful sources of information for both instructors and researchers to track the learning trajectories of individual students and the class as a whole (e.g. Kim & Canagarajah, 2021). Insights from these artifacts have played a major role in showing the non-linearity evident in SLA and the importance of context-specific performance (Godwin-Jones, 2019). What artifacts are created and displayed is dependent on the teacher and the class community and can be greatly affected by the institution in which the class is housed.

Wall space and classroom personalization

While pre-K through post-secondary L2 classrooms both contain teacher and student-created artifacts, there is one major difference between the two. In a typical school setting, many classrooms are assigned to a specific teacher. This means that they can decorate and enhance their space in any number of ways, like putting up student work, hanging grammatical tables and charts, having a library of texts for students to read and other things that promote what the teacher wants students to learn and also emphasize the accomplishments and products created by students and as a class.

For post-secondary instructors, this is not the case. Classrooms are usually assigned based on class size and technology needs, and instructors often teach in different rooms all across campus. This means that their classrooms do not get to act as showcases for their priorities and student accomplishments. In addition, any rearrangement of furniture needs to be done just before class starts and then undone after the class is over. For high school students, just entering the L2 classroom can prime them to shift to the L2 and be ready to use it; however, for post-secondary instructors, this shift puts a lot of the work on them to get students primed to use the L2.

People in the L2 Classroom Community

The L2 classroom would be nothing without the people that inhabit and traverse its space. This section covers the presence of students, instructors and more tertiary individuals who are often seen as visitors, at least from the perspective within the classroom, such as administrators, guest speakers and lecturers, and student teachers.

Students

Students are at the heart of ISLA. The breadth and depth of their personal experiences, needs, wants, ambitions, aptitudes, individual differences and goals are what make ISLA a complex educational and research environment. Their very nature disrupts attempts at organizing, analyzing and explaining their behaviors in and development from classroom-based interventions. For some researchers, this makes the lab learning environment all the more appealing, but for those of us interested in making sure that our theories, and methods based on those theories, work within the complex classroom environment, this challenge is all the more rewarding when we see positive results in spite of the challenges posed by an almost unknowable number of unanticipated behaviors, internal and external influences and wildly variable individual differences.

Delineating between the following groups of students, the next sections present important differences in psycholinguistic processing, general cognitive abilities, socially relevant constructs and communicative competencies that affect the way teachers should approach these groups.[2]

Elementary and middle school students

It is difficult to generalize about this group of students broadly, because they span such a wide range of developmental stages, including cognitive, social and physiological changes. However, the clearest point that can be made about this group of learners is exactly that they are changing, and drastically. They are simultaneously gaining L1 literacy skills and, especially for very young learners, still learning how to control the complex grammatical features of their L1.

It is important to point out that some researchers would also argue that language acquisition is easier for these pre-pubescent learners because of their developmental status, namely that they are still in a biological critical period of language learning. While I disagree with the critical period hypotheses as biological reality, I do agree that language learning tends to be easier for these students because they are focused on learning without many of the social requirements placed on older and adult learners, and L1 processes are not nearly as entrenched. However you wish to look at it, it does appear that starting L2 classes at these ages leads to more successful L2 acquisition (Birdsong, 2004; Chondrogianni, 2008).

Of utmost importance to keep in mind for these learners is that they are still navigating what it means to be a student, what expectations teachers have, how to balance academic and social learning, and therefore in the L2 classroom, how to learn how to do all of these things at the same time as they are learning a new language.

High school students

High school students are also going through significant cognitive and social development. For those researchers who believe in a critical period, they would argue that certain aspects of the L2 are now no longer acquirable, in the sense they would use for child learners, and that access to universal grammar (UG) may be limited or cut off all together (see Rothman & Slabakova, 2018). I would argue that the social and L1 processes have been entrenched to the point where making changes to these processes is significantly harder, and that operating in the L2 itself is also seen differently by these students in terms of the purpose of learning the L2. However, with age also comes more cognitive maturity and knowledge of learning strategies that they can apply to new knowledge.

College and university students

While developmental changes, especially within the brain, are still occurring within these students (e.g. Casey et al., 2000), they are cognitively mature, and in a US context, considered adults. This means that parents no longer have the right to look at their grades or schoolwork (without special permissions), or to be part of the language learning community. For many students, this transition from parental involvement in school to a context in which they are solely responsible for their own education can be very difficult (Cullaty, 2011). For the L2 classroom, students likely need time to adjust, as with other courses, to learning more self-management skills. These social changes can impact the L2 class in a number of ways, including student readiness and preparedness for class, how assignments are structured and how students learn to work together outside of class and engage in different kinds of extracurricular activities that help them explore the L2 (Bland et al., 2012; Clark, 2005; Geller & Greenberg, 2009).

Adult students

By adult students, I mean students who are no longer in school, or who have gone back to school at a later age but have work and/or family responsibilities. These learners are fully cognitively mature and have deeply entrenched L1 (and other L2) processes. They also do not have the same time to dedicate to purely learning the language if they are balancing school, work and family (e.g. Kara et al., 2019).

The location of these classes also differs. While many colleges and universities offer language courses for commuter students or adult learners, they also often take courses at institutions that focus only on teaching the L2 and have specialized courses for different types of learning needs. The question of why these learners take this course, for what purpose and to what ends, is one that the L2 classroom instructor needs to grapple with as they select course materials, design lesson plans and activities, and pick appropriate assessment methods. Is it for personal enrichment? For business purposes? So that they can integrate into or interact with speakers of that language as part of a planned move to another country? So that they can integrate into or interact with the culture of the country they are now residing in? Or are they learning the language to help immigrants and refugees by speaking to them in their language(s)? What are the stakes if these students do not achieve their goals?

Heritage language students

Heritage language (HL) learners can be of all ages, but any course that groups them together recognizes that they have specialized needs. HL learners generally have more proficiency in speaking and listening skills, while they often fall behind in reading and writing (Fairclough & Beaudrie, 2016). This is a result of their context of learning. They likely use it for family and social purposes, but not as much for educational purposes, where more reading and especially writing occur. Their experience with their HL also likely did not contain formal educational training about grammar, compared to whatever language they used for schooling. For the HL classroom, this means a heavier focus on teaching reading and writing skills than one would likely encounter in an L2 classroom, where many teachers lean heavily toward oral language proficiency and communicative language practices for their students over academic language and writing.

Some of the mitigating factors that help to explain HL proficiency in this group of learners include the type of language behaviors they conduct on a daily basis (Valdés *et al.*, 1999), access to HL classes, such as Saturday/weekend culture and language schools (Chinen & Tucker, 2005; Otcu, 2010; Shibata, 2000), and their family's and their own motivations for continuing to speak the language, which was covered in Chapter 1 of this book.

The instructor(s)

Instructors, like students, come in all shapes and sizes. They have different reasons for becoming teachers, they have different teacher training experiences and they bring with them different beliefs about L2 development. Teachers of different age groups and student populations face similar and dissimilar challenges.

Elementary school teachers

The elementary school language teacher has a complex task in front of them. Unlike teachers of older students, they are tasked with teaching students what it means to be a student, what schooling is all about and how to act within a school, in addition to the content of their courses. For language teachers, they must balance their learning objectives with regards to language with the prior knowledge (or lack there of) that students bring with them to the classroom. This is not only related to linguistic knowledge, but also cultural knowledge about what it means to be a student and engage with the educational system. Therefore, confusion can arise not just from a lack of L2 knowledge and proficiency, but also a lack of understanding about what is expected of them as students.

Models that are highly effective for these learners are bilingual/dual-language immersion courses (Olivos & Lucero, 2018; Watzinger-Tharp *et al.*, 2018). Many students at this age don't have a solidified understanding of what 'language' itself is, and they have fewer beliefs about why they should or shouldn't be learning a foreign language. Discussions about motivation, career goals and uses of the L2 beyond the classroom don't really need to be had with this age group. With their parents, that's a different story.

Middle and high school teachers

Teachers at this level have to differentiate between students who come from elementary school feeder programs and students starting at the 'initial stage'. In some school systems, L2 teachers can start with more advanced activities and have higher expectations about what students can do from day one, if they know that the students coming to their classes have some base in the language from elementary school.

However, most US school systems do not start foreign language courses until middle or high school (American Councils for International Education, 2017). Therefore, the teacher has to design the curriculum over the course of four years to help students go from some initial state to at least some level of proficiency. They also need to keep in mind that some students may only be taking a language because it is a requirement for graduation or for college acceptance and will stop once the requirement is completed (American Councils for International Education, 2017). In this case, the teacher is not only tasked with how to make the two-year experience meaningful for those students who are not really motivated to learn another language, but must also try and change those motivations within those two years to have students continue learning the L2 throughout high school and hopefully beyond. Lastly, and most difficult for the L2 teacher, is how to balance students who come in at various proficiency levels. For example, within a school system, a particular elementary school might have a foreign language immersion program, while another does not. This means that the base level of understanding, even if incoming students with some proficiency are placed in a higher level, change the dynamics of the class and the teacher is in a position where they need to bring lower-proficiency students along and still challenge those with higher proficiency all in the same room, or manage a class with students who vary greatly in age.

College and university instructors

As mentioned above, students learning an L2 at an institution of higher education may encounter a wide variety of language instructors, such as adjuncts, visiting lecturers and assistant professors, language faculty, culture/literature faculty and graduate students. Each of these categories of instructors bring their own perspectives to the language classroom, especially when it comes to what students need to know and be able to do.

They also have different restrictions placed on them. For example, graduate student instructors operate much like student teachers. Adjunct and visiting faculty are often expected to teach in a particular way as laid out by the faculty or a language program coordinator. Other tenure-track and tenured faculty members usually have more freedom in what they do within their own classes, but hopefully they are coordinating across the curriculum and sections to make sure that certain learning objectives, as agreed upon by the department, are being met.

One other aspect that is somewhat unique to the higher education space is that many faculty are asked to consider how they can incorporate their research into their teaching, or how their research affects their teaching. This is a fairly common question in the current job market, so it is fair to assume that curricular content as well as modes of instruction within these instructors' classes is influenced by their own unique backgrounds.

Tutors

Tutors can operate at all levels of education and proficiency, be various ages and work at all types of institutions. A common theme with this type of instructor is that they usually work one on one or in small groups, inside or outside the classroom. They often help students understand what was covered within the class so that they can spend the time necessary to master it, which they likely were not able to do with the limited time and practice in class. They may also be involved in outreach programs with local schools (Davidheiser, 1999; Polansky, 2004). Even though they may not be in the physical classroom with the students, they still affect the in-class learning, and can be an outstanding resource that helps the teacher make sure all students are advancing, despite the fact that learners will understand the course content in the moment to varying degrees.

Heritage program instructors

Heritage program teachers operate at all levels and across all institution types, from elementary through high school programs, higher education and specialized HL schools. They may have specialized training or knowledge to focus on particular skills that heritage learners need (Potowski, 2003). They may also have very different backgrounds and training. For example, while those operating in schools might have formal training in foreign language education, those working at weekend schools might be volunteers from the community with limited L2 linguistic knowledge, but a deep understanding of important cultural issues related to the HL and its speakers (Shibata, 2000).

Other visitors and guests

This final section on people in the L2 classroom turns to what one might call visitors. People who come to the classroom for specific purposes, and for short or limited amounts of time, to perform various functions, such as assessing teaching, providing resources for the teacher or student, or learning about the profession. While none of these people would be considered part of the L2 classroom community, they can impact the normal learning and teaching patterns into which students and instructors have assimilated. The breaking of this normal mode of instruction can be beneficial or detrimental to the L2 classroom, and an analysis of each of the following visitors provides insight into what these disruptions might cause.

Guest speakers/target language speaker guests

Guest speakers, including L1 speakers, are an excellent source of inspiration and perspective for students. They bring with them narratives and experiences that many students have not yet encountered with the L2 culture or language. They also showcase what a person can do with the L2 and the different opportunities being bi-/multilingual can afford them. They also provide an opportunity for students to interact with someone who has mastered, or at least can use, the L2 to engage with L2 speakers through travel, study or work. While these people act as visitors and don't usually become part of the class community, they are still valuable sources of inspiration and motivation that can re-engage students with the L2.

Administrators

Administrators play very different roles based on the language learning class environment. Some classes are regularly visited by vice-principals and the like, while others never see an administrator grace their class. For example, in K-12 schools, it is common for administrators to sit in on an L2 class to assess the teacher. At the university level, it is usually a peer who does the classroom observations, and administrators do not really interact with the class.

The appearance of these people in the class is usually announced ahead of time by the teacher, because they may want to let students know they need to be on their best behavior, stay in the L2 and save any concerns that are not emergencies for after that person has left. The presence of an administrator may also increase teacher lesson planning and preparedness. In sum, the effect of this person visiting can cause the instructor a certain degree of anxiety, which is especially observable for teachers in training (Bilali, 2015). This anxiety, while maybe helpful in class planning, can be detrimental to the authentic teacher–student interactions that play out in typical, unobserved classes.

Exchange students

In discussing exchange students here, I'm specifically referring to students who come into the L2 classroom with the target language as an L1, or at least very advanced proficiency. A distinction needs to be made between L2-speaking exchange students who visit the L2 classroom and those who act as full participants in the class, attending every day. For the former, they act in similar ways as visitors and guest lecturers, where they provide an opportunity for students to get to know more about the culture of L2 speakers through personal narratives and questions and answers. For the latter, they play a very different role in the classroom, with its advantages and disadvantages. As L1 speakers of the language, they have an excellent feel for the language, even if they may not be able to explain why a grammatical feature or vocabulary item works the way it does. This can be a great help for teachers who can only interact with so many students at one time. However, having an L1 speaker in the L2 classroom can be intimidating to both students and the instructor if they are teaching the L2 as an L2. Hopefully, the inclusion of exchange students in the classroom enhances the L2 learning experience for everyone. Before moving on, it is important to note that these exchange students, just like L1-speaking guests, are only one person in a very large community of language speakers, and they should not be perceived as a monolith for the norms and dispositions of all the other speakers of that language.

Student teachers

Student teachers bring an amazingly complex dynamic to the L2 classroom. As their title indicates, they are in the unique position of inhabiting the role of the learner and the expert. They are usually barely older than their oldest students, and much younger than the rest of the teaching faculty. They are also still, in many cases, learning the L2, so mistakes or gaps in grammatical and cultural knowledge are to be expected. They are also being trained, aside from the L2, in theories about teaching, classroom management and, for the L2 teacher, how language instruction and learning differs from other types of teaching, as it is both the topic of the course as well as the mode of communication about the topic.

Student teaching is a humbling, emotional challenge, speaking from my own experience. The role that the host teacher plays significantly impacts the performance of the student teacher. When we talk about language learner anxiety as an inhibitory factor for language learning, it's a guarantee that the student teacher, speaking in their L2, expected to be the expert and being observed, recorded, critiqued and assessed by higher education faculty, their host teacher (and likely the principal or some other administrator), as well as themselves, is experiencing some amount of anxiety (Bilali, 2015). In addition to this stress, they are also performing mental gymnastics as they try to remember lesson plans, manage the classroom, explain, model and guide activities, give feedback and remember to talk about homework, communicate with parents, assign grades and all the other classroom internal and external duties that fall on teachers. This inevitably leads to production errors, especially since most majors in foreign languages do not graduate with proficiency above intermediate high/advanced low following the MLA guidelines, or a B2/C1 level in the Common European Framework of Reference (CEFR), and many graduates' proficiency is well below these levels (Carroll, 1967; Malone *et al.*, 2005; Tschirner, 2016). This means that there are still many grammatical features that require some amount of conscious attention in order for these learners/teachers to produce them correctly.

Structural and Systematic Influences

In the US context, most students, if they take a foreign language at all, never expand beyond the growing proficiency or active learning stages described in Chapter 4. Few develop into the stage of budding multilingualism, and it is the rare few who achieve advanced multilingualism. Why is this the case when multilingualism is more the norm globally than monolingualism? Why is this the case when so many other countries boast students who go on to pursue advanced degrees of study in one of their L2s? For this, we need to investigate how the greater social context, societal beliefs about language learning and the structural aspects of global economic and national educational systems play a role in the language learning outcomes of students.

Language requirements

The larger societal context, the goals of government and social organizations, and the beliefs circulating within the national consciousness all influence the emphasis placed on language education within national and private education systems, down to individual institutions and on through to administrators, faculty, students and parents who participate in the language learning community. In the US context, this national consciousness about the importance of language learning negatively impacts the breadth and depth of language education opportunities, and the funding earmarked to improve educational outcomes. There is a small ray of hope in the United States, with the current trend in better perceptions of learning and knowing other languages, maybe particularly because of the rise of Chinese as an economically competing language.

In the United States, language requirements vary immensely between grade/institution level, school district and state. According to Devlin (2019: n.p.), 'Throughout all 50 states and the District of Columbia, 20% of K-12 students are enrolled in foreign language classes'. Some of the states in this Pew survey reported that less than 10% of the students in their state were enrolled in an L2. This lack of language requirement is a clear reflection of the nation's and individual states' perceived importance of creating bi-/multilingual citizens and the worth of multiple language knowledge in the global, as well as local economy.

Frustratingly, it cannot even be said that the lack of L2 course participation is correlated to the language make-up of each state. For example, Arizona and New Mexico, which have some of the highest non-English-speaking populations of any state, have under 10% participation in L2 classes (Devlin, 2019). The better correlation between state and language learning requirements is political party control and distribution in the state. For example, a survey by the *Washington Post* on reactions to hearing someone speak a language besides English in the United States found that 'nearly half of white republicans say it bothers them' (Ingraham, 2019). With this contention dictated by political leaning versus the economic interests of the country, it is unclear whether a national policy, pro or contra national foreign language requirements, will ever be decided, especially with so much power over educational systems and decisions left to the state and local levels.

The shared belief in the worth of language learning and being bi-/multilingual is much different in non-English-speaking countries (Devlin, 2019). To some extent, these requirements are necessary because they serve the government by increasing the economic productivity of their citizens who, in order to work internationally, require some lingua franca.

Language offerings and student enrollments

The languages offered within the US national context are steeped in history. If this were not the case, the United States would see a much broader range of language offerings. Instead, the majority of foreign language course offerings in the United States come from historical relations between earlier diplomatic partners and countries from which large populations of immigrant came. Tables 5.1 and 5.2, taken from the National K-16 Foreign Language Enrollment Survey Report (American Councils for International Education, 2017), provide an overview of the majority languages offered at US high schools and higher education enrollment information about the languages offered and taken by students in the United States, respectively.

In terms of overall enrollment and changing demographics, from the data we see that Spanish and American sign language (ASL) remain the top choices for students, as well as European languages, although some are giving way to pressures from other globally important and widely used languages, such as Chinese, Korean, Arabic and Japanese.

If students, at least at the post-secondary level, are interested in taking a different language than the standard ones offered, there are other opportunities. Less commonly taught languages (LCTLs), as the name suggests, provide students with an opportunity to learn a language that is not generally offered by an institution, usually through the support of governmental programs that bring L1 speakers of other languages, usually geopolitically strategic ones, to the United States, so that a small number of US students might be able to gain a working capacity in that language in order to support federal institutions, like the National Security Agency (NSA), the Central Intelligence Agency (CIA) and the State Department. Selecting an LCTL has very different implications for that learner, including who they will be working with to learn the language, where they will be having class (many of these LCTLs are taught one on one or one on two and therefore are not assigned to a physical classroom) and the types of (often limited) materials they will have to support their learning (Godwin-Jones, 2013).

Table 5.1 Distribution of high school programs by language

Distribution of High School Programs by Language
Table 4 below shows the distribution of languages offered by high schools in each state and the District of Columbia as reported in the high school survey.

Table 4. Distribution of Foreign Language Programs (as reported)		
Language	Number of HS programs per language	Percent of HS programs per language
Arabic	161	0.91
ASL	621	3.49
Azeri	31	0.17
Chinese	1144	6.43
French	3738	21.03
German	1548	8.71
Greek	129	0.72
Hindi	19	0.11
Japanese	433	2.44
Korean	43	0.24
Latin	1513	8.51
Persian	10	0.06
Portuguese	37	0.21
Russian	147	0.83
Spanish	8177	46.00
Turkish	27	0.15

Table 5.2 Fall language enrollments and percentage change in US institutions of higher education (languages in descending order of 2016 totals)

	2006	2009	% Change, 2006–09	2013	% Change, 2009–13	2016	% Change, 2013–16
Spanish	822,148	861,015	4.7	789,888	–8.3	712,240	–9.8
French	206,019	215,244	4.5	197,679	–8.2	175,667	–11.1
American Sign Language	79,744	92,068	15.5	109,567	19.0	107,060	–2.3
German	94,146	95,613	1.6	86,782	–9.2	80,594	–7.1
Japanese	65,410	72,357	10.6	66,771	–7.7	68,810	3.1
Italian	78,176	80,322	2.7	70,982	–11.6	56,743	–20.1
Chinese	51,382	59,876	16.5	61,084	2.0	53,069	–13.1
Arabic[1]	24,010	35,228	46.7	33,526	–4.8	31,554	–5.9
Latin	32,164	32,446	0.9	27,209	–16.1	24,866	–8.6
Russian	24,784	26,740	7.9	21,979	–17.8	20,353	–7.4
Korean	7,146	8,449	18.2	12,256	45.1	13,936	13.7
Greek, Ancient[2]	22,842	21,515	–5.8	16,961	–21.2	13,264	–21.8
Portuguese	10,310	11,273	9.3	12,407	10.1	9,827	–20.8
Hebrew, Biblical[3]	14,137	13,764	–2.6	12,596	–8.5	9,587	–23.9
Hebrew, Modern	9,620	8,307	–13.6	6,698	–19.4	5,521	–17.6
Other Languages	33,800	39,349	16.4	34,746	–11.7	34,830	0.2
Total	1,575,838	1,673,566	6.2	1,561,131	–6.7	1,417,921	–9.2

Language exams

Language exams can also alter the way in which teachers and students interact in the classroom and what is taught (Cheng & Watanabe, 2004). For example, advanced placement (AP) language exams offered through the College Board in the United States can be used by students as college credit. These exams are expensive, so ensuring that students score well on them is incumbent on the teacher. Therefore, many teachers participate in AP exam prep courses and learn strategies to help their students do well on these exams, as well as begin to practice exam-type questions with their AP-level students. Whether and to what extent different universities honor these exams as credit are not always in line with what AP programs and teachers say they will upon admission, but many students can at least use these exam scores together with their previous coursework to springboard themselves into higher-level language classes. In fact, research conducted by AP language testing administrators has shown that students who participate in AP classes are more likely to continue their language of study and go on to major and minor in that language, than they are to use that test score as their language requirement and stop studying a foreign language at the post-secondary level.

Other high-stakes language exams, such as those needed to study in a foreign country, also affect teachers' approaches in the classroom. For example, most students who want to study in Germany are required to take and pass an exam at or above the CEFR B1 level in order to enroll as a student in a German university. This language exam can have a significant impact on students' futures; therefore, those tasked with teaching non-L1 German-speaking students are under immense pressure to make sure that students are prepared to pass this examination. Aligning their in-course practices with test expectations is absolutely logical.

Other emblematic awards, like the new seal of bilingualism available in many US states, don't necessarily have a huge impact on what is done in the classroom, but these programs do have certain requirements regarding aspects of the language course, so the way the curriculum is structured overall can also be impacted by these types of honors.

Extracurricular opportunities

The language classroom is also a space where students learn about and experience extracurricular opportunities to engage as a learning community, as well as with other classroom-external L2 events, opportunities and communities of practice (CoP) (e.g. Fraga-Cañadas, 2011). The following sections highlight three of these opportunities for class-external engagements that have positive flows back into the L2 classroom environment and the learning experiences of the entire L2 learning community.

Student clubs

Student language clubs are a staple of the middle/high school language learning experience. They offer ways for students to engage in language- and culture-related activities that cannot be completed within the normal time allotted in class and offer students links to students at other levels of the L2, maybe other teachers of the L2 that they have not yet met, and also a way to engage with the L2 as a member of the broader school and local community.

Just as the American Association of Languages offers a place for instructors from all different levels of teaching to come together to learn, share and connect, so too can language clubs. In the state of Georgia where I teach, many of the languages hold statewide conventions, where students from all across Georgia come together to meet, take part in language competitions, interview for scholarships and learn about opportunities to continue their language studies at many of Georgia's institutes of higher education through faculty and college students. Many of these higher education students participate in their own college's or university's language club, where they take on leadership roles, promote language events and serve as excellent recruiting tools for the language faculty. The experiences that these clubs provide for students are a larger sense of community (Cagle, 2011), as well as the opportunity to either provide help to students who are at a lower L2 proficiency or vice versa learn from more advanced students and see what they can accomplish (Krause & Beitter, 1983). For lower-proficiency students, they can see what they will be able to do with the language if they continue. For higher-proficiency students, the challenge of teaching another student can really solidify their L2 knowledge or highlight existing gaps.

Study abroad

Opportunities for international exchanges and study abroad are also key drivers for both content and language delivery in the US-based classroom as well as the classroom abroad, which can take many forms, like classes run by teachers and professors from a US institution, from the host country institution or third parties. For example, if you are teaching in the United States but have a popular summer study abroad program to, let's say, Vienna, then it is highly likely that your course content will include information about Austrian culture, geography and dialects. While another program, which has a program in Bremen, Germany, will likely spend much less time on Austria, comparatively, and more time on north German cultural and linguistic variations from the usual American perceptions of beer, bratwurst and lederhosen.

These study abroad experiences also translate into different classroom foci as students return (Freed, 1995; Isabelli-García *et al.*, 2018; Kinginger, 2011). They likely had multiple experiences with the target culture(s) and language(s) that did not match their preconceived notions of what the people and places would be like, or things they learned in their textbooks. From this new, critical, nuanced understanding of the locality of culture and language, and the non-conformity of language in use compared to the language found in written texts and descriptions of standard language, the teacher has an opportunity to help students continue to apply that criticality to new linguistic structures and cultural phenomena, as well as draw on the lived experiences of returning students to engage with them in meaningful ways.

Internships abroad

The third extracurricular opportunity is internships abroad. It is unclear how much this applies to students at the high school level, or even for beginning language learners at the college level, as many universities and companies require at least intermediate, if not advanced proficiency in the L2 in order to obtain an internship. However, for those who are successful and return in time to bring their experiences back to the classroom, they have had a unique experience of understanding what it means to work with and through another language and what skills it takes to manage and grow in that situation. In the L2 classroom, these students have much to offer in terms of how the L2 is actually used, both in social as well as professional settings, and can provide authentic language that may not be provided in class resources, or language that is used regularly by the faculty. International students often use the L2 for different purposes. They might find themselves working in a corporate position using their L2 to navigate a much different situation from the L2 classroom, but still complex, with its own unique factors.

Classroom Context Effects on Consciousness and Learning

The L2 (and HL) classroom intersects with each of the classroom variables described above – place, space, people, artifacts and the geopolitical, cultural and social systems in which they find themselves. I argue that much of this has been left out of the discussion of ISLA, in favor of looking at the effects of instruction and interventions on language-specific learning outcomes. However, a full picture of the environment in which ISLA takes place and the factors that influence instructors' and students' everyday engagement with L2 learning in an instructed environment need to be contextualized in order to be of use to instructors in the real world, and to make them aware of the language-related variables that influence the L2 class.

Notes

(1) For monolingual (not heritage learners) in some US locations, this raises an interesting question about the boundary between second and foreign language classes. Is Spanish in El Paso a 'foreign' language or 'second' language? Likewise for French in the Bayou, Arabic in Dearborn, MI, or Chinese in San Francisco?

(2) One group that can be found in all the age levels and types of students I outline here, that I fear I must leave out, are students with disabilities or accessibility issues. My personal background in psycholinguistics and SLA is not sufficient to do this very diverse group of learners justice. In fact, doing so really requires an entire book. For those interested, I happily point you to the following resources: Hearne (2000), Konyndyk and Snyder (2011) and Scott and Edwards (2018).

6 Curricular and Pedagogical Recommendations

In his 1997 book, Ellis described the state of second language acquisition's (SLA) impact on language teaching as follows:

> There has, in fact, been very little consideration of how SLA can be utilized in language pedagogy. In general, researchers have been busy with finding out how L2 learners acquire a second language, while teachers have been busy trying help them do it (…) there has been no comprehensive discussion of how this might best be achieved. (Ellis, 1997: 3)

And while some things have changed in the last 25 years in terms of SLA's impact on language teaching, outreach and connections have not been enough to make a significant impact for most teachers.

This is one of the chief tasks of instructed second language acquisition (ISLA). To connect research to the classroom, test its efficacy in multiple real-world contexts, with different languages, instructor and student populations, institutional, cultural and social contexts and programmatic goals, and to make well-founded recommendations for instructors based on their unique convergence of classroom internal and external factors. Much of this research still needs to be done, and concerted efforts to test theories and methods in a more coordinated way would go a long way toward establishing reliable results applicable to the second language (L2) classroom. The goal would be to tailor unique responses to individual instructors based on their needs.

With the knowledge that there is still much classroom research to be done, there is enough available today to propose evidence-based SLA solutions for instructors. In this chapter, I hope to be able to provide not only a pragmatic framework for curricular decisions and classroom practices, but also specific recommendations that any language instructor could pick up and implement in their own L2 classroom, keeping in mind their students' individual needs.

Designing a Curriculum

Designing a curriculum is difficult, to say the least. One must make a multitude of decisions about all of the factors discussed in this book and more! The following sections recommend a few general practices for curriculum design that can make the decision-making processes easier, and maybe even time-saving. We begin with a brief overview of backward design, which may be more familiar to the K-12-level and educational readership than post-secondary and SLA colleagues who are reading this book. Some language curriculum-specific considerations follow that may be different from the general approach to backward and curriculum design. The chapter concludes with three sections: where learners begin in a curriculum, where you want them to end up and where they go upon exiting your class and curriculum. What happens in between to get them to where you want them to go will be covered in the rest of the chapter.

Before we move on, I would like to make one final point. Curricular design is a lot like language learning: there really is no 'end'. There are familiarized patterns, entrenched ways of doing things, yes, but there is always room to change a curriculum, and if one is not actively doing so from year to year, then one is missing out on one of the best ways to keep a program not only fresh for students, but also on the cutting edge of pedagogy. So, rather than seeing this chapter as a work-through that will get you to an end product, you should think of it as a process for continued design, evaluation, redesign, re-evaluation. It is incumbent upon the person or people responsible for the curriculum to schedule times throughout the year to assess what's working well, what could be done better and how to implement these changes for the next group of learners.

Backward design

Backward design, as contrasted with forward design or central design, is a three-stage approach to curricular design, consisting of:

(1) identifying desired results;
(2) determining acceptable evidence;
(3) and planning learning experiences and instruction (Wiggins & McTighe, 2005).

In this approach, curriculum designers, be they teachers or administrators, are first asked to figure out where they want students to end up on completion of the curriculum. Then, they are asked to decide how they will track this learning, what will be considered evidence of progress and how they will assess this progress. And finally, we ask what is done in the classroom, now that we understand what themes, concepts and ideas we want to cover when, and how we plan to assess progress toward these goals.

The first step is arguably the most important, which is why a later section is dedicated to where we want our students to end up. The second step is arguably the most difficult to design, since many teachers can probably articulate what they want their students to do after they finish their curriculum and have a lot of experience in Stage 3, the actual day-to-day teaching. As Wiggins and McTighe (2005: 49) argue, 'Evidence of understanding requires that we test quite differently, then. We need evidence of students' ability to "extract" understandings and apply them in situated problems, in performance – something quite different from merely seeing if they can recall and plug in the underlying principles the teacher or textbook gave them'. Thus, the design of assessment materials requires a deeper analysis by designers and instructors to make sure that their assessments align and connect their Stage 3 daily activities to their Stage 1 goals. Korotchenko *et al.* (2015) propose the following four main principles that should be accounted for when evaluating students' knowledge and searching for optimal criteria:

(1) Inclusiveness. Knowledge and skills acquired by the students throughout the whole study period should be evaluated.
(2) Variety. Monitoring system has to contain different forms of training efficiency evaluation including traditional and innovative ones.
(3) Complexity. On awarding a final estimate, one needs to consider not only the number of points according to test results, but also student's portfolio, their performance within the course and subsequent activity.
(4) Reflection. A student's evaluation of the work presented in the form of 'self-evaluation'.

Ample evidence has shown that backward design is an effective way to plan a curriculum. For example, in a study on intermediate English as a foreign language (EFL) learners' reading development, Hodaeian and Biria (2015: 92) argue that 'backward design provided the opportunity for learners to achieve deep understanding of texts and desired outcome in real contexts and enjoyed the process of teaching, topics and materials implemented in the class'. They go on to describe the positive effect it had on the teacher: 'It also provided the opportunity for teacher to find her way in the process of teaching and design an appropriate method of teaching in accordance with learners' needs and interests' (Hodaeian & Biria, 2015: 92). Therefore, implementing a backward designed course is mutually beneficial to the students and the teacher.

It is also important to understand backward design as a general approach that can be continually applied. For example, Paesani (2017: 7) notes that 'backward design is enabled by an ongoing cycle of program evaluation, which underscores connections among the three components of the model'. So again, curricular design is not really work toward an end product, but rather a continual process of evaluation, design and implementation, cycled over and over toward an ever better, but never perfect curriculum.

Language curriculum considerations

The language curriculum needs some special considerations, even if the framework of backward design can be applied widely to many subjects. First, we have language learning institutions, such as the American Council of Teachers of Foreign Languages (ACTFL), which provide standards like the 5Cs (communication, communities, comparisons, connections, cultures [National Standards Collaborative Board, 2015]). This design process fits nicely over these ACTFL standards, as Dhonau and Cheatham (2012) demonstrate:

> The interconnectedness of the 5Cs, the [Integrated Performance Assessment (IPA)], and the stages of backward design form the foundation for this performance-based instructional and assessment model for [World Language] educators. (…) the 5Cs represent stage one (desired learning outcomes), (…) the IPA provides evidence in stage two (evidence of performance), and finally, the backward design model itself serves as a catalyst for 'end in mind' curriculum and lesson planning. (Dhonau & Cheatham, 2012: 155)

This design model can also accommodate other language instruction-specific teaching approaches. For example:

> Advocates of [Competency-based instruction] suggest it has similar advantages to the backward design approach proposed by Wiggins and McTighe (2005). Competency-based approaches to teaching and assessment offer teachers an opportunity to revitalize their education and training programs. Not only will the quality of assessment improve, but the quality of teaching and student learning will be enhanced by clear specification of expected outcomes and the continuous feedback that competency-based assessment can offer. (Docking, 1994: 15)

This is also true for task-based language teaching (TBLT). In designing tasks for the L2 class, Ellis (2017: 121) promotes 'an ordering of tasks in terms of their cognitive complexity determined by a set of "resource-directing factors"'. This can also be used to determine end goals, assessment and evidence of development, the appropriateness of various daily activities with an eye toward language-specific proficiencies and complex task development. Beyond backward design, other factors specific to the L2 classroom should be part of the curricular design process. For example, the selection of materials for students is always challenging.

Instructors must often pick and choose from what's available through textbooks or other L2 learner-specific materials designed for the L2 classroom, or do the harder, but often more meaningful work of finding and didacticizing authentic materials. Dewaele (2008: 490) promotes a variety, where 'instructed learning should ideally rely on a rich source of diverse types of written and visual authentic material (Ellis 1999; Weyers 1999) allowing learners to familiarise themselves with sociolinguistic, sociopragmatic, and sociocultural aspects of the TL'.

The incorporation of technology into the curriculum is also something that needs to be strongly considered, since 'when technology is introduced into the equation, it will have some impact on the ways in which learners interact with content, with other learners, or with the teacher' (Reinders & Stockwell, 2017: 370). Ultimately, technology must be used to support the goals of the program, assessment options and classroom activity. If the effects and purposes of technology are not considered along with all of the other considerations of the curriculum, as well as the technological familiarity of the students and instructors, it can often be a hindrance rather than a support.

Finally, a few specific populations need to be considered in the language learning classroom. First, heritage languages (HLs) need some special curricular considerations. HL learners typically bring a lot of cultural knowledge, oral proficiency and listening skills to the HL class, so many teachers tend to stress these skills. However, Montrul and Bowles (2017: 497) caution, 'Although research has repeatedly called attention to HL learners' weaker reading and writing skills, literacy should not be the sole focus of HL instruction'. So, for the HL classroom, the teacher needs to recognize that reading and writing skills may be lacking compared with other language skills and proficiencies, but they remain in need of instruction in all areas of language development. They may also have very different motivations and goals for studying the language, so it is just as essential for teachers to understand these factors as it is for L2 learners.

The other group I would call out here is child learners, since they are not cognitively mature and they have also not been as socialized as older students to the expectations of schooling. They are still learning what it means to be a student. Because of this, Oliver *et al.* (2017: 479) argue that 'teachers should account for task familiarity' and that 'it is advisable to train children to develop necessary task-related strategies such as clarification questions, repetition, and alternative ways of expressing meaning'. In addition to task familiarity, Oliver *et al.* (2017: 480) also call for careful planning for group and peer–peer interactions: 'teachers [should] carefully consider the way they group their students (…) putting L2 children into small groups can significantly reduce social threat and facilitate interaction'. And finally, Oliver *et al.* (2017) also recommend that feedback during a task may not be as effective. Specifically, 'using pretask examples as a way of whole-class scaffolding rather than providing on-task feedback for younger learners' (Oliver *et al.*, 2017: 480) might be more beneficial than interrupting young learners during an activity.

One final consideration for these learners is how to balance the first languages (L1s) and L2(s). Immersion or dual-language immersion programs are very effective for young learners, and having young students learn content rather than focusing on the language as the target can help them normalize the use of the L2 for educational purposes. Lyster *et al.* (2017: 103) argues that 'A notable strength of [Content Based Language Teaching] has been its effectiveness in the form of immersion programs and supporting a variety of languages'. So curriculum designers for young students should consider what types of non-language concepts they want to help students develop alongside L2 proficiency.

Where (your) learners start

When designing the first days/months of a curriculum, it is important to think about learners' initial states, as detailed in Chapter 4. Some characteristics of the initial state can apply generally, especially if we are assuming this is both the first formal course and real exposure to the L2. For example, learners likely have some beliefs about the importance of learning this language, who its speakers are and its relative perceived difficulty as compared with other languages. For very young learners, this may not be the case, but for most L2 learners in the United States who start a language in middle/high school or in college, this should hold true for the most part. These learners also bring with them motivations to learn the L2, be they external, like pressure from parents or opportunities for work, or internal, like curiosity or attempting something challenging. They may also bring with them concrete goals about what they want to do with the language, like talking to relatives who still live in a country that uses the L2.

That they have these beliefs, motivations and possible goals, is true, but exactly what these things are for each individual is diverse, even if many of the students in a class have similar family backgrounds, educational experiences and socioeconomic statuses. Because of this, it is necessary for instructors to spend time learning about these factors in their students, even if they are not immediately integrated into the course. Knowledge about what students bring to the table can provide a serious advantage down the road to customize lesson plans and daily activities to highlight the strengths and interests of students in the class, especially if any of those are shared by multiple students. One of the most important long-term investments that can be made at the initial state is understanding the complex nature of individual students' motivation to take the L2. Pushed by parents, or society, or peers to take an L2 is not a strong motivator in the long run compared to students who cite genuine curiosity, career opportunities and family connections, although they too need help forming a more robust motivational network as they progress in the L2. Students need to continually develop their motivations as they progress through the curriculum, and engage with activities that link them to real-world, effective motivators if they are going to continue to be lifelong learners. This can be done by using content and issues relevant to that student, which they may not realize are also being discussed and lived through by speakers of that L2.

In addition to beliefs, motivations and goals, students at the very beginning of their L2 learning journey also have L1 linguistic and metalinguistic knowledge, as well as entrenched language processes, and various proficiencies in reading, writing, listening and speaking. If any students have issues that require accommodations, it would of course be necessary to discuss these in private with the student and other legally involved parties, like administrators or parents. However, beyond any accommodation issues that fall under legal purview, it would also be good to get a sense of the class's general reading and text comprehension ability. We would also want to understand which students are more prone to speaking up and which students will need more time, structure or support to make speaking in the L2 and real-time engagement in class activities more possible. And finally, we need to give students who want to interact as part of the class the tools to do so in a manner that not only satisfies our expectations as instructors, but also provides ways for students to be engaged beyond speaking up in class. A final note on the initial state: instructors should be aware that skill transfer is often not automatic (Cárdenas-Hagan et al., 2007). This means that it might take work on the part of the instructor to help learners' consciously look for areas of transfer, like strategies for structuring a text or how to negotiate task needs with a partner or group.

Where do you want them to end up?

The question of where you want your particular group of students, or even individual students, to be at multiple possible exit points from your curriculum is one that I cannot answer for you. This is one of the reasons I put the section on backward design first. If properly done, using this methodology for curriculum design should not only give you the answers about where a group of students should be by the end of your curriculum, but also where they should be if they were to leave early, if, for example, your institution has a two-course language requirement. While you may have goals for students who go through the entire curriculum, taking advanced courses, traveling abroad, etc., it is still good to set up your curriculum with particular goal posts that align with major exit points. Some of these might be, as mentioned, the last required course for general education requirements, or the last course needed for a minor or major, or the most common course taken by students about to graduate.

Where do they go next?

If you've paid attention to not only the linguistic development of your students, but also their changing motivations, goals and reasons for continued study of the language(s) you teach, then, I have to say, this is the fun part. While teaching can be rewarding in its own right, it is immensely satisfying to know that students are out in the real world using the language to pursue career and personal goals that require the use of that language. Whether it be study abroad, advanced research, travel, graduate school, a career, friendship or love, it is important to help them realize that a richness in their life came from the study and use of a language that was completely foreign to them and opened doors to experiences that will shape them for the rest of their lives.

In order to facilitate these futures for your students, it is necessary to make them seem real for your students while they are still in your class. A number of more concrete opportunities should be back-loaded in your curriculum so that students are looking for opportunities for continued study and use of the language when they are actually able to apply for those opportunities. However, this in no way means that these opportunities should be absent from the rest of the curriculum. Rather than just providing a list of these opportunities, instructors should and can do two things. First, they can spend time in class preparing materials that would be necessary for applications, like CVs and resumes that are formatted to the cultural expectations of the countries that use the target language, writing cover letters and exploring opportunities together as a class.

Second, and one of the great feedback loops in the curriculum, is to have former students who have taken part in these opportunities back in the classroom to talk about their experiences, yes, but also to have real people that can act as ambassadors for these programs as well as real-world examples that current students can see themselves in. In prepping returning students, they should be encouraged to emphasize how they felt when they were at whatever point in the curriculum the current students are, so that the link between where they are and where they could go is seen as doable, rather than having some advanced person come in without showing that they too at one time was not proficient in the language and had to do a lot of work to get to where they are today.

Although we would love for all of our students to find a use for the L2 in their lives, we know that in the United States at least, this is likely not going to be the case. So, what do the next steps look like for these students? Hopefully, there are any number of things, not only language and cultural related, but also social and interpersonal, like working in teams and working through problems with communication, that students leave our classroom with, but if we have to be strategic, I suggest focusing on the transferability of skills and intercultural communication. Transferability is a very broad term. It could be a transfer of interactional competency, or learning how to navigate a confusing situation, or working with multilingual speakers, or pattern recognition. Whatever it may be, it is useful to help students learn that they should be paying attention, using their conscious mind, to look for areas of transfer generally, and how they can apply previously acquired knowledge to new problems.

Of all the transferable skills one could focus on, intercultural communication is probably the most unique to the L2 classroom and curriculum (McBride, 2010). Students in our classes have to learn how to use another language in which they are not proficient, to get their meaning across to someone who does not know the language, or does not want to use the language that the student speaks. They also learn how to support what they are saying through gestures, facial expressions, visual aids, circumlocution and other communicative tools. Finally, they know patience for others who are speaking another language and know how to support those speakers who are trying to get something across to them.

For the learners who do not continue using the language we taught them, who knows if they may one day need to learn another language for work or some other adventure. Knowing that they already learned another language successfully can be a great motivator for learning another L2 and provide confidence that no matter what age they are, they have the tools to learn how to become proficient users of that language.

Daily Instruction

Turning a high-level overview into daily activities is the most time-consuming part of a well-constructed language class. We know where we are in the curriculum, we know where we've been (what we can reliably assume is known or familiar to our students) and where we need to go in the immediate sense (what's the next thing we want our students to be able to do, what grammar and its functionality do we need to explain, what cultural issues are connected to it, which texts or other media are we going to use to connect students to real-world situations, how do we get students to practice this in meaningful ways?) and what we need to hint at coming up in the near and distant future (what does learning this have to do with other language functions we will learn later?). This section outlines the daily structure of the language classroom, with an emphasis on linking previous classes to today and the days after. In the subsequent section, we will look at ways to support L2-specific skill development within this daily framework.

Class structure

Every class has its own institutional restrictions, e.g. time, space and number of students, but a common framework can be applied to all. I suggest, and outline below, how creating daily lessons should be done in the mindset of a moment in a larger continuum of instruction, rather than seen as an independent lesson. This involves the incorporation of looking back and looking forward, at the start and end of class, respectively, as well as the role of the teacher to make students aware of how they can link and transfer known information to new information.

Warming up and linking classes

Warming up a class might be the most important thing an instructor can do to ensure that the lesson they planned for, the topics they want to cover and the activities they want to run through are accomplished. Not only in a high school setting, but also often in a college one, students are running from one course to the next. The faster you can get students into an L2 headspace the more effective your plan will be. As discussed in Chapter 5, this is often easier to do in a school than in a post-secondary setting, as teachers have more options to customize their classroom so that students are immediately cued upon entry to the room that they need to be shifting to the L2. Other ways to accomplish this task include playing music in the target language, having a prompt on the board ready for students to discuss and, as instructor, actively going around and engaging students in small talk in the L2.

In order to warm up the class effectively, it is important to get students to start using the language to do something that is familiar to the point that it is almost automatic for them at the start of class, in other words, a ritualized activity. Students could ask each other what they did over the weekend or answer a prompt with a quick-write activity. Whatever the activity, it should be something that students can accomplish easily without help from the instructor, so that all students start the class with a win and don't need extensive scaffolding or teacher support to accomplish it. This activity is not the goal of the lesson, it is just the activity to prepare them for something new that they can't do yet and this priming will support a cognitive shift toward readiness for operating in the L2.

In addition to a warm-up, an effective course is connected to the past and what was just learned, so that students make clear connections with how to build off prior knowledge. This could include discussing homework for that day or explicit information given by the instructor, but using an activity that requires knowledge from a prior lesson with a small primer for the students to reflect on their own is also a great way for students to make and see connections across the curriculum on their own. That being said, even though we structure these activities in a way that assumes students are making these connections, it is still the prerogative of the instructor to ensure that students are making these connections.

Explaining, scaffolding, modelling and supporting classroom activities

As students gain more and more experience with a particular instructor, they also gain familiarity with the different types of activities that they are expected to be able to carry out in the classroom, such as partner interviews, storytelling and summarizing and reading aloud. However, each of these activities will quickly become second nature if they are clearly explained, scaffolded and modelled by the instructor and/or a few courageous volunteers. To be effective, explanations, especially if conducted in the L2[1] need to be simple, even if you are working with students you've taught before. It is much more important that the activities are scaffolded, i.e. presented in such a way that each smaller step allows students to reach a more complicated end goal, and that they are modelled (i.e. the instructor, with the help of another student or students, if necessary, performs the activity in front of the class). As any teacher can attest, there are times when you explain an activity at length, only to have groups of students miss the point of the activity. By extension, the tendency is to feel that the fault lies in the explanation of the activity, but with scaffolding and modelling, students are more likely to understand and complete the activity as intended.

One important way to think about scaffolding activities so that they have their desired effect is to utilize a pre-during-post model. This model works especially well when working with complex texts. In the pre-phase, e.g. pre-reading, pre-listening or pre-viewing, instructors should prepare students for the text by asking for prior knowledge about the topic so that the students can connect their experiences to what they are going to read, hear or see. It is also helpful to have them provide a list of vocabulary that they anticipate hearing, in the L2 if they can, but also in the L1 and then they can work on translating those words. Focus-on-form could also be part of the pre-phase, if particular linguistic structures are going to appear in the genre of the text. They can also make assumptions about what they expect to encounter in the text and then use those as comprehension checks in the during-phase.

In this next phase, students would have different expectations based on proficiency level and text complexity. For example, beginning learners might be asked to list words they recognize, others they just hear but don't know what they mean. More proficient learners could be asked to take notes as they go, and also note times/places in the text that do not make sense to them so that they can pay more attention to them on the next pass, because activities like these also require repetition. It is usually not effective for learners to hear a text one time and be able to get anything more than a gist. If, however, they are given multiple opportunities with a text, they often have the opportunity to apply their conscious attention to aspects beyond word recognition and text comprehension, like grammatical forms, author choice and text structure.

In the post-phase, beginning learners might be asked to compare the list of words they made in the during-phase to the list of words they made in the pre-phase to see if their predictions about vocabulary usage overlap. More advanced learners could provide a summary of what they heard or check whether their pre-phase assumptions were true or not. Another option is to ask students to do some type of form-focused activity, like a dictogloss, which 'is a reconstruction activity whose basic procedure consists in the learner simply listening to or reading a short text once or twice in its entirely and reconstruct it from memory (individually or in pairs/groups). The reconstructed text is then compared with the original' (Wajnryb, 1990: 398). Mayo (2008: 398) argues that a dictogloss is a 'task that could be used to make learners aware of the gap between their production and the target language'.

Another highly popular activity in the L2 classroom is peer-to-peer and small-group discussion. Loewen (2020: 57) argues, 'In addition to providing opportunities for interaction and modified output, teachers can raise learners' awareness of the benefits of peer interaction'. For beginning learners, it might be more effective to have very short (one minute or less) activities, because of the limited amount of L2 knowledge and ability they currently possess. As students gain more proficiency, they can be put in situations where they are required to process and produce extended discourse. Not only are the students in a position where this extended talk pushes them to use broader and more complex language, assuming you emphasize that all discussion needs to be in the L2, but this also helps them construct interactional competencies in the L2. In some frameworks, there may appear to be an assumption that an expert must work with a novice to drive development, such as the dynamic needed to create the zone of proximal development (ZPD). However, Loewen (2020: 98) assures us that 'expert-novice pairings for the purposes of learning may be unnecessary because learners have the ability to move in and out of expert and novice roles during collaborative activities'. The idea that they can switch between expert and novice roles is also a skill we would want to foster in our students.

Guided reflection and incidental learning

Beyond the planned class activities, it is also essential to make space for students to bring in their own observations. Some of these may not fit nicely into the curriculum, or they were a topic for another day, but we need to remind ourselves that language learning is not linear and no two students follow the same path. So, despite our best laid plans for how and when different linguistic features or cultural knowledge should be focused on, if a student is bringing it up to you and the class for discussion, then they might likely be ready to learn (about) it, even if you think that it is something for which they are not ready. It is important to give students space to explore what they have incidentally learned, either in class or as homework. For example, students could note for homework things they saw in class that they did not understand or noticed for the first time and the instructor can use that information to inform and build activities for future classes.

Following your plan and allowing for this type of student-driven learning is a balance, especially when students' questions arise in the middle of an activity. So, how do you answer the question without disrupting the flow of the class? Before I recommend any option, the instructor needs to consider three factors:

(1) Is this something that I can answer quickly or might it take some time?
(2) Is this something that I think only this student noticed or is it something that many students in the class have commented on or are likely questioning?
(3) Will it lose meaning if I don't explain it now in this context or will it still be relevant later?

If the answer falls more on the side of a short explanation, relevant to only that student, and important in this context, then I would take time in the moment to provide an *ad hoc* explanation. If the answer falls more on the side of a complex explanation, and this exact context isn't so important, I recommend having students or the instructor make a note of it and work it in as part of the next class. However, if many students in the class are noticing and bringing something to your attention, it makes sense to pause and take this opportunity for joint class attention.

Homework, assignments and looking ahead

Finally, ending a class should also be an opportunity to make connections to future learning, just as the warm-up and the beginning of class were an opportunity to make connections to prior knowledge. Besides recapping on the lesson, it is important for the instructor to be deliberate about linking what was done in the class today with how it will be important tomorrow, the day after and long down the road. Homework and assignments should also be designed in this way. They should contain aspects relevant to the class, not act as something external, and instructors should be straightforward about how they plan to grade these assignments and integrate them into class. In this way, assignments come to be viewed not only as a way for the instructor and student to judge their understanding and ability, but also as a tool for learning. This is important for all classes, but maybe especially for language classes. Language learning is a process and it is not about the grade, but rather tracking progress over time, and if used appropriately, it can be a great way to track and display this progress for students.

Feedback

Feedback in the L2 classroom has been extensively studied, and as such, it deserves its own section on its application in the L2 classroom. The use of feedback in the L2 classroom is meant to help learners come to the realization that something they have produced is, as deemed by the instructor, incorrect. What counts as correct or incorrect, or what receives feedback and what does not is highly dependent on the instructor and these expectations should be made clear to students.

Numerous studies have investigated the impact of diverse types of classroom feedback: implicit or explicit, repetition or partial repetition, written versus oral, immediately upon error or after the student is finished or after class or in the next class. All this research attempted to come to a specific answer about which type of corrective feedback was most helpful in the aggregate. Unfortunately, as Kim (2017: 138) summarizes, 'no one type has been identified as the most effective type'. So, what are instructors supposed to do from here?

I propose a new way to think about feedback, combining what we want from our students regarding conscious attention, dynamic assessment and an important role for the instructor as a master of their craft who brings art to the science of teaching. First, if we re-imagine the types of classroom feedback from a psycholinguistic perspective, we can ask questions: What do the different types of feedback in the classroom elicit in terms of conscious and unconscious processes? Do we want them to have explicit knowledge of what they got wrong, or do we want them just to be able to do it implicitly? How much attention do we need to draw to the mistake for the learner to notice it? The answers to these questions can be addressed by dynamic assessment to promote language teachers' understanding of how to use a repertoire of feedback options rather than assume a particular method is 'best' overall.

Dynamic assessment is a method of assessment from sociocultural theory (SCT) that helps us tailor feedback in the most developmentally useful way possible (Lantolf, 2009). Within SCT, assessment is not only seen as a way for the teacher to probe the understanding of the individual, but also a place where learning can and does happen. The process of providing differential feedback with increasingly specific information does just that. Using dynamic assessment, a teacher provides different feedback that first attempts to draw attention only to the fact that an error was produced by the student. If the student corrects their error, this shows not only that they have knowledge of the correct form, but also that they are able to identify the error without outside help. If the student produces an incorrect form again or does not seem to notice that the teacher was directing them to an error in their production, the teacher provides more explicit information about where the error occurred, which may include pointing directly to the error. If the student can then correct their utterance, it shows that they have knowledge of the correct form, but maybe do not have the momentary proficiency or processing capacity to recognize it without assistance. If the student is not able to produce the correct form, the teacher moves on to increasingly explicit feedback, which might include a reminder of a rule or pattern that needs to be applied, or a reminder about a previous mistake. Finally, if the student is still not able to produce the correct form, the teacher can provide the correct answer for the student.

To reiterate, this is only one method. An entire day could be dedicated to a classroom full of intermediate language learners this way. It can be an effective tool for particular instances, such as one-on-one conversations or small-group discussions where the teacher moves from group to group, or in a large class setting where the teacher has observed multiple students making a similar mistake. The question though, is, why not just give the student the correct answer through feedback the first time? The answer may be straightforward and almost intuitive, but the less explicit the feedback, the more useful it is to the learner. When a learner has to put in the work of identifying their own error, it helps them in future cases to do the same. They are also learning the tools to help themselves in future circumstances. When they make similar errors, they can form a habit to be more aware of their language and they can rely on linguistic knowledge about the language. And in the case where students are unable to correct their own language and need the exact answer, it is important evidence for the teacher in assessing what they think students should know and what students actually know.

This might seem like a long process, so one adjustment that could be made, especially for experienced L2 teachers, is using their insight into their students to skip some of the steps of dynamic assessment to speed up arriving at the most beneficial level of intervention for the student. Teaching is an art, in addition to a science, and it takes experience for teachers to know how to apply their craft with the tools at their disposal. For feedback, this means that instructors could recognize that simply pointing to the error in a particular situation is not going to do the trick, and a more explicit gesture toward or explanation of the mistake is going to be necessary for the student to become aware of and repair their mistake. This would save significant time in the classroom, which is a small critique of dynamic assessment, in that it can be time-consuming, and not always an option within a classroom environment where time is limited and the teacher needs to attend to many students at once.

L2 Skills and Knowledge

This section moves from a more general overview of language teaching that could apply to any number of other classrooms to content, knowledge and skills specific to L2 learning. Each of these sub-skills of SLA have their own cognitive, social and cultural underpinnings, which make them important to discuss individually, but they all operate together as part of the multilingual mind, so it is important to keep in mind that these subsystems all affect one another. Acquisition in one area might result in changes in another area.

Vocabulary

Vocabulary is the first thing that students need to start understanding, processing and producing in the L2. One can understand a non-inflected list of memorized vocabulary words, but one cannot understand morphology applied to nonsense words.

There are two major approaches to vocabulary acquisition in L2 pedagogy, and both incorporate the recycling of vocabulary in multiple meaningful contexts. Of primary importance to both approaches is Laufer's (2010) assertion that, 'there is very little chance for a word to be learned after first exposure'. So, in order to promote real acquisition, González-Fernández and Schmitt (2017: 291) argue that 'recycling is fundamental to effective vocabulary instruction, and teachers should provide opportunities/activities that allow students to encounter a word repeatedly and in varied contexts, to both consolidate and enhance their understanding of it'.

As mentioned, there are two approaches to getting students to encounter vocabulary in this meaningful way: extended reading and planned lexical instruction (PLI). On the one hand, it has been shown that providing students with opportunities to read longer texts can be very beneficial, even at the beginning stages of learning (Maxim, 2002). Unlike shorter texts, students are exposed to common as well as topic-specific vocabulary again and again throughout the text. They encounter vocabulary not only in its standard form as one might find in a dictionary, but also in its various inflected forms (e.g. plural, past-tense, progressive and declined). This helps students gain a deeper understanding of vocabulary in addition to broadening their vocabulary, since what it means to know a word goes well beyond just its meaning to include collocational information, inflected forms, context-appropriate uses and idiomatic expressions.

The other approach to language instruction is based on the fact that while L1 learners do gain a large portion of their vocabulary through reading, L2 learners do not receive nearly the same amount of exposure, even with extended reading. Laufer (2005: 320) notes that 'Empirical data on learners' vocabulary size in different countries show that L2 learners know small amounts of words in spite of many hours of instruction (Laufer, 1999)'. This means that the recycling of vocabulary needs to be planned to occur within the classroom, rather than left to chance. This sentiment is visible in Laufer's (2005: 323) plea for more PLI instruction for L2 vocabulary acquisition: 'One feature of PLI is providing additional exposures to new words in planned input, rather than leaving such exposure to mere chance'.

I suggest a combination of both extended reading and PLI. For vocabulary that teachers want and need students to have, PLI is the better option because it ensures that all students will have some common footing. I would limit the amount of vocabulary, however, to that which is essential for the goals set in the curriculum and which will be assessed. This is because, again, each language learner is on their own path, and one cannot predict what words they will definitely need in the future. That depends on their individual goals. To aid them, as well as provide opportunities for them to engage in independent learning, I recommend the use of long texts, which provide a broader range of vocabulary than is needed and used in the classroom, as well as opportunities for further depth in vocabulary knowledge through the use of vocabulary in multiple contexts, both topically and linguistically.

A final question about vocabulary is what type, common or uncommon or a mix, one should teach or highlight? Some pedagogues are strongly in favor of teaching common vocabulary, for example, from lists of the most common 100 words as found in a corpus of language use (e.g. Rankin, 2018). This is effective in providing students with a solid base that makes up most of the words one needs to know for everyday communication as well as covering a large vocabulary needed to understand texts and successfully guess the meaning of unfamiliar vocabulary. On the other hand, common vocabulary words are more likely to be irregular, while uncommon words are likely to follow regular patterns and have more complex morphology. This type of vocabulary provides more 'grist for the mill' as I discussed earlier. I do not think that the field is currently in any position to say which one is better to teach, or which should be taught first. My recommendation is to strike a balance between common and uncommon words in both PLI and extended reading approaches.

Morphology and syntax, aka grammar

Frequent exposure to and usage of some grammar may be sufficient to ensure acquisition. In a study on the acquisition of grammatical forms by varying degrees of input frequency, Gor and Chernigovskaya (2008: 128) found that the 'importance of the statistical characteristics of the language used in the classroom for the internalization of the target language system and for the development of native-like processing strategies in L2 learners'. However, no matter how much input one receives or practice one gets, some grammatical features are so complex that it is unlikely that the majority of learners will be able to understand their function without explicit instruction.

The instruction and acquisition of grammar is one of the most widely studied aspects of SLA, which is interesting when one reads the following from Loewen (2020: 82): 'research suggest that no single type of focus on form on its own is the best solution for the classroom; rather multiple types of focus on form (…) can be employed to bring about L2 development'. This makes it both easy and challenging for me. Easy because there are a plethora of ways to teach grammar to discuss but challenging because there is no clear-cut 'right' approach to promote. All approaches have their way of teaching grammar, be it communicative language teaching (CLT), TBLT, content-based language instruction (C-BLI), content-based language teaching (CBLT), content and language integrated learning (CLIL) or any other acronym framework.

One general method to teaching grammar that can be applied in multiple instructional frameworks is focus-on-form, conducted during meaningful tasks, to link grammatical forms to functions. Toward that end, VanPatten (2017: 171) argues that 'interventions that help with the creation of mental representation ought to be processing-oriented pedagogical interventions'. In other words, learners need to be put in situations in which the processing of grammar is required to process meaning. One can also make noticing grammatical features in context easier or harder by altering task complexity. As Kim (2017: 138) suggests, 'when task complexity is increased in a way that encourages learners to use target features, learners might pay more attention to target linguistic features while carrying out collaborative tasks (Kim, 2012)'. Loewen (2020: 98) proposes that 'C-BLI may be appropriate for teaching difficult concepts to adults, since adults are cognitively mature and have existing knowledge to build on (Walter and van Compernolle, 2017)'.

For the L2 instructor, I suggest that one thinks of activity distributions over time spans longer than a single class. Sometimes you may have more reading, other days you may have more task-based or interactional activities. It's more important to think about the instructional experiences your students have over a few lessons, than trying to pack everything into one. With that, I suggest taking the recommendation proposed by Loewen (2020: 122), who says 'it seems that the best type of L2 instruction may be that which integrates both implicit and explicit types of instruction (Nassaji & Fotos, 2011; Swan, 2005)'. It is not that every activity needs to have both an implicit and explicit part, nor does that need to happen every day, but the instructor should work to balance instructional methodology so that students see and use grammar in multiple dimensions.

Pragmatics

Pragmatics is another area that requires extensive instruction based on the lack of exposure to the target language, interlocutor and culture.

One way to adjust for this deficiency, which has been noted in other areas such as vocabulary and grammar instruction, is the use of authentic texts. Loewen (2020: 178) argues that 'Teachers should strive to incorporate authentic materials as much as possible, because the classroom represents a constrained and limited environment in terms of social roles and routines'. These texts contain pragmatic aspects of L2 interactions that may not be contained in materials made for L2 learners.

Another way to provide learners with pragmatic knowledge is to incorporate corpus approaches. Bardovi-Harlig *et al.* (2019: 75) found that 'teacher-developed corpus materials improved learners' production of speech acts and pragmatic routines and (…) corpus searches engaged learners in discovery and improved pragmatic routines even more than corpus materials did'. So, not only can the teacher use a corpus to highlight language in context for students, but with fairly simple training, students can also be asked to use a corpus to find their own instances of language in use.

Pragmatics can also be effectively approached through C-BLI. A number of studies on the use of C-BLI to teach concepts related to formality have been shown to be effective for teaching address forms (Van Compernolle *et al.*, 2016). In a recent study on Korean verbal honorifics instruction, Yoon *et al.* (in preparation) showed C-BLI to be effective for HL learners, as well. HL learners may have developed everyday concepts through experiences with family members and friends, but often do not have as much as L1 learners and can benefit from systematic conceptual information to cement their understanding. One reason for the effectiveness of C-BLI for pragmatics is that there is often no 'right' answer, only a match between the language used by the learner and their intended meaning within a context toward another person or other people.

Metalinguistic knowledge

According to Erlam (2013):

> Metalinguistic knowledge is a learner's explicit knowledge about the syntactic, morphological, phonological and pragmatic features of the L2 (Roehr & Gánem-Gutiérrez, 2009). It is knowledge that is analyzed, requires deliberate focus and, as Elder (2009) claims, learners know when they are drawing on it, in, for example, making judgements about the grammaticality of sentences or in edited writing. (Erlam, 2013: 72)

The usefulness of metalinguistic knowledge, especially specific terminology, is hotly debated in SLA. More and more research is falling on the side of the importance of teaching metalinguistic knowledge as part of the L2 curriculum. Fortune (2013: 73) argues that 'metalingual knowledge can play a significant role in L2 development (e.g. Hu, 2010) and that learner metalanguage awareness training (Berry, 2009) may be worthwhile'. And in response to opponents of metalinguistic knowledge, Azarola (2013: 221) notes that 'the critique against teaching metalinguistic knowledge in the L2 classroom, or any over teaching of grammar for that matter, emerges when grammar (metalanguage, forms, rules of use) becomes the main, and sometimes exclusive focus of the classroom time (Hadley & Reiken, 1993)'.

Metalinguistic knowledge and its use to talk about language support both passive and active language behaviors and do much to help students focus their consciousness on a wide array of language and language-related features. Azarola (2013: 221) argues that 'metalinguistic knowledge has the potential of becoming functional knowledge for second language (L2) learners'. For example, it has been shown that 'good metalinguistic ability allows the use of abstract and decontextualized language, which is an asset in successful reading skills learning', and that specifically metalinguistic syntactic awareness (MSA) 'contributes significantly to the construction of reading comprehension' (Simard et al., 2013: 62). The effect of metalinguistic knowledge is also influenced by proficiency level and context. In a study on learners' use of metalanguage, Fortune (2013) reported that:

> there is strong evidence that advanced learners not only attend to form more often than their intermediate counterparts while engaged in similar series of tasks, but also that they employ metalanguage far more often than their intermediate counterparts while engaged in a similar series of tasks, but also that they employ metalanguage far more often when jointly reflecting about their output. (Fortune, 2013: 180)

More advanced learners might make more ready use of metalinguistic knowledge, and this might be more common in activities that involve reflecting on work with other students than on their own language production.

Some instructors may be apprehensive about using metalanguage in the classroom, as they assume it comes with complex terminology that may not be age appropriate or is too complex for the needs of their students. Erlam's (2013: 72) position about the use of metalanguage should soothe any apprehension related to the need for jargon: 'Metalanguage is any language used to talk or write about language (Berry, 2005). It is not restricted to the use of linguistic or grammatical terminology only, because one can "talk" about language without using such terminology'. So, even if the students and instructor do not have the official verbiage used in linguistics textbooks to describe what is happening in a language, doing so in a vernacular, understandable way is often just as effective.

Instructors can do more to be systematic in the way they talk about different language features. The use of metalanguage, including scientific concepts, is often necessitated because, as Azarola (2013: 221) judges, 'The quality of explanations available through textbooks is not consistent or systematic'. The use of metalanguage around concepts can be an extremely powerful tool 'to help L2 learners to consciously use conceptual categories of meaning to orient linguistic choices (Negueruela-Azarola, 2011)' (Azarola, 2013: 221). He goes on to argue that 'Transforming metalinguistic knowledge into conceptual categories with functional relevance in communicative activity requires the merging of communication with conceptualization' (Azarola, 2013: 221). Therefore, it is incumbent upon the instructor to design activities in which these concepts are of use to learners, not simply taught as explicit knowledge without helping students understand how to apply the conceptual knowledge to functional use.

Listening and aural comprehension

Listening skills and oral comprehension can be supported by extensive use of the L2 in the classroom by the instructor, as well as an expectation set for students that the L2 should be the L1 in which they attempt to communicate. In saying this, I am not a proponent of 100% immersion in the L2, and I think there is a place for the L1, as we are helping students become multilinguals, not L1 speakers of the target language (e.g. see Walter, 2019). That being said, L2 learners often have limited access to target language material outside of the class (unless they are learning English of course), and therefore the L2 classroom is their primary resource for hearing the L2. For this reason, instructors need to be intentional about when and why they would use the class's L1 (or another shared lingua franca).

One of the pitfalls of teaching a language is that students often get used to the dialect, pace and sound of the instructor's voice, and have trouble when they encounter other speakers of the language with other accents or dialects, or soft or low voices, or a quick pace of speech. For example, Zárate-Sández (2019) points to how teaching multiple varieties of Spanish can have important considerations for teachers and learners alike. Other factors that can be problematic for learners are contexts in which there is a lot of peripheral noise, there are multiple speakers talking at once or there is no help from visual aids, such as phone conversations. As Scharenborg and van Os (2019) emphasize, listening in the presence of background noise is harder for non-native speakers of a language. It is therefore important to provide opportunities for students to engage in these difficult contexts, which are very common in real-world communication, through the use of other media, or the inclusion of guest speakers.

Speaking and oral fluency

In order to get students talking as soon as possible, it is essential to help them acquire chunks that they can easily apply to a number of activities, and also learn to formulate productive chunks and slot-and-frame constructions. Here is an example of a common transition from a static to a productive chunk that my students in German go through very early on.

They begin by learning the phrase:

Was machen Sie heute?
What do you-formal today
'What are you doing today?'

Soon after they come to realize a frame, *Was machen Sie* X, where X can be replaced by any number of time-adverbials already learned (e.g. *nach der Schule* – after school). As students gain more proficiency and are able to apply various grammatical information on the fly, students should be pushed to use more complex grammar by increasing the task complexity and extending the length of discourse they are required produce. As Kida (2008) points out, it is significant that learners' experience the teacher's use of discourse to promote their own extended discourse: 'The teacher's discourse in a classroom can have positive effects on the learners' discourse in such a way that learners produce meaningful and complex discourse that promotes discourse acquisition'. Speaking for longer amounts of time, which requires more vocabulary and grammatical knowledge while integrating pragmatic and contextual information, can be very difficult so extensive modelling by the teacher is highly beneficial.

Another instructional method that can support speaking at all levels is building in time for practice. De Jong and Perfetti (2011) showed that providing time for practice before speaking improved fluency for all levels of learners. This is a great habit to get students used to, as it cycles the L2 constantly through learners' minds, therein creating processing loops that will later support spontaneous oral language production that can make use of these proceduralized grammatical application/production processes.

The question of providing feedback during spoken production by students is also important to consider. Date (2015: 202) notes that 'Form instruction during task repetition will raise learner's consciousness of language forms and lead to correct modifications while speaking. However, the consciousness of forms will also have a negative impact, leading to shorter fluent runs and less attention to target forms among other others'. Therefore, it is up to the instructor to decide if it is more important to highlight mistakes for students to notice, or if this activity is more about building fluency. For more advanced learners, they can be pushed to deal with interruptions while still maintaining fluent speech and integrating corrections in real time.

Pronunciation

Pronunciation requires instruction, but to what degree? I propose two steps for language instructors to follow. First, I fully agree with Loewen

(2020: 161), who states that 'teachers may wish to emphasize to learners that native-like proficiency is not a realistic goal for most learners, and that intelligibility is a better goal to strive for (Levis, 2005; Saito, 2011)'. That said, I would also argue that learners, considering their goals, should focus on a target group of speakers, since every speaker has an accent and dialect, and no one speaks the standard language presented in textbooks.

Second, I recommend the use of corpora or region-specific authentic materials. These materials can help students find a reason to acquire a particular style of speech and adapt it, for a specific reason, to their pronunciation. For actual instruction on pronunciation, it is effective to be concise, and provide ample modelling, as well as any strategies that can help students with sounds not present in their own language(s).[2] Loewen (2020: 162) notes that, 'If teachers already employ numerous meaning-focused tasks, it can be an efficient use of class time to incorporate brief attention to specific phonological features, as well as to address those that occur incidentally during the tasks'. Other ways to support pronunciation include the use of visual aids (Suzuki & Miyamoto, 2016), or spectrographs of accurate pronunciation compared to learners' own output (Lantolf, 1976), or functional magnetic resonance imaging (fMRI) videos of mouth-internal movement, if feasible. They can also compare recordings of themselves with L1 speakers after whom they want to model themselves. For tonal languages, the use of visual aids (like up or down arrows) or embodied cognition and the use of hands to model tone patterns can be highly effective (Baills *et al.*, 2019). Not only should teachers use these methods when instructing on the pronunciation of various tones, but learners should also be taught to use these tools to aid in their pronunciation. This has been shown to be effective for pronunciation, as well as listening, as reported previously in this chapter.

Reading and text comprehension

Reading is a multifaceted skill and its development is reliant on a number of factors, such as grapheme–sound mapping ability, vocabulary knowledge, grammatical processing, predictive language skills and context, genre and audience awareness, as more fully described in Chapters 2 and 4. To support the multiple types of knowledge that need to be built up to increase L2 reading competency, it is important to balance activities that help students learn to read and read to learn. This is especially true for learners who already have literacy skills in their L1 which are going to transfer assumptions about the point and purpose of reading to the L2, even if they don't have the L2 knowledge to make sense of the text.

I highly recommend, as I have for other skills, the use of authentic texts to teach reading. There are too many cultural practices involved in the writing process. Learner-focused texts simply won't map correctly, no matter how much they attempt to do so, from text structure and genre expectations, to grammatical, functional and pragmatic choices made by the author within the system of the target language to create the effect for the reader that they are seeking.

I also support extended reading as part of class, as well as outside of class. When reading a text together in class, it is helpful to have students read aloud, either as a whole class, where one student reads a portion of a text at a time, or in small groups or with a partner. This is useful for the instructor because it is a way to ensure correct sound–grapheme mapping. When reading aloud in class, it is important to recognize this as a very vulnerable situation for students who will inevitably make mistakes as they are just learning to map graphemes to sounds in real time. It is important to ensure that students respect one another, and no one makes degrading comments when any one student mispronounces or stumbles, as is important with any activity in which one or a few students are performing in front of the rest of the class. In a healthy class environment, students will either support the student who made the mistake by offering help via a correction or clue, or recognize that the instructor has a plan for the amount and type of feedback each student needs and wants without overwhelming them. I do not recommend, on the part of the instructor, correcting all mistakes, as this will significantly slow down the amount of reading done in class and, more importantly, could have negative effects on the motivation of that student to participate and increase their anxiety in future situations. Psycholinguistically, this decreases processing ability and fluent speech while trying to map words to their sound symbols. Ethically, it is right to support students' emotional and mental well-being in our classes.

In addition to reading together, I recommend assigning reading outside of class, especially longer texts, like novels, that can only be read in part in class. By assigning reading outside of class, students are able to work at their own pace. There are two hurdles to overcome when assigning reading outside of class. The first is making sure students do it. This is more of a classroom management issue than an SLA issue, but it is still important to build trust and ensure that students are doing the beneficial things we plan for them. The tool I use to get over the second hurdle may help with this as well.

The second hurdle that the instructor needs to overcome is how to scaffold the reading assignment when the teacher isn't present. As with in-class work with texts, I recommend pre-during-post reading activities. The pre-reading work is done in class and the during-reading and some post-reading work is done as homework. Then, to link the previous class and homework to the next class, more post-reading work is included as part of the next class.

The use of a reading journal with composite parts related to comprehension, vocabulary, grammar and interpretation skills can be highly effective. Adapted from Dr Jennifer Redmann's work, it is described here: The first section consists of comprehension questions, in the L2, along with what page the students should be able to find the answer on. The students are asked to answer these questions in a complete sentence. Then, students are asked to provide a four to five sentence summary of the entire reading. The journal provides the first half of the first sentence, which can be used to force students into particular syntactic or grammatical constructions. Then, there is a list of new vocabulary words in the L2 that have been identified as essential to understanding the reading. Usually, students work through the comprehension questions and this list at the same time, and they have reported that just by identifying the new vocabulary they can glean at least a general understanding of what is going on in the text. Afterwards, students are asked to use three or four of the words in their own sentences on a topic related to the text. Next are interpretation questions. These are questions that do not have an answer in the text, but students can use what they read to make propositions about what might happen. These interpretation questions also allow the opportunity to ask students about specific vocabulary or grammar choices made by the author. Finally, students are asked to provide their opinion on the text as a whole or a specific topic that arises in the text.

As learners grow more proficient, the structure of these reading journals changes. For example, one can remove page numbers as hints from the comprehension questions or ask for a longer summary or interpretation answers. I also recommend using techniques from systemic functional linguistics (SFL) and other text-based approaches to language teaching that help students recognize a text as a series of choices by an author or authors, and to learn how to analyze why these choices were made and to what effect (e.g. Troyan, 2016). Through analysis of author choice across and within different genres, they can see how grammar and vocabulary are used to support stylistic moves by the author. And from a multiliteracies standpoint (e.g. Kumagai *et al.*, 2015), this can be applied to multiple types of media and content, not just stories or poems. Students need to learn how to read and analyze all kinds of texts in multiple modalities if they are going to be able to use the L2 to learn about their L2 world. This is very important in the development of writing as well.

Writing and text construction

I purposefully placed the reading and writing instruction pedagogy suggestions near each other because they really do go hand in hand (Paesani, 2016). Just like reading, students need to consider aspects related to genre, audience, style, L1 skills transfer and cultural expectations, not to mention vocabulary and grammar choices to support these higher-level text features (Gebhard *et al.*, 2013). Therefore, it is essential to raise these issues during reading instruction, not just as part of writing. Students can use what they see in other texts as models for their own texts.

In addition to the texts they are reading as part of the class, corpus approaches to supporting L2 writing can be very effective, especially if learners are given the tools to navigate a corpus (Park, 2012; Poole, 2016). They can find examples from the same genre they are trying to write in and have multiple options from which to choose. An important balance is struck through discussion between the instructor and students about appropriate uses, and what counts as plagiarism versus using a particular linguistic structure that is more general.

Another effective tool for instructors is activating L1 writing knowledge. While there are obvious differences in writing styles and expectations by culture, many textual considerations and writing processes can be applied to L2 writing. That being said, some stark differences between teachers' expectations and students' cultural knowledge about the norms of writing can lead to significant issues. For those who teach (and grade) the writing of L2 English learners, this is often evident in L2 English learners' use (or lack of use) of citations. In such cases, teachers might suspect that students are plagiarizing, when in reality, they have no cultural understanding of the use of citations in academic writing in English. This is especially true if their own cultural does not make much use of the practice of citation.

Finally, instructors need to decide how and when students can use technology, and to what extent. Some questions that teachers need to ask themselves are:

- Where should students be doing writing? In the class, where I can have a better handle on the types of resources they are using or outside the class, assuming they are all following the agreed-upon terms of use?
- What resources are allowed? Only dictionaries? Which ones? Also, other tools like verb conjugators, or whole translation systems like Google Translate?
- How many words in a row can students look up? Only single words? Short phrases? What counts as a phrase?
- How can I make sure that students are learning how to be technologically literate and not using it as a crutch?

I recommend that instructors focus on aligning the answers to these questions with the goals of assessment. For example, do I want to know what students can do on their own? Then I would suggest in-class writing with, of course, appropriate scaffolding of pre-writing assignments. Or do I want to see what they can create with all the resources at their disposal? Then, something out of class with some clear rules for technology use would be appropriate. In any case, it is important to make sure that students understand that you are there to assess and work on their L2 writing, not Google's.

Assessment

Entire books can and have been written about how to assess language learning outcomes, so suffice to say for this book that assessment needs to both match student expectations and build toward the skills and activities we want out students to be able to do. If assessments are to help us gain insight into how our students would do outside our classroom, then we need to do the best we can to mirror those actions in our assessments.

Assessment says a lot about an instructor's view on language instruction, which can be helpful for self-reflection by the instructor, as well as people who are conducting program assessment. A teacher's methodological toolbox reveals their language learning and teaching ideologies and the frameworks that govern their assessment of language development.

Two of the mainstream frameworks that teachers have access to are the Common European Framework of Reference for Languages (CEFR) and the ACTFL. The ideologies that inform these scales of assessment have particular foci that lead teachers' attention to particular language skills. The types of skills assessed are part of the way that assignments are both created and graded. Again, I would point to the effectiveness of dynamic assessment. As Knoch and Macqueen (2017: 192) point out 'Outcomes of dynamic assessments can provide educators with much more information than the raw scores of conventional assessments'. In other words, rather than one number, we get a range of outcomes based on the varying levels of support and students' variable performance at each of these levels. On a standard assessment, two students who get the same score may actually be farther apart developmentally than two students who have much different scores, but the lack of understanding how scaffolded interaction affects their performance can lead to misunderstandings about student readiness for new material.

Rubrics are also important artifacts for assessing language learning ideologies and they do so in two ways. First, the categories that teachers select reflect divisions within language functions and language forms. For example, a rubric for a short essay may contain categories for style, organization, appropriateness of the argument or inclusion of examples, in addition to categories with a heavier linguistic focus, like spelling, vocabulary choice and grammar. Second, the weight given to these different categories also reveals teachers' standards. For the same fictional short essay, one teacher may assign more weight to the content and essay design categories, while another may assign more weight to the more linguistically focused categories. The debate about which approach is better, however, is meaningless unless we look at this assignment within the broader curriculum. Is the grading scheme supported by the teaching focus and the way students are prepared? There is also no reason for assessments to be static. By this, I mean that for one assignment, there might be a heavier focus on content over language, and vice versa for another. These decisions have to be made based on the long-term developmental goals established within the language learning classroom.

Integrating assessment back into the classroom

Students need to see that assessment isn't only for the teacher's eyes. To make this happen, instructors need to ensure that assessments are seen as part of the curriculum. If backward design has been followed, then doing so is easier since the connections between the assessments and class activities should be transparent. This should also raise students' awareness of the integration of the curriculum as a whole, and prime students to know what to expect after finishing assessments.

Building a Language Learning Community to Support Multilingual Identity Development

To reinforce the motivation to continue learning the L2 that the instructor is able to establish inside the classroom, it is extremely beneficial to connect students across curriculum and proficiency levels, as well as provide opportunities for students to see and engage with the L2 as a tool for communication in both local and global contexts. In this way, students can gain the perspective that they are multilingual and have an identity that is constructed by and through the use of multiple languages. It cannot be left solely to the individual to develop their multilingual identity. It must come with support from the teacher. Mantero (2006: 377) emphasizes, 'It is clear that instructors have the tools to construct, produce, reform and sustain identity development in second language learners'. One of these tools is the intentional construction of a language learning (and using) community, since, as Mantero (2006: 9) argues 'our identities come to life as "language learners" when we participate in meaning-driven discourse in authentic contexts', and that 'identity is constructed (consciously and subconsciously) by semiotic activity in communities of practice where individuals engage in the negotiation of meaning'.

It is also important to emphasize that these identities are not static, as Mantero (2006) further explains:

> Identities are always in an emergent state and the world around us does impact our language, but context does not always dictate what or how we interact in society. The meaning that emerges through linguistic activities carries with it our voice (...) Our voices give us the power to change not only how others view us, but also, how we view ourselves. (Mantero, 2006: 9)

This section outlines some of the ways in which instructors can enable class-external resources.

The L2 class as a learning community

While I think that developing a strong classroom community is crucial for all effective classes, I emphasize this even more so for the L2 class. For all L2 classes, this is a space where the topic becomes part of a new multilingual identity that emerges as learners explore the L2 and create new meanings with their classmates. Aronin and Jessner (2016: 31) describe this phenomenon as follows: 'In the multilingualism domain, emergent phenomena could be the atmosphere in a particular multilingual school, identities of multilinguals, a mini-community of a multilingual family, and certainly, the contexts in which new speakers emerge (spacetimes) and new speakers themselves'. The emergence of these identities is tightly linked to the actual practices and interactions that students take part in together, and they need to see each other as a resource.

This might be most important for two groups of learners in particular. First, it may be developmentally important for young student who are still learning how to interact with classmates and to see each other as sources of knowledge. Second, for post-secondary students, especially those whose college or university involves a residential component. For many college students, this language learning community might be one of the only academically based groups of friends and close peers they develop in their first years of study due to the usually smaller class size of language classes. This may also be a result of the frequency of activities that involve peer-to-peer interaction that can be found in most US language classrooms today, with their emphasis on communicative approaches to L2 teaching and learning.

Learners grow to see their classmates as more than just peers (in many cases competition) and instead a community of learners of which they are a part, with all its members supporting one another. In class, they can have more comfortable conversations with each other and see each other as both a resource for support and as someone who contributes their own unique perspective and understanding of what it means to become multilingual. Outside of class, students have a tighter, more extensive network of support than a single teacher or professor can provide, and students keep hours for homework and study when only other students would be available to provide immediate help.

Building a community across L2 proficiency, grade levels and courses

There are many ways to get students across the curriculum engaged with one another, including language clubs, regional and national events, charity work, engagement with local target language community groups and tutoring.

I highlight one example of cross-curricular community building that spanned grade, age and proficiency levels that came about as a result of my work at Michigan State University during my MA program where I worked as the assistant director of outreach for the Center for Language Teaching Advancement (CeLTA). In this position, I worked with my director, Dr Angelika Kraemer, to develop a peer-mentoring program between the upper-level and lower-level German students. The result of this program (reported in Walter & Kraemer, 2013) showed that both parties valued the exchange. Lower-proficiency students obviously gained understanding of German as an L2 from exposure to more advanced speakers and their active role as tutors, and advanced students also reported gains in understanding because, for the first time, they were put in the position where they had to explain their knowledge to someone else, which refined their thinking and conceptualization about different aspects of German grammar. In addition, all groups reported a higher level of community engagement with the German program, because they had built ties to students beyond their own class.

Whatever decision instructors or program leads make about the best way to increase cross-curricular engagement, the major point is that students have the opportunity to see themselves as part of a learning community that is larger than their classroom and can look forward to students who are where they are going, and also give back by tutoring and mentoring lower-proficiency or younger learners. This can be an effective tool for consciousness raising. For lower-proficiency learners, they see how they can develop and the way that they can use the language as their proficiency increases. And, maybe more importantly, for those advanced learners who no longer see the large jumps in skill and proficiency they did when they first started the language, they can use this opportunity to reflect on how far they have come.

Connecting learners and the class to the L2 in the local community

Many students, especially monolingual students, are not aware of the broad range of languages used within their communities because they are often hidden away by those speakers in public spaces, so helping students become aware of the use of the L2 in the local community can go a long way to making the language immediately applicable for them. They not only have a chance to practice their language in meaningful ways beyond the four walls of their classroom, but they can also use these opportunities to build meaningful connections within the community and learn to see these speakers not only as a resource that can help them on their language learning journey, but also as community partners who can work together, as well as a population of people for whom they could also be of service.

To help students become more aware of what languages are used in the everyday lives of people in their communities, even if not the L2, using techniques from linguistic landscape research can be an effective tool. In linguistic landscape research, the objects of study are the material artifacts emblazoned with language that one can find in public – shared spaces that provide insights into the different languages used in the community. For the L2 classroom, this can be a useful and less intrusive way to figure out where the L2 is being used, in what ways and by whom. From there, outreach can begin by visiting these areas, locales and businesses, looking for opportunities for students to use the language or getting these community members interested in supporting their language through contributions to these new learners.

Navigating this relationship can be tricky, especially for younger learners. For older learners, there is still a definite need for guidance by teachers, community leaders and other community-facing resources and support structures offered through the institution. For college students, I highly recommend trying this type of engagement with the local community for a few reasons. First, there is often tension between students who move to a college and live in somewhat of a bubble but also contact local residents in sometimes disagreeable ways. Second, college students are often unaware of the populations and needs of the people in the towns they inhabit because their time and energy is so locally focused on the campus. These reasons vary, of course, based on the type of institution, the student population and other institutional endeavors to connect students with the broader community. It is also important to state that many students do work to engage with their new community. Here, I am simply pointing to the role that the L2 class can play in making these connections both salient and meaningful for all involved parties.

Connecting learners and the class to the L2 in the global community

In addition to L2 learners seeing themselves as part of a classroom, programmatic and local language community, they also need to see themselves as part of a global network of speakers where the applicability and usage of the target language play a role in the broader global context. Dewaele (2008: 490) echoes this need, stating, 'Formal instruction should be complemented by a period in the TL community in order to stimulate the process of temporary resocialization into a foreign culture and its practices and beliefs'. Through interactions with L1 and L2 speakers of their L2, they build everyday knowledge of how the language is used in the real world, and how the language itself varies across geographic space, from one cultural context to another, and among speakers.

While there is more than one way to accomplish this goal, the most common form is study abroad. However, not all study abroad experiences are alike. No specific time allotment has been proven most beneficial for study abroad; however, very short trips that are more like vacations abroad don't really provide learners with the opportunity to face the real challenges of living within a new culture and context, being forced to use an incompletely acquired language to navigate their daily lives.

One consideration that may help though, is to provide students with opportunities to engage with the local community as much as possible. This can be done through sporting and gaming clubs, interest groups, participation in authentic L1 educational contexts and living with target language-speaking peers. Students who travel together as a group tend to stick together, which limits their opportunities to engage in meaningful and extended use of the L2. I like to think of study abroad as the ultimate opportunity for large gains in L2 proficiency and cultural understanding. It is not a guarantee.

In an increasingly globalized world, students need to recognize that having knowledge of a widely used lingua franca like English will get general access to people across the world, but knowing a language that is used by particular communities will get you intimate access to people and open doors to cultural understanding that remain closed to those who do not speak the language.

Next steps for continued L2 development and engagement: Questions to consider

Finally, it is important to help students think of next steps after they graduate from your program. After all those years spent gaining proficiency and learning about the L2 and the people who use it, it would be a shame to leave students completely to their own devices to figure out what to do with all of the skills and knowledge. However, students have all kinds of different goals, so no one plan is applicable to all students. For this reason, I recommend presenting some specific programs that former students have gone through and try to get them back to talk about their experiences in detail, providing a narrative to which the class can connect. In addition, one-on-one work with advanced students that allows learners to see how their other interests align with continued study of the language is necessary. Much of this work can be given to students to complete and they can be responsible for bringing their findings back to the rest of the class.

Putting It All Together

Looking back on the study of the individual learner's development, we can use it as a guide for planning our learning outcomes by year. A simple way to do this is by using backward design or starting at the end. The question about what the 'end' is and what students should be able to do, is highly dependent on the type of program, of course. The learning outcomes of a program that begins in elementary school or that has bilingual course offerings in other subjects will be much different from one that begins in high school or college. The age of the learners also has an impact, but if we think in terms of psycholinguistic processes, we can tackle cognitive needs, such as age-appropriate topics, through our choice of materials.

Returning to the curriculum, let's start with the typical four to five year high school program, with elementary language courses being offered in eighth grade running through advanced placement (AP) in twelfth grade. What should our realistic learning outcomes be for a student who completes all five years of study? A 5 on the AP exam is one way to measure it, but there are 10 learning outcomes to aim for after extended language study. The first five have to do with using the language itself. Learners:

(1) Not only survive but thrive if put in a completely L2 context.
(2) Use their L2 to guide their thought.
(3) Take part in extended discourse, both understanding multiple interlocutors and making themselves understood, even if they are missing vocabulary or some other grammatical feature through circumlocution.
(4) Operate across genres, contexts and interlocutors, adjusting pragmatic choices to fit their intended meanings and the way they want to interact with others to the extent they have control over that.
(5) Make informed conscious choices about how and when they want to code-switch, mix languages and play with languages.

The next five have to do with metalinguistic and metacognitive skills that can and should be developed while learning an L2. Learners:

(6) Have an awareness of how another language operates and how that language operates differently from their own language.
(7) Express the importance of culture and its interconnected nature with languages used to express that culture.
(8) Desire to continue learning the language and have developed concrete plans for its continued use, be it through plans for study, travel or work abroad, and connections to groups of target language speakers, as well as language artifacts like books, news, music, television shows, movies and other media.
(9) Know why they are motivated to learn the language, what their goals are and the steps to reach those goals.

(10) Know where to find and how to use tools to support their continued language development, including dictionaries, web-based tools and other support materials, especially when teacher support is unavailable.

Each curriculum coordinator would also want to build in intermediary goals, as described in the section on backward design and curriculum construction, for end goals for students who only complete two or three years of the program. This is very important for contexts in which there is a minimum language requirement in place, for example by various states and universities. For those students who go through two years of study, reasonable expectations might include surviving in an L2 context, knowing how to work with multilingual individuals and being aware of cultural differences. In fact, for these learners, the latter five outcomes above on metalinguistic and metacognitive skills might be more important to emphasize, as some L2 skills require a proficiency that is not attainable within two years of study.

More than Methods: The Art in L2 Teaching

The design of a curriculum must be more than a question of which method is best. The belief in the effectiveness of a single method of instruction, such as CLT, can handcuff teachers into providing a monotonous, single-layered style of teaching. Methods need to be tailored to the goals of instruction, as well as implemented with the development of various psycholinguistic processes in mind, sociocultural processes of interaction and understandings of the ebbs and flows of L2 development in time, space and context.

This balance is not something that any scientific study, be it a case study of a classroom, a multivariate analysis of classroom factors in learning or the most detailed, ethno-quantitative mixed-method study with years of individual learners' daily changes and millions of pages of classroom data along with their minute-by-minute biofeedback. The point is that the classroom instructor is in charge of balancing all the factors that they see affecting their class with the most detailed, well-planned, organized course they can provide, which no method, on its own, can accomplish. It is the instructor who makes their methods effective through their belief and their training in them. They also make these methods effective via their preparation and planning for each unit, lesson and activity. Instructors make the L2 relatable and learnable, not the materials. Through language, instructors show students connections across cultures that enhance students' engagement with the language.

It is important to recognize that not only is SLA non-linear, but so is teaching, and each instructor must navigate the optimal path for their students, with their own background and knowledge, and their comfort and training with different methods. As teachers hopefully continue to develop, they should be able to feel more comfortable with a variety of tools to make the L2 learning process smoother for their students.

Conclusion: A Robust Language Learning Experience

For anyone in charge of designing a curriculum, I pose the following question: Am I designing a curriculum in which I engage my students in a robust language learning experience that involves multiple levels of linguistic, cultural and conceptual representation? If the research shows us anything, SLA is a composition of skills and knowledge shared widely across brain regions. Language serves different functions and involves different linguistic resources. There is no singular approach that will not overemphasize one area, leaving others to wither or starve. If you only practice total physical response (TPR), how will your students learn to understand author choices? If you never allow the L1 to be used in your class under any circumstance and never talk about it, will students realize that they are becoming multilinguals, not 'native-speakers'? Activities that require a combination of diverse skills and knowledge are best suited to accomplish this goal, but this cannot always be done from the get go. Some skills need to be developed to a certain proficiency independently before a student has the cognitive resources or capacity necessary to integrate that skill into a more complex task. Any attempt to conform to a unified L2 learning experience for all students across a curriculum is a futile effort. There are too many variables, too many mediating factors, too many individual differences and an established fact of non-linearity in L2 acquisition. This does not mean that the language teacher is powerless over the development of their students. Rather, it means that teachers are provided with a myriad of choices to ensure that learners are experiencing a well-rounded curriculum with the L2 that allows for all students to find ways to engage with learning using their own experiences, their own consciousness and their own identity.

Notes

(1) Whether you want to explain activities in the L1 or the L2 depends on your approach to teaching, the time you have, the difficulty of the task and other factors.
(2) For example, the /ch/ grapheme in German has two forms, neither of which we have in English. For /ç/, I tell them to sound like a pissed off cat, and for /x/, to hock a loogie.

References

Abu-Rabia, S. (2001) The role of vowels in reading Semitic scripts: Data from Arabic and Hebrew. *Reading and Writing* 14, 39–59.

Abu Khattala, I. (2014) Introducing the communicative approach in Libya: Resistance and conflict. *Faculty of Arts Journal* 4 (8), 8–21.

Alhumaid, K., Ali, S., Waheed, A., Zahid, E. and Habes, M. (2020) COVID-19 & Elearning: Perceptions & attitudes of teachers towards e-learning acceptance in the developing countries. *Multicultural Education* 6 (2), 100–115.

American Councils for International Education (2017) The national K-12 foreign language enrollment survey report. ACIE. Retrieved from https://www.americancouncils.org/sites/default/files/FLE-report-June17.pdf.

American Council on the Teaching of Foreign Languages (2012) *ACTFL Proficiency Guidelines 2012*. Retrieved from http://www.actfl.org/sites/default/files/pdfs/public/ACTFLProficiencyGuidelines2012_FINAL.pdf.

Anderson, J.R. (2005) *Cognitive Psychology and its Implications*. London: Macmillan.

Anderson, J.R. (1983) A spreading activation theory of memory. *Journal of Verbal Learning and Verbal Behavior* 22 (3), 261–295.

Anya, U. (2011) Connecting with communities of learners and speakers: Integrative ideals, experiences, and motivations of successful black second language learners. *Foreign Language Annals* 44 (3), 441–466.

Arbib, M.A. (2001) Co-evolution of human consciousness and language. *Annals of the New York Academy of Sciences* 929 (1), 195–220.

Armstrong, T.C. (2013) 'Why won't you speak to me in Gaelic?' Authenticity, integration, and the HL learning project. *Journal of Language, Identity & Education* 12 (5), 340–356.

Aronin, L. and Jessner, U. (2016) Spacetimes of multilingualism. In D. Gałajda, P. Zakrajewski and M. Pawlak (eds) *Researching Second Language Learning and Teaching from a Psycholinguistic Perspective* (pp. 27–35). Cham: Springer.

Asher, J.J. (1969a) The total physical response approach to second language learning. *The Modern Language Journal* 53 (1), 3–17.

Asher, J.J. (1969b) The total physical response technique of learning. *The Journal of Special Education* 3 (3), 253–262.

Atkinson, D. (2002) Toward a sociocognitive approach to second language acquisition. *The Modern Language Journal* 86 (4), 525–545.

Awwad, A. and Tavakoli, P. (2019) Task complexity, language proficiency and working memory: Interaction effects on second language speech performance. *International Review of Applied Linguistics in Language Teaching* 60 (2), 169–196.

Ayoun, D. (2018) Grammatical gender assignment in French: Dispelling the native speaker myth. *Journal of French Language Studies* 28 (1), 113–148.

Azarola, E.N. (2013) The being and becoming of metalinguistic knowledge: Rules and categories of grammatical description as functional tools of the mind. In K. Roeher and G.A. Gánem-Gutiérrez (eds) *The Metalinguistic Dimension in Instructed Second Language Learning* (pp. 221–242). London: Bloomsbury Academic.

Aziz, A.A., Ibrahim, M.A., Shaker, M.H. and Nor, A.M. (2016) Teaching technique of Islamic studies in higher learning institutions for non-Arabic speakers: Experience of faculty of Quranic and Sunnah Studies and Tamhidi Centre, Universiti Sains Islam Malaysia. *Universal Journal of Educational Research* 4 (4), 755–760.

Baddeley, A. (1998) The central executive: A concept and some misconceptions. *Journal of the International Neuropsychological Society* 4 (5), 523–526.

Baddeley, A. (2000) The episodic buffer: A new component of working memory? *Trends in Cognitive Sciences* 4 (11), 417–423.

Baddeley, A. (2017) *Exploring Working Memory: Selected Works of Alan Baddeley.* Abingdon: Routledge.

Bailey, D.R. and Lee, A.R. (2020) Learning from experience in the midst of COVID-19: Benefits, challenges, and strategies in online teaching. *Computer-Assisted Language Learning Electronic Journal* 21 (2), 178–198.

Bailey, P.J. and Snowling, M.J. (2002) Auditory processing and the development of language and literacy. *British Medical Bulletin* 63 (1), 135–146.

Baills, F., Suárez-González, N., González-Fuente, S. and Prieto, P. (2019) Observing and producing pitch gestures facilitates the learning of Mandarin Chinese tones and words. *Studies in Second Language Acquisition* 41 (1), 33–58.

Bardovi-Harlig, K. (2012) Pragmatics and second language acquisition. In R.B. Kaplan (ed.) *The Oxford Handbook of Applied Linguistics* (2nd edn; pp. 147–167). New York: Oxford University Press.

Bardovi-Harlig, K., Mossman, S., Rothgerber, J., Su, Y. and Swanson, K. (2019) Revisiting clarifications: Self- and other-clarifications in corpus-based pragmatics instruction. In M. Sato and S. Loewen (eds) *Evidence-Based Second Language Pedagogy* (pp. 52–80). New York: Routledge.

Bargh, J.A. (2014) Our unconscious mind. *Scientific American* 310 (1), 30–37.

Barton, A., Matthews, B., Farmer, E. and Belyavin, A. (1995) Revealing the basic properties of the visuospatial sketchpad: The use of complete spatial arrays. *Acta Psychologica* 89 (3), 197–216.

Bauer, T., Epstein, G.S. and Gang, I.N. (2005) Enclaves, language, and the location choice of migrants. *Journal of Population Economics* 18 (4), 649–662.

Beattie, J. (1788) *The Theory of Language: In Two Parts. Part I. Of the Origin and General Nature of Speech. Part II. Of Universal Grammar* (No. 10). London: A. Strahan.

Bell, N. (2012) Formulaic language, creativity, and language play in a second language. *Annual Review of Applied Linguistics* 32, 189–205.

Benati, A. (2013) The input processing theory in second language acquisition. In M.d.P. García Mayo, M.J. Gutiérrez Mangado and M. Martínez-Adrián (eds) *Contemporary Approaches to Second Language Acquisition* (pp. 93–110). Amsterdam: John Benjamins.

Benson, P. (2019) Ways of seeing: The individual and the social in applied linguistics research methodologies. *Language Teaching* 52 (1), 60–70.

Benson, P., Lang, T., Baynes, M.A. and Aribisala, W. (2010) How are non-native-English-speaking authors coping with requirements to publish in English-language journals. *Science Editor* 33 (6), 189.

Berk, L.E. (1986) Relationship of elementary school children's private speech to behavioral accompaniment to task, attention, and task performance. *Developmental Psychology* 22 (5), 671–680.

Bernacer, J., Lombo, J.A. and Murillo, J.I. (2015) Habits: Plasticity, learning and freedom. *Frontiers in Human Neuroscience* 9, 468.

Berry, R. (2005) Making the most of metalanguage. *Language Awareness* 14 (1), 3–20.

Berry, R. (2009) EFL majors' knowledge of metalinguistic terminology: A comparative study. *Language Awareness* 18 (2), 113–128.

Bilali, O. (2015) Factors influencing the appearance of teaching anxiety to student teachers. *European Journal of Social Science Education and Research* 2 (2), 90–94.

Birdsong, D. (2004) Second language acquisition and ultimate attainment. In A. Davies and C. Elder (eds) *Handbook of Applied Linguistics* (pp. 82–105). Oxford: Blackwell Publishing Ltd.

Bischoff, B. (1961) The study of foreign languages in the Middle Ages. *Speculum* 36 (2), 209–224.

Blake, C.D. and Walter, D.R. (2020) HL labor market returns: The importance of speaker density at the state level. *Journal of Economics, Race, and Policy* 1–19.

Bland, H.W., Melton, B.F., Welle, P. and Bigham, L. (2012) Stress tolerance: New challenges for millennial college students. *College Student Journal* 46 (2), 362–376.

Block, D. (2000) Revisiting the gap between SLA researchers and language teachers. *Links & Letters* (7), 129–143.

Block, D. (2003) *The Social Turn in Second Language Acquisition*. Washington, DC: Georgetown University Press.

Bokamba, E.G. (2018) Multilingualism and theories of second language acquisition in Africa. *World Englishes* 37 (3), 432–446.

Bolinger, D. (1976) Meaning and memory. *Forum Linguisticum* 1 (1), 1–14.

Bongers, K.C.A. and Dijksterhuis, A. (2009) Consciousness as a troubleshooting device? The role of consciousness in goal pursuit. In E. Morsella, J.A. Bargh and P.M. Gollwitzer (eds) *Oxford Handbook of Human Action* (pp. 587–602). New York: Oxford University Press.

Borzykowski, B. (2017) The international companies using only English. See https://www.bbc.com/worklife/article/20170317-the-international-companies-using-only-english. Accessed 07/23/2022.

Bowden, H.W., Steinhauer, K., Sanz, C. and Ullman, M.T. (2013) Native-like brain processing of syntax can be attained by university foreign language learners. *Neuropsychologia* 51 (13), 2492–2511.

Boring, E.G. (1946) The perception of objects. *American Journal of Physics* 14 (2), 99–107.

Boyadzhieva, E. (2014) Theory and practice in foreign language teaching-Past and present. *Journal of Modern Education Review* 4 (10), 776–788.

Brigham Young University (2022) BYU center for language studies. See https://cls.byu.edu/about. Accessed 10/15/2022.

Brown, C.L. (2011) Maintaining HL: Perspectives of Korean parents. *Multicultural Education* 9 (1), 31–37.

Bruyer, R. and Scailquin, J.C. (1998) The visuospatial sketchpad for mental images: Testing the multicomponent model of working memory. *Acta Psychologica* 98 (1), 17–36.

Burnaby, B. and Sun, Y. (1989) Chinese teachers' views of western language teaching: Context informs paradigms. *TESOL Quarterly* 23 (2), 219–238.

Bybee, J. (2008) Usage-based grammar and second language acquisition. In P. Robinson and N. Ellis (eds) *Handbook of Cognitive Linguistics and Second Language Acquisition* (pp. 226–246). New York: Routledge.

Bybee, J.L. (2013) Usage-based theory and exemplar representations of constructions. In T. Hoffmann and G. Trousdale (eds) *The Oxford Handbook of Construction Grammar* (pp. 49–69). Oxford: Oxford University Press.

Byon, A.S. (2005) Apologizing in Korean: Cross-cultural analysis in classroom settings. *Korean Studies* 29, 137–166.

Byrnes, H. (2019) Affirming the context of instructed SLA: The potential of curricular thinking. *Language Teaching Research* 23 (4), 514–532.

Caffarra, S., Molinaro, N., Davidson, D. and Carreiras, M. (2015) Second language syntactic processing revealed through event-related potentials: An empirical review. *Neuroscience & Biobehavioral Reviews* 51, 31–47.

Cagle, L. (2011) Community building: Study abroad and the small German program. *Die Unterrichtspraxis/Teaching German* 44 (1), 12–19.

Canan, A. (2022) Contributions of cognitive theory to the problem of automatization of grammatical structures in teaching foreign language. *Educational Research and Reviews* 17 (4), 131–137.

Cárdenas-Hagan, E., Carlson, C.D. and Pollard-Durodola, S.D. (2007) The cross-linguistic transfer of early literacy skills: The role of initial L1 and L2 skills and language of instruction. *Language, Speech, and Hearing Services in Schools* 38 (3), 249–259.

Carey, R. (2013) On the other side: Formulaic organizing chunks in spoken and written academic ELF. *Journal of English as a Lingua Franca* 2 (2), 207–228.

Carpenter, B.D., Achugar, M., Walter, D. and Earhart, M. (2015) Developing teachers' critical language awareness: A case study of guided participation. *Linguistics and Education* 32, 82–97.

Carroll, J.B. (1967) Foreign language proficiency levels attained by language majors near graduation from college. *Foreign Language Annals* 1 (2), 131–151.

Carstens, A. (2016) Translanguaging as a vehicle for L2 acquisition and L1 development: Students' perceptions. *Language Matters* 47 (2), 203–222.

Casey, B.J., Giedd, J.N. and Thomas, K.M. (2000) Structural and functional brain development and its relation to cognitive development. *Biological Psychology* 54 (1–3), 241–257.

Cattell, R. (2006) *An Introduction to Mind, Consciousness and Language*. London: Bloomsbury.

Cavanna, A.E. and Nani, A. (2014) John Eccles and Karl Popper. In J. Rakhmat (ed.) *Consciousness* (pp. 123–126). Berlin/Heidelberg: Springer.

Cenoz, J. and Gorter, D. (2020) Teaching English through pedagogical translanguaging. *World Englishes* 39 (2), 300–311.

Chaput, P.R. (1997) Culture in grammar. *The Slavic and East European Journal* 41 (3), 403–414.

Cheng, L. and Watanabe, Y. (eds) (2004) *Washback in Language Testing: Research Contexts and Methods*. New York: Routledge.

Chinen, K. and Tucker, G.R. (2005) Heritage language development: Understanding the roles of ethnic identity and Saturday school participation. *Heritage Language Journal* 3 (1), 27–59.

Cho, G., Cho, K.S. and Tse, L. (1997) Why ethnic minorities want to develop their HL: The case of Korean-Americans. *Language, Culture and Curriculum* 10 (2), 106–112.

Chomsky, N. (1986) *Knowledge of Language: Its Nature, Origin, and Use*. Westport, CT: Greenwood Publishing Group.

Chomsky, N. (2013) A review of BF Skinner's verbal behavior. *Readings in Philosophy of Psychology* 1, 48–64.

Chomsky, N. (2017) The Galilean challenge: Architecture and evolution of language. *Journal of Physics: Conference Series* 880 (1), 012015.

Chondrogianni, V. (2008) Comparing child and adult L2 acquisition of the Greek DP. In B. Haznedar and E. Gavruseva (eds) *Current Trends in Child Second Language Acquisition: A Generative Perspective* (pp. 97–142). Amsterdam: John Benjamins.

Chorrojprasert, L. (2020) Learner readiness: Why and how should they be ready? *LEARN Journal: Language Education and Acquisition Research Network* 13 (1), 268–274.

Christiansen, M.H., Onnis, L. and Hockema, S.A. (2009) The secret is in the sound: From unsegmented speech to lexical categories. *Developmental Science* 12 (3), 388–395.

The Chronicle of Higher Education (2021) Which colleges grant the most bachelor's degrees in foreign languages? See https://www.chronicle.com/article/which-colleges-grant-the-most-bachelors-degrees-in-foreign-languages/. Accessed 05/12/2022.

Clark, M.R. (2005) Negotiating the freshman year: Challenges and strategies among first-year college students. *Journal of College Student Development* 46 (3), 296–316.

Clark, B., Wagner, J., Lindemalm, K. and Bendt, O. (2011) Språkskap: Supporting second language learning 'in the wild'. *Språkskap: Supporting Second Language Learning "In The Wild". 2011 Proceedings* (pp. 985–994). London: Royal College of Art.

College Factual (2021) Best colleges for foreign languages and linguistics, 2021. See https://www.collegefactual.com/majors/foreign-languages-linguistics/rankings/top-ranked/. Accessed 10/20/2021.

Conteh, J. (2018) Translanguaging. *ELT Journal* 72 (4), 445–447.

Conway, A.R., Kane, M.J., Bunting, M.F., Hambrick, D.Z., Wilhelm, O. and Engle, R.W. (2005) Working memory span tasks: A methodological review and user's guide. *Psychonomic Bulletin & Review* 12 (5), 769–786.

Cook, V.J. (1998) Relating SLA research to language teaching materials. *Canadian Journal of Applied Linguistics* 1 (1–2), 9–27.

Corder, S.P. (1967) The significance of learner's errors. *International Review of Applied Linguistics in Language Teaching* 5 (4), 161–170.

Crivos, M.B. and Luchini, P.L. (2012) A pedagogical proposal for teaching grammar using consciousness-raising tasks. *MJAL* 4 (3), 141–153.

Croft, W. (2007) Construction grammar. In D. Geeraerts and H. Cuyckens (eds) *The Oxford Handbook of Cognitive Linguistics* (pp. 463–508). New York: Oxford University Press.

Crystal, D. (1997) *The Cambridge Encyclopedia of Language, 2nd Edition*. New York: Cambridge University Press.

Cullaty, B. (2011) The role of parental involvement in the autonomy development of traditional-age college students. *Journal of College Student Development* 52 (4), 425–439.

Curry, M.J. and Lillis, T. (2018) *Global Academic Publishing: Policies, Perspectives and Pedagogies*. Bristol: Multilingual Matters.

Daive, L. (1997) Facilitating reflection through interactive journal writing in an online graduate course: A qualitative study. *Journal of Distance Education* 1 (12), 103–126.

Date, M. (2015) Does form instruction during task repetition facilitate proceduralization and accuracy of linguistic knowledge? *ARELE: Annual Review of English Language Education in Japan* 26, 189–204.

Davidheiser, J.C. (1999) Attracting and retaining students in small undergraduate German programs. *Die Unterrichtspraxis/Teaching German* 60–65.

Davidson, D.E. and Lekic, M.D. (2010) The overseas immersion setting as contextual variable in adult SLA: Learner behaviors associated with language gain to level-3 proficiency in Russian. *Russian Language Journal/Русский язык* 60, 53–76.

Davies, A. (2003) *The Native Speaker: Myth and Reality*. Clevedon: Multilingual Matters.

De Bot, K., Lowie, W. and Verspoor, M. (2007) A dynamic systems theory approach to second language acquisition. *Bilingualism: Language and Cognition* 10 (1), 7–21.

de Cordoba, C. (1978) The silent way: An introduction to an approach to teaching foreign and second languages in the schools. Unpublished master's thesis. California State University, Fullerton.

De Guerrero, M.C. (2006) *Inner Speech-L2: Thinking Words in a Second Language* (Vol. 6). New York: Springer Science & Business Media.

De Jong, N. and Perfetti, C.A. (2011) Fluency training in the ESL classroom: An experimental study of fluency development and proceduralization. *Language Learning* 61 (2), 533–568.

de Masson D'Autume, C., Ruder, S., Kong, L. and Yogatama, D. (2019) Episodic memory in lifelong language learning. *Advances in Neural Information Processing Systems* 32, 1–10.

DeKeyser, R. (2017) Knowledge and skill in ISLA. In S. Loewen and M. Sato (eds) *The Routledge Handbook of Instructed Second Language Acquisition* (pp. 15–32). New York: Routledge.

Del Pin, S.H., Skóra, Z., Sandberg, K., Overgaard, M. and Wierzchoń, M. (2021) Comparing theories of consciousness: Why it matters and how to do it. *Neuroscience of Consciousness* 2021 (2), niab019.

Demirezen, M. (2014) Cognitive-code learning theory and foreign language learning relations. *International Online Journal of Education and Teaching (IOJET)* 1 (5).

Dennett, D.C. (1993) *Consciousness Explained*. London: Penguin UK.

Devlin, K. (2018) Most European students are learning a foreign language in school while Americans lag. *Pew Research Center*. https://www.pewresearch.org/fact-tank/2018/08/06/most-european-students-are-learning-a-foreign-language-in-school-while-americans-lag/. Accessed 4/12/2022.

Dewaele, J.M. (2008) The effect of type of acquisition context on perception and self-reported use of swearwords in L2, L3, L4 and L5. In A. Housen and M. Pierrard (eds) *Investigations in Instructed Second Language Acquisition* (pp. 531–560). Berlin: Mouton De Gruyter.

Dhonau, S.A. and Cheatham, R.M. (2012) Backward design: Enduring learning for 21st century world language instruction. *Touch the World: 2012 Report of the Central States Conference on the Teaching of Foreign Languages* (pp. 149–161).

Diessel, H. (2015) Usage-based construction grammar. In E. Dabrowska and D. Divjak (eds) *Handbook of Cognitive Linguistics* (pp. 296–322). Berlin: De Gruyter Mouton.

Docking, R. (1994) Competency-based curricula: The big picture. *Prospect* 9 (2), 8–17.

Doehler, S.P. (2013) Social-interactional approaches to SLA: A state of the art and some future perspectives. *Language, Interaction and Acquisition* 4 (2), 134–160.

Doehler, S.P. (2019) On the nature and the development of L2 interactional competence: State of the art and implications for praxis. In M.R. Salaberry and S. Kunitz (eds) *Teaching and Testing L2 Interactional Competence* (pp. 25–59). New York: Routledge.

Doiz, A. and Lasagabaster, D. (2017) Teachers' beliefs about translanguaging practices. In C.M. Mazak and K.S. Carroll (eds) *Translanguaging in Higher Education: Beyond Monolingual Ideologies* (pp. 157–176). Bristol: Multilingual Matters.

Douglas Fir Group (2016) A transdisciplinary framework for SLA in a multilingual world. *The Modern Language Journal* 100 (S1), 19–47.

Ducar, C.M. (2008) Student voices: The missing link in the Spanish HL debate. *Foreign Language Annals* 41 (3), 415–433.

Dunn, W.E. and Lantolf, J.P. (1998) Vygotsky's zone of proximal development and Krashen's i + 1: Incommensurable constructs; incommensurable theories. *Language Learning* 48 (3), 411–442.

Efklides, A. (2014) How does metacognition contribute to the regulation of learning? An integrative approach. *Psihologijske Teme* 23 (1), 1–30.

Elder, C. (2009) Validating a test of metalinguistic knowledge. In R. Ellis, S. Loewen, C. Elder, R. Erlam, J. Philp and H. Reinders *Implicit and Explicit Knowledge in Second Language Learning, Testing and Teaching* (pp. 113–138). Bristol: Multilingual Matters.

Ellis, N. (1999) Cognitive approaches to SLA. *Annual Review of Applied Linguistics* 19, 22–42.

Ellis, N. (2011) Implicit and explicit SLA and their interface. In C. Sanz and R. Leow (eds) *Implicit and Explicit Language Learning: Conditions, Processes, and Knowledge in SLA and Bilingualism* (pp. 35–47). Washington, DC: Georgetown University Press.

Ellis, N. (2013) Construction grammar and second language acquisition. In T. Hoffmann and G. Trousdale (eds) *The Oxford Handbook of Construction Grammar* (pp. 365–378). Oxford: Oxford University Press.

Ellis, R. (1997) *SLA Research and Language Teaching*. Oxford: Oxford University Press.

Ellis, R. (1999) *Learning a Second Language Through Interaction* (Vol. 17). Amsterdam: John Benjamins Publishing.

Ellis, N. and Wulff, S. (2014) Usage-based approaches to SLA. In B. VanPatten, G.D. Keating and S. Wulff (eds) *Theories in Second Language Acquisition* (pp. 87–105). New York: Routledge.

Ellis, R. (2014) Evaluating and researching grammar consciousness-raising tasks. In P. Rea Dickins and K. Germaine (eds) *Managing Evaluation and Innovation in Language Teaching: Building Bridges* (pp. 220–252). New York: Routledge.

Ellis, R. (2017) Task-based language teaching. In S. Loewen and M. Sato (eds) *The Routledge Handbook of Instructed Second Language Acquisition* (pp. 108–125). New York: Routledge.

Ellis, R. (2021) A short history of SLA: Where have we come from and where are we going? *Language Teaching* 54 (2), 190–205.

Epstein, W. (1973) The process of "taking-into-account" in visual perception. *Perception* 2 (3), 67–85.

Erlam, R. (2013) Effects of instruction on learners' acquisition of metalinguistic knowledge. In K. Roeher and G.A. Gánem-Gutiérrez (eds) *The Metalinguistic Dimension in Instructed Second Language Learning* (pp. 71–94). London: Bloomsbury Academic.

Eskey, D.E. (1983) Meanwhile, back in the real world...: Accuracy and fluency in second language teaching. *TESOL Quarterly* 17 (2), 315–323.

Eskildsen, S.W. (2009) Constructing another language: Usage-based linguistics in second language acquisition. *Applied Linguistics* 30 (3), 335–357.

Eskildsen, S.W. (2018) Building a semiotic repertoire for social action: Interactional competence as biographical discovery. *Classroom Discourse* 9 (1), 68–76.

Evans, D.R. (2019) Bifurcations, fractals, and non-linearity in second language development: A complex dynamic systems perspective. Unpublished doctoral dissertation. State University of New York at Buffalo.

Ezra, O., Cohen, A., Bronshtein, A., Gabbay, H. and Baruth, O. (2021) Equity factors during the COVID-19 pandemic: Difficulties in emergency remote teaching (ERT) through online learning. *Education and Information Technologies* 26, 7657–7681.

Fairclough, M.A. and Beaudrie, S.M. (2016) *Innovative Strategies for Heritage Language Teaching: A Practical Guide for the Classroom*. Washington, DC: Georgetown University Press.

Faryadi, Q. (2007) Techniques of teaching Arabic as a foreign language through constructivist paradigm: Malaysian perspective. *Online Submission*.

Fazilatfar, A.M., Elhambakhsh, S.E. and Allami, H. (2018) An investigation of the effects of citation instruction to avoid plagiarism in EFL academic writing assignments. *Sage Open* 8 (2), 2158244018769958.

Fenoll, A.A. and Kuehn, Z. (2021) *The Bilingual Advantage*. Turin: Collegio Carlo Alberto.

Firth, A. and Wagner, J. (1997) On discourse, communication, and (some) fundamental concepts in SLA research. *The Modern Language Journal* 81 (3), 285–300.

Firth, A. and Wagner, J. (2007) Second/foreign language learning as a social accomplishment: Elaborations on a reconceptualized SLA. *The Modern Language Journal* 91, 800–819.

Flowerdew, J. (1999) Writing for scholarly publication in English: The case of Hong Kong. *Journal of Second Language Writing* 8 (2), 123–145.

Fodor, J.A. and Pylyshyn, Z.W. (1988) Connectionism and cognitive architecture: A critical analysis. *Cognition* 28 (1–2), 3–71.

Ford, M. (1985) Mental models: Towards a cognitive science of language, inference, and consciousness. *Language* 61 (4), 897–903.

Forgas, J.P., Williams, K.D., Laham, S.M. and Von Hippel, W. (eds) (2005) *Social Motivation: Conscious and Unconscious Processes* (Vol. 5). Cambridge: Cambridge University Press.

Fortune, A. (2013) The role of metalanguage in the performance of a sequence of collaborative output tasks by five L2 learner dyads. In K. Roeher and G.A. Gánem-Gutiérrez (eds) *The Metalinguistic Dimension in Instructed Second Language Learning* (pp. 171–194). London: Bloomsbury Academic.

Fox, E. and Alexander, P.A. (2011) Learning to read. In R.E. Mayer and P.A. Alexander (eds) *Handbook of Research on Learning and Instruction* (pp. 21–45). New York: Routledge.

Fraga-Cañadas, C.P. (2011) Building communities of practice for foreign language teachers. *The Modern Language Journal* 95 (2), 296–300.

Fredborg, K.M. (1980) Universal grammar According to some 12th century grammarians. *Historiographia Linguistica* 7 (1–2), 69–84.

Freed, B.F. (1995) *Second Language Acquisition in a Study Abroad Context*. Amsterdam: John Benjamins.

Frick, R.W. (1988) Issues of representation and limited capacity in the visuospatial sketchpad. *British Journal of Psychology* 79 (3), 289–308.

Fried, I., Haggard, P., He, B.J. and Schurger, A. (2017) Volition and action in the human brain: Processes, pathologies, and reasons. *Journal of Neuroscience* 37 (45), 10842–10847.

Friedman, A. (2015) America's lacking language skills. *The Atlantic*. https://www.theatlantic.com/education/archive/2015/05/filling-americas-language-education-potholes/392876/. Accessed 4/22/2022.

Fries, C.C. (1952) *The Structure of English*. London: Longmans.

Garrote, P.R. (2014) Second language learning in a multilingual classroom: Didactic interaction development. *Journal of Educational and Social Research* 4 (3), 429–429.

Gass, S.M. (1993) Second language acquisition: Past, present and future. *Second Language Research* 9 (2), 99–117.

Gass, S.M. (2017) *Input, Interaction, and the Second Language Learner*. New York: Routledge.

Gass, S.M. and Mackey, A. (2006) Input, interaction and output: An overview. *AILA Review* 19 (1), 3–17.

Gattegno, C. (2010) *Teaching Foreign Languages in Schools: The Silent Way*. New York: Educational Solutions World.

Gebhard, M., Chen, I.A., Graham, H. and Gunawan, W. (2013) Teaching to mean, writing to mean: SFL, L2 literacy, and teacher education. *Journal of Second Language Writing* 22 (2), 107–124.

Geller, L.L. and Greenberg, M. (2009) Managing the transition process from high school to college and beyond: Challenges for individuals, families, and society. *Social Work in Mental Health* 8 (1), 92–116.

Gette, C.R., Kryjevskaia, M., Stetzer, M.R. and Heron, P.R. (2018) Probing student reasoning approaches through the lens of dual-process theories: A case study in buoyancy. *Physical Review Physics Education Research* 14 (1), 010113.

Gibson, J.J. (1966) *The Senses Considered as Perceptual Systems*. Boston, MA: Houghton Mifflin.

Gibson, J.J. (1979) *The Ecological Approach to Visual Perception*. Boston, MA: Houghton Mifflin.

Ghilzai, S.A. (2020) Overgeneralization and under-generalization in SLA: Evidence from Japanese. *European Academic Research* 8 (2), 753–762.

Giang, V. (2012) *The Reason So Many Business Deals Go Wrong in China*. Business Insider. May, 2. https://www.businessinsider.com/language-barriers-are-costing-companies-tons-of-money-2012-5. Accessed 08/12/2022.

Giering, J.A. and Fitzgerald, H. (2019) The Language Commons: An innovative space supporting second language acquisition. *Journal of Teaching and Learning with Technology* 8, 33–41.

Gkaintartzi, A., Kiliari, A. and Tsokalidou, R. (2016) HL maintenance and education in the Greek sociolinguistic context: Albanian immigrant parents' views. *Cogent Education* 3 (1), 1155259.

Glaser, J. and Kihlstrom, J.F. (2005) Compensatory automaticity: Unconscious volition is not an oxymoron. In R.R. Hassin, J.S. Uleman and J.J. Bargh (eds) *The New Unconscious* (pp. 171–195). New York: Oxford University Press.

Gleason, J.B. (1967, June) Do children imitate. In International conference on oral education of the deaf. New York: Lexington School for the Deaf.

Godwin-Jones, R. (2013) The technological imperative in teaching and learning less commonly taught languages. *Language Learning & Technology* 17 (1), 7–19.

Godwin-Jones, R. (2019) Riding the digital wilds: Learner autonomy and informal language learning. *Language Learning & Technology* 23 (1), 8–25.

Goldberg, A.E. (1995) *Constructions: A Construction Grammar Approach to Argument Structure*. Chicago, IL: University of Chicago Press.

González-Fernández, B. and Schmitt, N. (2017) Vocabulary acquisition. In S. Loewen and M. Sato (eds) *The Routledge Handbook of Instructed Second Language Acquisition* (pp. 280–298). New York: Routledge.

Gor, K. and Chernigovskaya, T. (2008) Formal instruction and the acquisition of verbal morphology. In A. Housen and M. Pierrard (eds) *Investigations in Instructed Second Language Acquisition* (pp. 131–166). Berlin: De Gruyter Mouton.

Gordon, D. (2011) Trauma and second language learning among Laotian refugees. *Journal of Southeast Asian American Education and Advancement* 6 (1), 13.

Gordon, R., Smith-Spark, J.H., Newton, E.J. and Henry, L.A. (2020) Working memory and high-level cognition in children: An analysis of timing and accuracy in complex span tasks. *Journal of Experimental Child Psychology* 191, 104736.

Grabe, W. and Kaplan, R. (1992). *Introduction to Applied Linguistics*. Reading, MA: Addison-Wesley.

Graybiel, A.M. (2008) Habits, rituals, and the evaluative brain. *Annual Review of Neuroscience* 31, 359–387.

Greenwald, A.G. (1992) New Look 3: Unconscious cognition reclaimed. *American Psychologist* 47 (6), 766.

Gregg, K.R. (2006) Taking a social turn for the worse: The language socialization paradigm for second language acquisition. *Second Language Research* 22 (4), 413–442.

Gregory, R.L. (1993) Seeing and thinking. *Giornale Italiano di Psicologia* 20 (5), 749–769.

Groome, L.J., Mooney, D.M., Holland, S.B., Smith, Y.D., Atterbury, J.L. and Dykman, R.A. (2000) Temporal pattern and spectral complexity as stimulus parameters for eliciting a cardiacorienting reflex inhuman fetuses. *Perception & Psychophysics* 62 (2), 313–320.

Gross, N. (2016) Dual-language programs on the rise across the US (Web log post). Education Writers Association, Washington, DC. See https://www.ewa.org/blog-latino-edbeat/dual-language-programs-rise-across-us (accessed 12 April 2016).

Guo, R. and Ellis, N.C. (2021) Language usage and second language morphosyntax: Effects of availability, reliability, and formulaicity. *Frontiers in Psychology* 12, 582259.

Gurney, L. and Díaz, A. (2020) Coloniality, neoliberalism and the language textbook: Unravelling the symbiosis in Spanish as a foreign language. *Language, Culture and Society* 2 (2), 149–173.

Gyi, K.K. (1994) Teaching English as a second language: The Silent Way. *ABAC Journal* 14 (3), 39–46.

Hadley, A.O. and Reiken, E. (1993) *Teaching Language in Context, and Teaching Language in Context: Workbook*. Cincinnati, OH: Heinle & Heinle.

Haggard, P. (2008) Human volition: Towards a neuroscience of will. *Nature Reviews Neuroscience* 9 (12), 934–946.

Hall, J.K. (2016) A usage-based view of multicompetence. In V. Cook and L. Wei (eds) *Cambridge Handbook of Linguistic Multicompetence* (pp. 183–206). Cambridge: Cambridge University Press.

Hall, J.K. (2018) From L2 interactional competence to L2 interactional repertoires: Reconceptualising the objects of L2 learning. *Classroom Discourse* 9 (1), 25–39.

Hall, J.K., Cheng, A. and Carlson, M.T. (2006) Reconceptualizing multicompetence as a theory of language knowledge. *Applied Linguistics* 27 (2), 220–240.

Hall, L. (2019) Literacy myth: Learning-to-read vs. reading-to-learn. See https://www.youtube.com/watch?v=ZbIsXueiynU. Accessed 06/24/2022.

Hamidah, H. (2019) Arabic language: Between learning necessity and responsibility (ar). *Al-Ta'rib: Jurnal Ilmiah Program Studi Pendidikan Bahasa Arab IAIN Palangka Raya* 7 (1), 35–44.

Hammerly, H. (1991) *Fluency and Accuracy: Toward Balance in Language Teaching and Learning*. Clevedon: Multilingual Matters.

Han, Z. (2004) To be a native speaker means not to be a nonnative speaker. *Second Language Research* 20 (2), 166–187.

Harris, K.R. (1990) Developing self-regulated learners: The role of private speech and self-instructions. *Educational Psychologist* 25 (1), 35–49.

Hasan, R. (1992) Speech genre, semiotic mediation and the development of higher mental functions. *Language Sciences* 14 (4), 489–528.

Hashimoto, K. and Lee, J.S. (2011) Heritage-language literacy practices: A case study of three Japanese American families. *Bilingual Research Journal* 34 (2), 161–184.

Hassin, R.R. (2013) Yes it can: On the functional abilities of the human unconscious. *Perspectives on Psychological Science* 8 (2), 195–207.

Hayashi, H. (2013) Dual goal orientation in the Japanese context: A case study of two EFL learners. In M.T. Apple, D. Da Silva and T. Fellner (eds) *Language Learning Motivation in Japan* (pp. 75–92). Bristol: Multilingual Matters.

Hayes, J.R. and Flower, L.S. (1981) *Uncovering Cognitive Processes in Writing: An Introduction to Protocol Analysis*. ERIC Clearinghouse.

Hayes, J.R. and Flowers, L.S. (2016) Identifying the organization of writing processes. In L.W. Gregg and E.R. Steinberg (eds) *Cognitive Processes in Writing* (pp. 3–30). New York: Routledge.

Hearne, J.D. (2000) *Teaching Second Language Learners with Learning Disabilities: Strategies for Effective Practice*. Oceanside, CA: Academic Communication Associates.

Henrich, J., Heine, S.J. and Norenzayan, A. (2010) The weirdest people in the world? *Behavioral and Brain Sciences* 33 (2–3), 61–83.

Henry, N., Culman, H. and VanPatten, B. (2009) More on the effects of explicit information in instructed SLA: A partial replication and a response to Fernández (2008). *Studies in Second Language Acquisition* 31 (4), 559–575.

Hernandez, A., Li, P. and MacWhinney, B. (2005) The emergence of competing modules in bilingualism. *Trends in Cognitive Sciences* 9 (5), 220–225.

Hesselmann, G. and Moors, P. (2015) Definitely maybe: Can unconscious processes perform the same functions as conscious processes? *Frontiers in Psychology* 6, 584.

Hidri, S. and Coombe, C. (eds) (2016) *Evaluation in Foreign Language Education in the Middle East and North Africa*. London: Springer.

Ho, C. (2010) HL loss in the Chinese community in Argentina. Senior honours thesis. Swarthmore College.

Hodaeian, M. and Biria, R. (2015) The effect of backward design on intermediate EFL learners' L2 reading comprehension: Focusing on learners' attitudes. *Journal of Applied Linguistics and Language Research* 2 (7), 80–93.

Holm, A. and Dodd, B. (1996) The effect of first written language on the acquisition of English literacy. *Cognition* 59 (2), 119–147.

Hopp, H. (2016) Learning (not) to predict: Grammatical gender processing in second language acquisition. *Second Language Research* 32 (2), 277–307.

Hopper, P. (1987) Emergent Grammar. *Proceedings of the Thirteenth Annual Meeting of the Berkeley Linguistics Society* (pp. 139–157). Berkeley, CA: The Berkeley Linguistics Society.

Hopper, P. (2002) Emergent grammar: Gathering together the fragments. Talk at the Institute for Applied Linguistics, Penn State University.

Housen, A., Kuiken, F. and Vedder, I. (eds) (2012) *Dimensions of L2 Performance and Proficiency: Complexity, Accuracy and Fluency in SLA* (Vol. 32). Amsterdam: John Benjamins Publishing.

Hu, G. (2002) Potential cultural resistance to pedagogical imports: The case of communicative language teaching in China. *Language Culture and Curriculum* 15 (2), 93–105.

Hu, G. (2010) Revisiting the role of metalanguage in L2 teaching and learning. *English Australia Journal* 26 (1), 61–70.

Huettig, F. and Pickering, M.J. (2019) Literacy advantages beyond reading: Prediction of spoken language. *Trends in Cognitive Sciences* 23 (6), 464–475.

Hulstijn, J.H. (2011) Language proficiency in native and nonnative speakers: An agenda for research and suggestions for second-language assessment. *Language Assessment Quarterly* 8 (3), 229–249.

Hulstijn, J.H. (2013) Incidental learning in second language acquisition. *The Encyclopedia of Applied Linguistics* 5, 2632–2640.

Hung, T.Y., Seow, V.K., Chong, C.F., Wang, T.L. and Chen, C.C. (2008) Gabapentin toxicity: An important cause of altered consciousness in patients with uraemia. *Emergency Medicine Journal* 25 (3), 178–179.

Hussain, Z.I. and Asad, M. (2017) A look at the potential of big data in nurturing intuition in organizational decision makers. British Academy of Management Annual Conference. BAM2017, 5–7 September 2017. Warwick Business School, Warwick, UK.

Ikhwanuddin, M. and Hashim, C.N. (2014) Relationship between memorization technique, mastery of the Arabic language and understanding of the Qur'an. *IIUM Journal of Educational Studies* 2 (2), 84–97.

Ingraham, C. (2019) Nearly half of white republicans say it bothers them to hear people speaking foreign languages. *The Washington Post*. See https://www.washingtonpost.com/business/2019/05/08/nearly-half-white-republicans-say-it-bothers-them-hear-people-speaking-foreign-languages/. Accessed 10/15/2021.

Isabelli-García, C., Bown, J., Plews, J.L. and Dewey, D.P. (2018) Language learning and study abroad. *Language Teaching* 51 (4), 439–484.

Ishikawa, T. (2006) The effect of task complexity and language proficiency on task-based language performance. *Journal of Asia TEFL* 3 (4).

Iwashita, N., McNamara, T. and Elder, C. (2001) Can we predict task difficulty in an oral proficiency test? Exploring the potential of an information-processing approach to task design. *Language Learning* 51 (3), 401–436.

Jackendoff, R.S. (2009) *Language, Consciousness, Culture: Essays on Mental Structure*. Cambridge, MA: MIT Press.

Jakiela, P. and Ozier, O. (2018) Gendered language. *World Bank Policy Research Working Paper* (8464).

Jin, B. (2020) English language requirements in the current international scientific publishing world: A content analysis of submission guidelines in chemical engineering. *Iberica* 40, 59–74.

Kachinske, I. (2021) Skill acquisition theory and the role of rule and example learning. *Journal of Contemporary Philology* 4 (2), 25–41.

Kagan, O. (2010) Russian HL speakers in the US: A profile. *Russian Language Journal/Русский язык* 60, 213–228.

Kara, M., Erdogdu, F., Kokoç, M. and Cagiltay, K. (2019) Challenges faced by adult learners in online distance education: A literature review. *Open Praxis* 11 (1), 5–22.

Karbakhsh, R. and Ahmadi Safa, M. (2020) Basic psychological needs satisfaction, goal orientation, willingness to communicate, self-efficacy, and learning strategy use as predictors of second language achievement: A structural equation modeling approach. *Journal of Psycholinguistic Research* 49 (5), 803–822.

Karim, K. and Nassaji, H. (2013) First language transfer in second language writing: An examination of current research. *Iranian Journal of Language Teaching Research* 1 (1), 117–134.

Karimi, M.N. (2013) Enhancing L2 students' listening transcription ability through a focus on morphological awareness. *Journal of Psycholinguistic Research* 42 (5), 451–459.
Keane, W. (1997) Religious language. *Annual Review of Anthropology* 26 (1), 47–71.
Kelleher, A. (2010) What is an HL program? *Heritage Briefs* 3, 1–4.
Kemmerer, D. (2014) *Cognitive Neuroscience of Language*. Oxford: Psychology Press.
Kester, L., Kirschner, P.A. and Van Merriënboer, J.J. (2004) Timing of information presentation in learning statistics. *Instructional Science* 32 (3), 233–252.
Khng, K.H. (2017) A better state-of-mind: Deep breathing reduces state anxiety and enhances test performance through regulating test cognitions in children. *Cognition and Emotion* 31 (7), 1502–1510.
Kida, T. (2008) Effects of teacher discourse on learner discourse in a second language classroom. In A. Housen and M. Pierrard (eds) *Investigations in Instructed Second Language Acquisition* (pp. 457–494). Berlin: De Gruyter Mouton.
Kiefer, M. (2012) Executive control over unconscious cognition: Attentional sensitization of unconscious information processing. *Frontiers in Human Neuroscience* 6, 61.
Kihlstrom, J.F. (1999) Conscious versus unconscious cognition. In R.J. Sternberg (ed.) *The Nature of Cognition* (pp. 173–203). Cambridge, MA: MIT Press.
Kihlstrom, J.F. (2018) The rediscovery of the unconscious. In H.J. Morowitz (ed.) *The Mind, the Brain, and Complex Adaptive Systems* (pp. 123–144). New York: Routledge.
Kim, Y. (2012) Task complexity, learning opportunities, and Korean EFL learners' question development. *Studies in Second Language Acquisition* 34 (4), 627–658.
Kim, Y. (2017) Cognitive-interactionist approaches to L2 instruction. In S. Loewen and M. Sato (eds) *The Routledge Handbook of Instructed Second Language Acquisition* (pp. 126–145). New York: Routledge.
Kim, M. and Canagarajah, S. (2021) Student artifacts as language learning materials: A new materialist analysis of South Korean job seekers' student-generated materials use. *The Modern Language Journal*, 105 (S1), 21–38.
Kinginger, C. (2002) Defining the zone of proximal development in US foreign language education. *Applied Linguistics* 23 (2), 240–261.
Kinginger, C. (2011) Enhancing language learning in study abroad. *Annual Review of Applied Linguistics* 31, 58–73.
Kleinmann, H.H. (1977) Avoidance behavior in adult second language acquisition. *Language Learning*, 27 (1), 93–107.
Kluver, R. (2014) The sage as strategy: Nodes, networks, and the quest for geopolitical power in the Confucius Institute. *Communication, Culture & Critique* 7 (2), 192–209.
Knoch, U. and Macqueen, S. (2017) Assessment in the L2 classroom. In S. Loewen and M. Sato (eds) *The Routledge Handbook of Instructed Second Language Acquisition* (pp. 181–202). New York: Routledge.
Koda, K. (2005) *Insights into Second Language Reading: A Cross-linguistic Approach*. Cambridge: Cambridge University Press.
Konyndyk, I.B. and Snyder, L.S. (2011) *Foreign Languages for Everyone: How I Learned to Teach Second Languages to Students with Learning Disabilities*. Grand Rapids, MI: Edenridge Press.
Kormos, J. and Kiddle, T. (2011) Systems of goals, attitudes, and self-related beliefs in second-language-learning motivation. *Applied Linguistics* 32 (5), 495–516.
Korotchenko, T.V., Matveenko, I.A., Strelnikova, A.B. and Phillips, C. (2015) Backward design method in foreign language curriculum development. *Procedia-Social and Behavioral Sciences* 215, 213–217.
Kozaki, Y. and Ross, S.J. (2011) Contextual dynamics in foreign language learning motivation. *Language Learning* 61 (4), 1328–1354.
Kramer, S., Miller, D. and Newberger, J. (2008) *The Linguists*. Ironbound Films, Garrison, N.Y.

Kramsch, C. (1998) *Language and Culture*. Oxford: Oxford University Press.
Kramsch, C. (ed.) (2003) *Language Acquisition and Language Socialization: Ecological Perspectives*. London: Bloomsbury Publishing.
Krashen, S. (1978) Individual variation in the use of the monitor. In W.C. Ritchie (ed.) *Second Language Acquisition Research: Issues and Implications* (pp. 175–183). London: Academic Press.
Krause, M.T. and Beitter, U.E. (1983) Beyond entertainment: Organizing a college German club. *Die Unterrichtspraxis/Teaching German* 16 (1), 34–42.
Kroll, J.F., Michael, E., Tokowicz, N. and Dufour, R. (2002) The development of lexical fluency in a second language. *Second Language Research* 18 (2), 137–171.
Kuiken, F., Mos, M. and Vedder, I. (2005) Cognitive task complexity and second language writing performance. *EuroSLA Yearbook* 5 (1), 195–222.
Kumagai, Y., López-Sánchez, A. and Wu, S. (2015) *Multiliteracies in World Language Education*. New York: Routledge.
Kuo, F.R., Hsu, C.C., Fang, W.C. and Chen, N.S. (2014) The effects of embodiment-based TPR approach on student English vocabulary learning achievement, retention and acceptance. *Journal of King Saud University-Computer and Information Sciences* 26 (1), 63–70.
Kwon, J. (2017) Immigrant mothers' beliefs and transnational strategies for their children's HL maintenance. *Language and Education* 31 (6), 495–508.
Lado, R. (1970) *English Pattern Practices: Establishing the Patterns as Habits*. Ann Arbor, MI: University of Michigan Press.
Lado, R. and Fries, C. (1957) *Linguistics Across Cultures: Applied Linguistics for Language Teachers*. Ann Arbor, MI: University of Michigan Press.
Lallier, M., Carreiras, M., Tainturier, M.J., Savill, N. and Thierry, G. (2013) Orthographic transparency modulates the grain size of orthographic processing: Behavioral and ERP evidence from bilingualism. *Brain Research* 1505, 47–60.
Lamy, M. and Hampel, R. (2007) *Online Communication in Language Learning and Teaching*. London: Palgrave MacMillan.
Lantolf, J.P. (1976) On teaching intonation. *Modern Language Journal* 60, 267–274.
Lantolf, J.P. (2009) Dynamic assessment: The dialectic integration of instruction and assessment. *Language Teaching* 42 (3), 355–368.
Lantolf, J.P. and Beckett, T.G. (2009) Sociocultural theory and second language acquisition. *Language Teaching* 42 (4), 459–475.
Larsen-Freeman, D. (1997) Chaos/complexity science and second language acquisition. *Applied Linguistics* 18 (2), 141–165.
Larsen-Freeman, D. (2007) Reflecting on the cognitive–social debate in second language acquisition. *The Modern Language Journal* 91, 773–787.
Larsen-Freeman, D. (2009) Adjusting expectations: The study of complexity, accuracy, and fluency in second language acquisition. *Applied Linguistics* 30 (4), 579–589.
Larsen-Freeman, D. (2015) Ten 'lessons' from complex dynamic systems theory: What is on offer. In Z. Dörnyei, P.D. MacIntyre and A. Henry (eds) *Motivational Dynamics in Language Learning* (pp. 11–19). Bristol: Multilingual Matters.
Larsen-Freeman, D. (2018) Looking ahead: Future directions in, and future research into, second language acquisition. *Foreign Language Annals* 51 (1), 55–72.
Laufer, B. (1999) Task effect on instructed vocabulary learning: the hypothesis of 'involvement'. Key-note address presented at AILA Congress, Tokyo.
Laufer, B. (2005) Instructed second language vocabulary learning: The fault in the 'default hypothesis'. In A. Housen and M. Pierrard (eds) *Investigations in Instructed Second Language Acquisition* (pp. 311–332). Berlin: De Gruyter Mouton.
Laufer, B. (2010) Form-focused instruction in second language vocabulary learning. In R. Chacón-Beltrán, C. Abello-Contesse and M. del Mar Torreblanca-López (eds) *Insights into Non-native Vocabulary Teaching and Learning* (pp. 15–27). Bristol: Multilingual Matters. https://doi.org/10.21832/9781847692900-003

Lecanuet, J.P., Graniere-Deferre, C., Jacquet, A.Y. and DeCasper, A.J. (2000) Fetal discrimination of low-pitched musical notes. *Developmental Psychobiology: The Journal of the International Society for Developmental Psychobiology* 36 (1), 29–39.

LeDoux, J.E. and Lau, H. (2020) Seeing consciousness through the lens of memory. *Current Biology* 30 (18), R1018–R1022.

Lee, I.J. (2011) *Language Habits in Human Affairs*. New York: Harper & Row.

Lee, J.S. (2002) The Korean language in America: The role of cultural identity in HL learning. *Language Culture and Curriculum* 15 (2), 117–133.

Lee, J. (2019) Task complexity, cognitive load, and L1 speech. *Applied Linguistics* 40 (3), 506–539.

Leite, J. and Cook, R. (2015) Utah: Making immersion mainstream. In P. Mehisto and F. Genesee (eds) *Building Bilingual Education Systems: Forces, Mechanisms and Counterweights* (pp. 83–96). Cambridge: Cambridge University Press.

Lenzing, A., Plesser, A., Hagenfeld, K. and Pienemann, M. (2013) Transfer at the initial state. *Zeitschrift für Anglistik und Amerikanistik* 61 (3), 265–286.

Leung, C. (2007) Dynamic assessment: Assessment for and as teaching? *Language Assessment Quarterly* 4 (3), 257–278.

Leung, C. and Valdés, G. (2019) Translanguaging and the transdisciplinary framework for language teaching and learning in a multilingual world. *The Modern Language Journal* 103 (2), 348–370.

Levis, J.M. (2005) Changing contexts and shifting paradigms in pronunciation teaching. *TESOL Quarterly* 39 (3), 369–377.

Lewis, G., Jones, B. and Baker, C. (2012) Translanguaging: Origins and development from school to street and beyond. *Educational Research and Evaluation: An International Journal on Theory and Practice* 18 (7), 641–654.

Liang, F. (2018) Parental perceptions toward and practices of HL maintenance: Focusing on the United States and Canada. *Online Submission* 12 (2), 65–86.

Lie, A. (2017) Learning Chinese as an HL by two multilingual youths in Indonesia. In G. Li and W. Ma (eds) *Educating Chinese–Heritage Students in the Global–Local Nexus* (pp. 47–66). Abingdon: Routledge.

Liljenström, H. (2022) Consciousness, decision making, and volition: Freedom beyond chance and necessity. *Theory in Biosciences* 141 (2), 125–140.

Lisman, J. and Sternberg, E.J. (2013) Habit and nonhabit systems for unconscious and conscious behavior: Implications for multitasking. *Journal of Cognitive Neuroscience* 25 (2), 273–283.

LivingTongues.org. Kallawaya. See http://livingtongues.org/kallawaya/.

Llinares, A. and McCabe, A. (2020) Systemic functional linguistics: The perfect match for content and language integrated learning. *International Journal of Bilingual Education and Bilingualism* 1–6.

Loewen, S. (2020) *Introduction to Instructed Second Language Acquisition*. Abingdon: Routledge.

Lombardi, R. (2003) Mental models and language registers in the psychoanalysis of psychosis: An overview of a thirteen-year analysis 2. *The International Journal of Psychoanalysis* 84 (4), 843–863.

Long, M. (1981) Input, interaction and second language acquisition. *Annals of the New York Academy of Sciences* 379, 259–278.

Long, M.H. (1985) A role for instruction in second language acquisition: Task-based language teaching. *Modelling and Assessing Second Language Acquisition* 18, 77–99.

Long, M.H. and Doughty, C.J. (eds) (2011) *The Handbook of Language Teaching* (Vol. 63). Malden, MA: John Wiley & Sons.

Lu, Y.C. and Berg, D.R. (2008) ESL learners' learning motivations and strategies. *International Journal of Learning* 15 (1).

Lyster, R. (2017) Content-based language teaching. In S. Loewen and M. Sato (eds) *The Routledge Handbook of Instructed Second Language Acquisition* (pp. 87–107). New York: Routledge.

Lyster, R. and Sato, M. (2013) Skill acquisition theory and the role of practice in L2 development. In M.G. Mayo, J. Gutierrez-Mangado and M.M. Adrián (eds) *Multiple Perspectives on Second Language Acquisition* (pp. 71–92). Amsterdam: Benjamins.

MacIntyre, P.D. and Vincze, L. (2017) Positive and negative emotions underlie motivation for L2 learning. *Studies in Second Language Learning and Teaching* 7 (1), 61–88.

Mackey, A. (1999) Input, interaction, and second language development: An empirical study of question formation in ESL. *Studies in Second Language Acquisition* 21 (4), 557–587.

MacWhinney, B. (1978) *The Acquisition of Morphophonology* (Monographs of the Society for Research in Child Development 43). Chicago, IL: Society for Research in Child Development.

MacWhinney, B. (2005a) Extending the competition model. *International Journal of Bilingualism* 9 (1), 69–84.

MacWhinney, B. (2005b) The emergence of linguistic form in time. *Connection Science* 17 (3–4), 191–211.

MacWhinney, B. (2006) Emergentism: Use often and with care. *Applied Linguistics* 27 (4), 729–740.

MacWhinney, B. (2008) How mental models encode embodied linguistic perspectives. In R. Klatzky, B. MacWhinney and M. Behrmann (eds) *Embodiment, Ego-Space, and Action* (pp. 385–426). New York: Psychology Press.

MacWhinney, B. (2022) The competition model: Past and future. In J. Gervain, G. Csibra and K. Kovács (eds) *A Life in Cognition: Studies in Cognitive Science in Honor of Csaba Pléh* (pp. 3–16). Cham: Springer Nature.

MacWhinney, B. and Bates, E. (1987) Competition, variation, and language learning. In B. MacWhinney (ed.) *Mechanisms of Language Acquisition* (pp. 157–193). New York: Routledge.

MacWhinney, B., Leinbach, J., Taraban, R. and McDonald, J. (1989) Language learning: Cues or rules? *Journal of Memory and Language* 28 (3), 255–277.

Mahboob, A. (2005) Beyond the native speaker in TESOL. *Culture, Context and Communication* 30, 60–93.

Majhanovich, S. (2013) English as a tool of neo-colonialism and globalization in Asian contexts. In Y. Hébert and A.A. Abdi (eds) *Critical Perspectives on International Education* (pp. 249–261). Uitgever: Brill Sense.

Mallikarjun, A., Newman, R.S. and Novick, J.M. (2017) Exploiting the interconnected lexicon: Bootstrapping English language learning in young Spanish speakers. *Translational Issues in Psychological Science* 3 (1), 34.

Malone, M.E., Rifkin, B., Christian, D. and Johnson, D.E. (2005) Attaining high levels of proficiency: Challenges for foreign language education in the United States. Center for Applied Linguistics Digest. CALdigest. https://www.cal.org/resource-center/resource-archive/digests. Accessed 1/5/2023.

Manhart, K. (2004) The limits of multitasking. *Scientific American Mind* 14 (5), 62–67.

Mantero, M. (ed.) (2006) *Identity and Second Language Learning: Culture, Inquiry, and Dialogic Activity in Educational Contexts*. Charlotte, NC: Information Age Publishing.

Marcel, A.J. (1983) Conscious and unconscious perception: An approach to the relations between phenomenal experience and perceptual processes. *Cognitive Psychology* 15 (2), 238–300.

Marr, A.J. (2001) In the zone: A biobehavioral theory of the flow experience. *Athletic Insight: Online Journal of Sport Psychology* 3 (1).

Mat, H. and Abas, W.U.W. (2016) The relevance of Arabic language in Islamic studies program: A case study of Open University Malaysia (OUM). *Journal of Education and Social Sciences* 5 (2), 205–209.

Mattson, M.P. (2014) Superior pattern processing is the essence of the evolved human brain. *Frontiers in Neuroscience* 8, 265.

Maxim, III, H. (2002) A study into the feasibility and effects of reading extended authentic discourse in the beginning German language classroom. *The Modern Language Journal* 86 (1), 20–35.

Maxim, H.H. (2006) Integrating textual thinking into the introductory college-level foreign language classroom. *The Modern Language Journal* 90 (1), 19–32.

Maxim, H.H. (2014) Curricular integration and faculty development: Teaching language-based content across the foreign language curriculum. In J. Swaffer and P. Urlaub (eds) *Transforming Postsecondary Foreign Language Teaching in the United States* (pp. 79–101). Dordrecht: Springer.

Maxim, H.H., Höyng, P., Lancaster, M., Schaumann, C. and Aue, M. (2013) Overcoming curricular bifurcation: A departmental approach to curriculum reform. *Die Unterrichtspraxis/Teaching German* 46 (1), 1–26.

May, S. (2014) Disciplinary divides, knowledge construction, and the multilingual turn. In S. May (ed.) *The Multilingual Turn: Implications for SLA, TESOL and Bilingual Education* (pp. 7–31). Abingdon: Routledge.

Mayo, M.D.P.G. (2008) Interactional strategies for interlanguage communication: Do they provide evidence for attention to form? In A. Housen and M. Pierrard (eds) *Investigations in Instructed Second Language Acquisition* (pp. 383–406). Berlin: De Gruyter Mouton.

McBride, K. (2010, August) Reciprocity in service learning: Intercultural competence through SLA studies. In *Proceedings of Intercultural Competence Conference* (Vol. 1; pp. 235–261).

McCauley, S.M. and Christiansen, M.H. (2017) Computational investigations of multiword chunks in language learning. *Topics in Cognitive Science* 9 (3), 637–652.

McCulloch, S. (2019) How language barriers affect international business. https://familyenterprisefHowLanguageBarriersAffectInternationalBusinessundation.org/resources/resources/our-insights/articles/2019/july/how-language-barriers-affect-international-business/. Accessed 05/23/2022.

McGurk, H. and MacDonald, J. (1976) Hearing lips and seeing voices. *Nature* 264, 746–748.

McLaughlin, B. (1992) Myths and misconceptions about second language learning: What every teacher needs to unlearn. *Educational Practice Report* 5, 3–17.

McNicoll, J. and Lee, J.H. (2011) Collaborative consciousness-raising tasks in EAL classrooms. *English Teaching: Practice and Critique* 10 (4), 127–138.

Meneghini, R. and Packer, A.L. (2007) Is there science beyond English? Initiatives to increase the quality and visibility of non-English publications might help to break down language barriers in scientific communication. *EMBO Reports* 8 (2), 112–116.

Merleau-Ponty, M. (1973) *Consciousness and the Acquisition of Language*. Evanston, IL: Northwestern University Press.

Michel, M.C. (2011) Effects of task complexity and interaction on L2 performance. In P. Robinson (ed.) *Second Language Task Complexity: Researching the Cognition Hypothesis of Language Learning and Performance* (pp. 141–173). Amsterdam: John Benjamins.

Miller, G.A. (1956) The magical number seven, plus or minus two: Some limits on our capacity for processing information. *Psychological Review* 63 (2), 81–97.

Miller, G.A. (2003) The cognitive revolution: A historical perspective. *Trends in Cognitive Sciences* 7 (3), 141–144.

Moeller, A.J., Theiler, J.M. and Wu, C. (2012) Goal setting and student achievement: A longitudinal study. *The Modern Language Journal* 96 (2), 153–169.

Mohebi, S.G. and Khodadady, E. (2011) Investigating university students' beliefs about language learning. *RELC Journal* 42 (3), 291–304.

Montague, R. (1970) Universal grammar. In J. Gutiérrez-Rexach (ed.) *Semantics: Critical Concepts in Linguistics 1: Foundational Issues* (pp. 90–109). London: Routledge.

Montero, B.G. (2015) Thinking in the zone: The expert mind in action. *The Southern Journal of Philosophy* 53, 126–140.

Montrul, S. and Bowles, M. (2017) Instructed HL acquisition. In S. Loewen and M. Sato (eds) *The Routledge Handbook of Instructed Second Language Acquisition* (pp. 488–502). New York: Routledge.

Moore, A.W. (2019) *Language, World, and Limits: Essays in the Philosophy of Language and Metaphysics*. Oxford: Oxford University Press.

Moore, L.C., Echu, G. and Obeng, S.G. (2004) Multilingualism and second language acquisition in the northern Mandara Mountains. In G. Echu and S.G. Obeng (eds) *Africa Meets Europe: Language Contact in West Africa* (pp. 131–148). New York: Nova Science.

Mucchi-Faina, A. (2005) Visible or influential? Language reforms and gender (in) equality. *Social Science Information* 44 (1), 189–215.

Murakami, A. and Ellis, N.C. (2022) Effects of availability, contingency, and formulaicity on the accuracy of English grammatical morphemes in second language writing. *Language Learning*.

Murphy, J.J. (1980) The teaching of Latin as a second language in the 12th century. *Historiographia Linguistica* 7 (1–2), 159–175.

Musumeci, D. (2009) History of language teaching. In M.H. Long and C.J. Doughty (eds) *The Handbook of Language Teaching* (pp. 42–62). Chichester: John Wiley & Sons.

Nagano, T., Ketcham, E. and Funk, A. (2019) Why do HL speakers opt out of their own HL? A survey-based study of HL learners at community colleges. *HL Journal* 16 (3), 318–339.

Narayan, C.R. (2019) An acoustic perspective on 45 years of infant speech perception, Part 1: Consonants. *Language and Linguistics Compass* 13 (10), e12352.

Nassaji, H. and Fotos, S.S. (2011) *Teaching Grammar in Second Language Classrooms: Integrating Form-focused Instruction in Communicative Context*. New York: Routledge.

National Standards Collaborative Board (2015) *World-Readiness Standards for Learning Languages* (4th edn). Alexandria, VA: Author. See https://www.actfl.org/resources/world-readiness-standards-learning-languages (accessed 30 August 2021).

Negueruela, E. (2003) A sociocultural approach to teaching and researching second languages: Systemic-theoretical instruction and second language development. Unpublished doctoral dissertation. The Pennsylvania State University.

Negueruela-Azarola, E. (2011) Beliefs as conceptualizing activity: A dialectical approach for the second language classroom. *System* 39 (3), 359–369.

New American Economy (2017) Not Lost in Translation: The Growing Importance of Foreign Language Skills in the US Job Market. Report. https://research.newamericaneconomy.org/report/not-lost-in-translation-the-growing-importance-of-foreign-language-skills-in-the-u-s-job-market/

Newmeyer, F.J. (2017) Form and function in the evolution of grammar. *Cognitive Science* 41, 259–276.

Nixon, J.S. (2020) Of mice and men: Speech sound acquisition as discriminative learning from prediction error, not just statistical tracking. *Cognition* 197, 104081.

Nolan, S.J. (2022) Foreign language acquisition before graduation. Unpublished doctoral dissertation. Roberts Wesleyan College (Rochester).

Norton, B. (2013) Identity, literacy, and the multilingual classroom. In S. May (ed.) *The Multilingual Turn: Implications for SLA, TESOL and Bilingual Education* (pp. 113–132). Abingdon: Routledge.

Nunan, D. (1998) Teaching grammar in context. *ELT Journal* 52 (2), 101–109.

Ochi, G., Kanazawa, Y., Hyodo, K., Suwabe, K., Shimizu, T., Fukuie, T. ... and Soya, H. (2018) Hypoxia-induced lowered executive function depends on arterial oxygen desaturation. *The Journal of Physiological Sciences* 68 (6), 847–853.

Oh, J.S. and Au, T.K.F. (2005) Learning Spanish as an HL: The role of sociocultural background variables. *Language, Culture and Curriculum* 18 (3), 229–241.

Oliver, R., Nguyen, B. and Sato, M. (2017) Child ISLA. In S. Loewen and M. Sato (eds) *The Routledge Handbook of Instructed Second Language Acquisition* (pp. 468–487). New York: Routledge.

Olivos, E.M. and Lucero, A. (2018) Latino parents in dual language immersion programs: Why are they so satisfied? *International Journal of Bilingual Education and Bilingualism* 23 (10), 1211–1224.

Ortega, L. (2011) SLA after the social turn: Where cognitivism and its alternatives stand. In D. Atkins (ed.) *Alternative Approaches to Second Language Acquisition* (pp. 179–192). Abingdon: Routledge.

Ortega, L. (2013) Ways forward for a bi/multilingual turn in SLA. In S. May (ed.) *The Multilingual Turn: Implications for SLA, TESOL and Bilingual Education* (pp. 42–63). Abingdon: Routledge.

Ortega, L. and Byrnes, H. (2009) *The Longitudinal Study of Advanced L2 Capacities*. New York: Routledge.

Oshita, H. (2014) U-shaped development. *Georgetown University Round Table on Languages and Linguistics* 155–170.

Otcu, B. (2010) Heritage language maintenance and cultural identity formation: The case of a Turkish Saturday school in New York City. *Heritage Language Journal* 7 (2), 273–298.

Ouyang, H. (2003) Resistance to the communicative method of language instruction within a progressive Chinese university. In K.M. Anderson-Levitt (ed.) *Local Meanings, Global Schooling* (pp. 121–140). New York: Palgrave Macmillan.

Ozsevik, Z. (2010) The use of communicative language teaching (CLT): Turkish EFL teachers' perceived difficulties in implementing CLT in Turkey. Unpublished master's thesis. University of Illinois at Urbana-Champaign.

Paesani, K. (2016) Investigating connections among reading, writing, and language development: A multiliteracies perspective. *Reading in a Foreign Language* 28 (2), 266–289.

Paesani, K. (2017) Redesigning an introductory language curriculum: A backward design approach. *L2 Journal* 9 (1), 1–20.

Paikeday, T.M. and Chomsky, N. (1985) *The Native Speaker is Dead! An Informal Discussion of a Linguistic Myth with Noam Chomsky and Other Linguists, Philosophers, Psychologists, and Lexicographers*. Toronto: Paikeday Publishers.

Palmer, E.C., David, A.S. and Fleming, S.M. (2014) Effects of age on metacognitive efficiency. *Consciousness and Cognition* 28, 151–160.

Paloma, F.G. (2017) Embodied cognition and second language teaching/learning. In F.G. Paloma, D. Ianes and D. Tafuri (eds) *Embodied Cognition: Theories and Applications in Education Science* (pp. 89–106). New York: Nova Science Publishers.

Papalia, A. (1978) Students' beliefs on the importance of foreign languages in the school curriculum. *Foreign Language Annals* 11 (1), 21–23.

Paradis, M. (2009) *Declarative and Procedural Determinants of Second Languages*. Amsterdam: John Benjamins Publishing.

Park, K. (2012) Learner–corpus interaction: A locus of microgenesis in corpus-assisted L2 writing. *Applied Linguistics* 33 (4), 361–385.

Park, S.M. and Sarkar, M. (2007) Parents' attitudes toward HL maintenance for their children and their efforts to help their children maintain the HL: A case study of Korean-Canadian immigrants. *Language, Culture and Curriculum* 20 (3), 223–235.

Parvini, K. (2017) Implementing Holy Quran in teaching Arabic for Iranian students of bachelor's degree in Arabic language and literature (listening skill model). *Studies in Arabic Teaching and Learning* 1 (2), 53–70.

Passey, A., Rubio, F. and Campbell, S. (2004) Grammar in disguise: The hidden agenda of communicative language teaching textbooks. *RAEL: Revista Electrónica de Lingüística Aplicada* 3, 158–176.

Pavlenko, A. (ed.) (2011) *Thinking and Speaking in Two Languages*. Bristol: Multilingual Matters.

Pennycook, A. (2007) ELT and colonialism. In J. Cummins and C. Davison (eds) *International Handbook of English Language Teaching* (pp. 13–24). Boston, MA: Springer.

Pérez-Serrano, M., Nogueroles-López, M. and Duñabeitia, J.A. (2021) Incidental vocabulary learning with subtitles in a new language: Orthographic markedness and number of exposures. *PloS One* 16 (2), e0246933.

Pienemann, M. (1985) Learnability and syllabus. In K. Hyltenstam and M. Pienemann (eds) *Modelling and Assessing Second Language Acquisition* (pp. 23–76). Clevedon: Multilingual Matters.

Pienemann, M. (1998) *Language Processing and Second Language Development: Processability Theory*. Amsterdam: John Benjamins Publishing.

Pinker, S. and Prince, A. (1988) On language and connectionism: Analysis of a parallel distributed processing model of language acquisition. *Cognition* 28 (1–2), 73–193.

Polansky, S.G. (2004) Tutoring for community outreach: A course model for language learning and bridge building between universities and public schools. *Foreign Language Annals* 37 (3), 367–373.

Polat, B. and Kim, Y. (2014) Dynamics of complexity and accuracy: A longitudinal case study of advanced untutored development. *Applied Linguistics* 35 (2), 184–207.

Polio, C. and Fleck, C. (1998) 'If I only had more time': ESL learners' changes in linguistic accuracy on essay revisions. *Journal of Second Language Writing* 7 (1), 43–68.

Poole, R. (2016) A corpus-aided approach for the teaching and learning of rhetoric in an undergraduate composition course for L2 writers. *Journal of English for Academic Purposes* 21, 99–109.

Potowski, K. (2003) Chicago's 'Heritage Language Teacher Corps': A model for improving Spanish teacher development. *Hispania* 86 (2), 302–311.

Prensky, M. (2009) H. sapiens digital: From digital immigrants and digital natives to digital wisdom. *Innovate: Journal of Online Education* 5 (3).

Pressley, M. and Harris, K.R. (2009) Cognitive strategies instruction: From basic research to classroom instruction. *Journal of Education* 189 (1–2), 77–94.

Price, C.J. (2010) The anatomy of language: A review of 100 fMRI studies published in 2009. *Annals of the New York Academy of Sciences* 1191 (1), 62–88.

Proctor, R.W., Vu, K.P.L. and Seel, N.M. (2012) Human information processing. In N.M. Seel (ed.) *Encyclopedia of the Sciences of Learning* (pp. 1458–1460). Heidelberg: Springer.

Pufahl, I. and Rhodes, N.C. (2011) Foreign language instruction in US schools: Results of a national survey of elementary and secondary schools. *Foreign Language Annals* 44 (2), 258–288.

Quarmyne, G.A. (2018) Lost language: Exploring HL loss among children of Ghanian immigrants in Calgary, Alberta. Unpublished master's thesis. University of Alberta.

Rankin, J. (2018) der| die| das: Integrating vocabulary acquisition research into an L2 German curriculum. In J. Watzinger-Tharp, K. Paesani, P. Ecke and S. Rott (eds) *AAUSC 2018: Understanding Vocabulary Learning and Teaching: Implications for Language Program Development* (pp. 99–120). Boston, MA: Cengage.

Rao, Z. (2013) Teaching English as a foreign language in China: Looking back and forward: Reconciling modern methodologies with traditional ways of language teaching. *English Today* 29 (3), 34–39.

Ratcliffe, J. and Tokarchuk, L. (2020, August) Evidence for embodied cognition in immersive virtual environments using a second language learning environment. In *2020 IEEE Conference on Games (CoG)* (pp. 471–478). Piscataway, NJ: IEEE.

Reinders, H. and Stockwell, G. (2017) Computer-assisted SLA. In S. Loewen and M. Sato (eds) *The Routledge Handbook of Instructed Second Language Acquisition* (pp. 361–375). New York: Routledge.

Robinson, P. (1997) Individual differences and the fundamental similarity of implicit and explicit adult second language learning. *Language Learning* 47 (1), 45–99.

Robinson, P. (2001) Task complexity, task difficulty, and task production: Exploring interactions in a componential framework. *Applied Linguistics* 22 (1), 27–57.

Robinson, P. and Gilabert, R. (2007) Task complexity, the cognition hypothesis and second language learning and performance. *International Review of Applied Linguistics* 45, 161–176.

Robinson, P. and Ellis, N.C. (eds) (2008) *Handbook of Cognitive Linguistics and Second Language Acquisition*. New York: Routledge.

Rock, I. (1977) In defense of unconscious inference. In W. Epstein (ed.) *Stability and Constancy in Visual Perception: Mechanisms and Processes* (pp. 321–373). New York, NY: Wiley.

Rock, I. (1983) *The Logic of Perception*. Cambridge, MA: MIT Press.

Rock, I. (ed.) (1997) *Indirect Perception*. Cambridge, MA: MIT Press.

Roehr, K. and Gánem-Gutiérrez, G.A. (2009) The status of metalinguistic knowledge in instructed adult L2 learning. *Language Awareness* 18 (2), 165–181.

Roehr-Brackin, K. (2018) *Metalinguistic Awareness and Second Language Acquisition*. London: Routledge.

Rogers, J. (2017) Awareness and learning under incidental learning conditions. *Language Awareness* 26 (2), 113–133.

Romanowski, P. (2021) A deliberate language policy or a perceived lack of agency: HL maintenance in the Polish community in Melbourne. *International Journal of Bilingualism* 25 (5), 1214–1234.

Rosmawati, R. (2014) Second language developmental dynamics: How dynamic systems theory accounts for issues in second language learning. *The Educational and Developmental Psychologist* 31 (1), 66–80.

Rossi, S., Gugler, M.F., Friederici, A.D. and Hahne, A. (2006) The impact of proficiency on syntactic second-language processing of German and Italian: Evidence from event-related potentials. *Journal of Cognitive Neuroscience* 18 (12), 2030–2048.

Rothman, J. and Slabakova, R. (2018) The generative approach to SLA and its place in modern second language studies. *Studies in Second Language Acquisition* 40 (2), 417–442.

Rubin, D.C. (2022) A conceptual space for episodic and semantic memory. *Memory & Cognition* 50 (3), 464–477.

Rumelhart, D.E. and McClelland, J.L. (1985) *On Learning the Past Tenses of English Verbs*. San Diego, CA: California University of San Diego La Jolla Institute for Cognitive Science.

Russell, V. and Murphy-Judy, K. (2020) *Teaching Language Online: A Guide to Designing, Developing, and Delivering Online, Blended, and Flipped Language Courses*. New York: Routledge.

Saito, K. (2011) Examining the role of explicit phonetic instruction in native-like and comprehensible pronunciation development: An instructed SLA approach to L2 phonology. *Language Awareness* 20 (1), 45–59.

Schachter, J. (1974) An error in error analysis 1. *Language Learning* 24 (2), 205–214.

Scharenborg, O. and van Os, M. (2019) Why listening in background noise is harder in a non-native language than in a native language: A review. *Speech Communication* 108, 53–64.

Schiff, R. and Ravid, D. (2004) Vowel representation in written Hebrew: Phonological, orthographic and morphological contexts. *Reading and Writing* 17 (3), 241–265.

Schinke-Llano, L. (1993) On the value of a Vygotskian framework for SLA theory and research. *Language Learning* 43 (1), 121–129.

Schmalz, X., Robidoux, S., Castles, A., Coltheart, M. and Marinus, E. (2017) German and English bodies: No evidence for cross-linguistic differences in preferred orthographic grain size. *Collabra: Psychology* 3 (1).

Schmidt, R. (1983) Interaction, acculturation, and the acquisition of communicative competence: A case study of an adult. In N. Wolfson and E. Judd (eds) *Sociolinguistics and Language Acquisition* (pp. 137–174). Rowley, MA: Newbury House.

Schmidt, R.W. (1990) The role of consciousness in second language learning. *Applied Linguistics* 11 (2), 129–158.

Schmidt-Renfree, N. (2020) He done done, or, He'd undone?: An investigation of second language listening processes with a particular focus on the processing of functional morphemes. Unpublished doctoral dissertation. University of Sussex.

Scott, S. and Edwards, W. (2018) *Disability and World Language Learning: Inclusive Teaching for Diverse Learners*. Lanham, MD: Rowman & Littlefield.

Searle, J.R. and Willis, S. (2002) *Consciousness and Language*. New York: Cambridge University Press.

Sebastián, C., Vergara, M. and Lissi, M.R. (2021) The Vygotskian contribution to the construction of a general theory of human learning. In P. Fossa (ed.) *Latin American Advances in Subjectivity and Development* (pp. 227–248). Cham: Springer.

Selinker, L. (1972) Interlanguage. *International Review of Applied Linguistics in Language Teaching* 10 (1–4), 209–232.

Seuren, P.A. (2004) How the cognitive revolution passed linguistics by. In F. Brisard, S. d'Hondt and T. Mortelmans (eds) *Language and Revolution: Language and Time* (pp. 63–77). Antwerp: Universiteit van Antwerpen.

Shanon, B. (1993) Why are we (at least sometimes) conscious of our thoughts?: Or: Why do we think in words (sometimes)? *Pragmatics & Cognition* 1 (1), 25–49.

Shibata, S. (2000) Opening a Japanese Saturday school in a small town in the United States: Community collaboration to teach Japanese as a heritage language. *Bilingual Research Journal* 24 (4), 465–474.

Shin, M. and Hickey, K. (2021) Needs a little TLC: Examining college students' emergency remote teaching and learning experiences during COVID-19. *Journal of Further and Higher Education* 45 (7), 973–986.

Siegesmund, A. (2017) Using self-assessment to develop metacognition and self-regulated learners. *FEMS Microbiology Letters* 364 (11).

Silverstein, B.H., Snodgrass, M., Shevrin, H. and Kushwaha, R. (2015) P3b, consciousness, and complex unconscious processing. *Cortex* 73, 216–227.

Simard, D., Foucambert, D. and Labelle, M. (2013) Examining the contribution of syntactic and metasyntactic abilities to reading comprehension among native and non-native speakers. In K. Roeher and G.A. Gánem-Gutiérrez (eds) *The Metalinguistic Dimension in Instructed L2 Learning* (pp. 45–70). London: Bloomsbury Academic.

Skinner, B.F. (1957) *Verbal Behavior*. New York: Appleton-Century-Crofts.

Slabakova, R. (2015) Is there a firewall between declarative knowledge and procedural knowledge of the functional morphology: A response to Paradis. *Foreign Language Teaching and Research* 47, 1–5.

Smith, B.H. (1975) On the margins of discourse. *Critical Inquiry* 1 (4), 769–798.

Smolucha, L. and Smolucha, F. (2021) Vygotsky's theory in-play: Early childhood education. *Early Child Development and Care* 191 (7–8), 1041–1055.

Sonaiya, R. (2002) Autonomous language learning in Africa: A mismatch of cultural assumptions. *Language Culture and Curriculum* 15 (2), 106–116.

Spada, N. (2007) Communicative language teaching. In J. Cummins and C. Davison (eds) *International Handbook of English Language Teaching* (pp. 271–288). Boston, MA: Springer.

Speelman, C.P. and Kirsner, K. (1997) The specificity of skill acquisition and transfer. *Australian Journal of Psychology* 49 (2), 91–100.

Spoelman, M. and Verspoor, M. (2010) Dynamic patterns in development of accuracy and complexity: A longitudinal case study in the acquisition of Finnish. *Applied Linguistics* 31 (4), 532–553.

Stata (2022) Market size of the global language services industry 2009–2022. https://www.statista.com/statistics/257656/size-of-the-global-language-services-market/. Accessed 03/14/2022.

Stevick, E.W. (1974) *Teaching Foreign Languages in Schools: The Silent Way*. New York: Educational Solutions Worldwide Inc.

Stevick, E.W. (1976) *Memory, Meaning and Method: Some Psychological Perspectives on Language Learning*. Boston, MA: Heinle & Heinle.

Stevick, E.W. (1980) *Teaching Languages: A Way and Ways*. Rowley, MA: Newbury House Publishers.

Sublett, C. (2020) Distant equity: The promise and pitfalls of online learning for students of color in higher education. *American Council on Education* https://www.equityinhighered.org/resources/ideas-and-insights/distant-equity-the-promise-and-pitfalls-of-online-learning-for-students-of-color-in-higher-education/.

Sueyoshi, A. and Hardison, D.M. (2005) The role of gestures and facial cues in second language listening comprehension. *Language Learning* 55 (4), 661–699.

Suter, R.W. (1976) Predictors of pronunciation accuracy in second language learning. *Language Learning* 26 (2), 233–253.

Suzuki, N. and Miyamoto, M. (2016) Effects of online repetition practice with animated visual aid on the acquisition of Japanese pitch accent and special moras. *Purdue Languages and Cultures Conference 2016*. Purdue University.

Suzuki, Y. (2021) The cognitive approach. In T. Gregersen and S. Mercer (eds) *The Routledge Handbook of the Psychology of Language Learning and Teaching* (pp. 7–21). New York: Routledge.

Suzuki, Y., Yokosawa, S. and Aline, D. (2020) The role of working memory in blocked and interleaved grammar practice: Proceduralization of L2 syntax. *Language Teaching Research*, 1362168820913985.

Swain, M. (1993) The output hypothesis: Just speaking and writing aren't enough. *Canadian Modern Language Review* 50 (1), 158–164.

Swain, M. (2000) The output hypothesis and beyond: Mediating acquisition through collaborative dialogue. In J.P. Lantolf (ed.) *Sociocultural Theory and Second Language Learning* (pp. 97–114). New York: Oxford University Press.

Swain, M. (2006) Languaging, agency and collaboration in advanced second language proficiency. In H. Byrnes (ed.) *Advanced Language Learning: The Contribution of Halliday and Vygotsky* (pp. 95–108). London: Continuum.

Swan, M. (2005) Legislation by hypothesis: The case of task-based instruction. *Applied Linguistics* 26 (3), 376–401.

Szilagyi, J. and Szecsi, T. (2020) Why and how to maintain the Hungarian language: Hungarian-American families' views on HL practices. *Heritage Language Journal* 17 (1), 114–115.

Taguchi, N. and Roever, C. (2017) *Second Language Pragmatics*. New York: Oxford University Press.

Tamaoka, K. (1991) Psycholinguistic nature of the Japanese orthography. *Studies in Language and Literature* 11 (1), 49–82.

Tamura, F. (1981) The development of the cognitive code-learning theory: Trends in language methodology in the United States. *Josai University Bulletin* 5 (3), 59–68.

Tate, T. and Warschauer, M. (2022) Equity in online learning. *Educational Psychologist* 57 (3), 192–206.

Taylor, I. and Taylor, M.M. (2014) *Writing and Literacy in Chinese, Korean and Japanese: Revised Edition*. Amsterdam: John Benjamins.

Thomas, M. (1995) Medieval and modern views of universal grammar and the nature of second language learning. *The Modern Language Journal* 79 (3), 345–355.

Thomas, M. (2002) Development of the concept of 'the poverty of the stimulus'. *The Linguistic Review* 19 (1–2), 51–71.

Todd, R.W. (2006) The myth of the native speaker as a model of English proficiency. *Reflections* 8, 1–7.

Tokowicz, N. and MacWhinney, B. (2005) Implicit and explicit measures of sensitivity to violations in second language grammar: An event-related potential investigation. *Studies in Second Language Acquisition* 27 (2), 173–204.

Tomić, A. and Kroff, J.V. (2021) Code-switching. In E. Kaan and T. Grüter (eds) *Prediction in Second Language Processing and Learning* (pp. 139–166). Amsterdam: Benjamins.

Tomlin, R.S. and Villa, V. (1994) Attention in cognitive science and second language acquisition. *Studies in Second Language Acquisition* 16 (2), 183–203.

Toribio, A.J. (2001) On the emergence of bilingual code-switching competence. *Bilingualism: Language and Cognition* 4 (3), 203–231.

Trautmann, N.M. (2008) Learning to teach: Alternatives to trial by fire. *Change* 40 (3), 40–45.

Trimbur, J. (2008) The Dartmouth conference and the geohistory of the native speaker. *College English* 71 (2), 142–169.

Troyan, F.J. (2016) Learning to mean in Spanish writing: A case study of a genre-based pedagogy for standards-based writing instruction. *Foreign Language Annals* 49 (2), 317–335.

Tschirner, E. (2016) Listening and reading proficiency levels of college students. *Foreign Language Annals* 49 (2), 201–223.

Tse, L. (2001) Resisting and reversing language shift: Heritage-language resilience among US native biliterates. *Harvard Educational Review* 71 (4), 676–709.

Tsuchiya, S. (2020) The native speaker fallacy in a US university Japanese and Chinese program. *Foreign Language Annals* 53 (3), 527–549.

Ullman, M.T. (2014) The declarative/procedural model: A neurobiologically motivated theory of first and second language. In B. VanPatten, G. Keating and S. Wulff (eds) *Theories in Second Language Acquisition: An Introduction* (pp. 147–172). New York: Routledge.

UNESCO (2016) If you don't understand, how can you learn? *Policy Paper 24 of Global Education Monitoring Report*. https://en.unesco.org/gem-report/if-you-don%E2%80%99t-understand-how-can-you-learn. Accessed 1/5/2023.

Unsworth, N., Redick, T.S., Heitz, R.P., Broadway, J.M. and Engle, R.W. (2009) Complex working memory span tasks and higher-order cognition: A latent-variable analysis of the relationship between processing and storage. *Memory* 17 (6), 635–654.

US News and World Report (2021) Best colleges: Brigham Young University–Provo. See https://www.usnews.com/best-colleges/byu-3670. Accessed 10/22/2021.

Vaezi, S. and Abbaspour, E. (2014) Implementing CLT in the Iranian context: 'Reality' versus theory. *Procedia-Social and Behavioral Sciences* 98, 1905–1911.

Vainapel, S., Shamir, O.Y., Tenenbaum, Y. and Gilam, G. (2015) The dark side of gendered language: The masculine-generic form as a cause for self-report bias. *Psychological Assessment* 27 (4), 1513.

Valdés, G., Peyton, J., Ranard, J. and McGinnis, S. (1999) Heritage language students: Profiles and possibilities. In J.K. Peyton, D.A. Ranard and S. McGinnis (eds) *Heritage Languages in America: Preserving a National Resource* (pp. 37–80). Washington, DC: Center for Applied Linguistics.

Van Compernolle, R.A. (2011) Developing second language sociopragmatic knowledge through concept-based instruction: A microgenetic case study. *Journal of Pragmatics* 43 (13), 3267–3283.

Van Compernolle, R.A., Gomez-Laich, M.P. and Weber, A. (2016) Teaching L2 Spanish sociopragmatics through concepts: A classroom-based study. *The Modern Language Journal* 100 (1), 341–361.

Vanderburg, R.M. (2006) Reviewing research on teaching writing based on Vygotsky's theories: What we can learn. *Reading & Writing Quarterly* 22 (4), 375–393.

VanPatten, B. (2004) Input processing in second language acquisition. In B. VanPatten (ed.) *Processing Instruction: Theory, Research, and Commentary* (pp. 5–31). New York: Routledge.
VanPatten, B. (2013) Input processing. In S. Gass and A. Mackey (eds) *The Routledge Handbook of Second Language Acquisition* (pp. 286–299). New York: Routledge.
VanPatten, B. (2017) Processing instruction. In S. Loewen and M. Sato (eds) *The Routledge Handbook of Instructed Second Language Acquisition* (pp. 166–180). New York: Routledge.
VanPatten, B. (2020) Input processing in adult L2 acquisition. In B. VanPatten, G. Keating and S. Wulff (eds) *Theories in Second Language Acquisition: An Introduction* (pp. 105–127). New York: Routledge.
VanPatten, B. and Cadierno, T. (1993) Input processing and second language acquisition: A role for instruction. *The Modern Language Journal* 77 (1), 45–57.
VanPatten, B. and Benati, A. (2011) Key terms in second language acquisition. See https://charttesl.wordpress.com/2011/02/21/key-terms-in-second-language-acquisition-van-patten-benati/. Accessed 10/15/2021.
VanPatten, B. and Borst, S. (2012) The roles of explicit information and grammatical sensitivity in processing instruction: Nominative-accusative case marking and word order in German L2. *Foreign Language Annals* 45 (1), 92–109.
VanPatten, B., Collopy, E., Price, J.E., Borst, S. and Qualin, A. (2013) Explicit information, grammatical sensitivity, and the first-noun principle: A cross-linguistic study in processing instruction. *The Modern Language Journal* 97 (2), 506–527.
Varvel, T. (1979) The silent way: Panacea or pipedream? *TESOL Quarterly* 13 (4), 483–494.
Viet, K.A. (2008) Imperialism of communicative language teaching and possible resistance against it from teachers in Vietnam as an English foreign languages context. *VNU Journal of Foreign Studies* 24 (3), 167–174.
Vygotsky, L. (1987) Thinking and speech. In R. Rieber and A. Carton (eds) *The Collected Works of Lev Vygotsky, Vol. 1* (N. Minick, trans.). New York: Plenum.
Vygotsky, L.S. (2012) *Thought and Language*. Cambridge, MA: MIT Press.
Wajnryb, R. (1990) *Grammar Dictation* (vol. 3). Oxford: Oxford University Press.
Wallace, M.P. (2022) Individual differences in second language listening: Examining the role of knowledge, metacognitive awareness, memory, and attention. *Language Learning* 72 (1), 5–44.
Walter, D. (2019) Student uses of the first language for L2 classroom interactions. In *2017 Second Language Research Forum* (pp. 200–214). Somerville, MA: Cascadilla Proceedings Project.
Walter, D.R. and Kraemer, A. (2013, Summer) SPRICH: Student provided enrichment: Building a language learning community. *Neues Curriculum*.
Walter, D.R. and van Compernolle, R.A. (2017) Teaching German declension as meaning: A concept-based approach. *Innovation in Language Learning and Teaching* 11 (1), 68–85.
Wamsley, E.J. (2014) Dreaming and offline memory consolidation. *Current Neurology and Neuroscience Reports* 14 (3), 1–7.
Watzinger-Tharp, J., Swenson, K. and Mayne, Z. (2018) Academic achievement of students in dual language immersion. *International Journal of Bilingual Education and Bilingualism* 21 (8), 913–928.
Weiland, B.J., Sabbineni, A., Calhoun, V.D., Welsh, R.C., Bryan, A.D., Jung, R.E. … Hutchison, K.E. (2014) Reduced left executive control network functional connectivity is associated with alcohol use disorders. *Alcoholism: Clinical and Experimental Research* 38 (9), 2445–2453.
Wexler, B.E. (1992) Experimental studies of higher cortical functions that proceed without conscious awareness. *Psychoanalytic Inquiry* 12 (3), 475–498.
Weyers, J.R. (1999) The effect of authentic video on communicative competence. *The Modern Language Journal* 83 (3), 339–349.

Whitney, D. and Levi, D.M. (2011) Visual crowding: A fundamental limit on conscious perception and object recognition. *Trends in Cognitive Sciences* 15 (4), 160–168.

Wiggins, G. and McTighe, J. (2005) *Understanding by Design*. Upper Saddle River, NJ: Pearson.

Williams, J. (2012) The potential role (s) of writing in second language development. *Journal of Second Language Writing* 21 (4), 321–331.

Williams, S. (2019) U-shaped trajectories in L2 learning: Testing the dual processing hypothesis – an experimental study of Norwegian L2 learners of English. Master's thesis. Norwegian University of Science and Technology.

Williams, S., Guijarro-Fuentes, P. and Vulchanova, M. (2022) U-shaped trajectories in an L2 context: Evidence from the acquisition of verb morphology. *Vigo International Journal of Applied Linguistics* (19), 223–266.

Wilson, I. (2018) A brief overview of psycholinguistic approaches to second language acquisition. *Applied Linguistics Research Journal* 2 (2), 1–7.

Wilson, A.D. and Golonka, S. (2013) Embodied cognition is not what you think it is. *Frontiers in Psychology* 4, 58.

Wittgenstein, L. (2010) *Philosophical Investigations*. Hoboken, NJ: John Wiley & Sons.

Wokke, M.E., van Gaal, S., Scholte, H.S., Ridderinkhof, K.R. and Lamme, V.A. (2011) The flexible nature of unconscious cognition. *PLoS One* 6 (9), e25789.

Wright, T. (2012) Managing the classroom. In A. Burns and J.C. Richards (eds) *The Cambridge Guide to Pedagogy and Practice in Second Language Teaching* (pp. 60–67). Cambridge: Cambridge University Press.

Yaghoubi, M. and Farrokh, P. (2022) Investigating Iranian English learners' private speech across proficiency levels and gender based on Vygotsky's sociocultural theory. *Journal of Psycholinguistic Research* 51 (2), 273–292.

Yalçın, Ş., Çeçen, S. and Erçetin, G. (2016) The relationship between aptitude and working memory: An instructed SLA context. *Language Awareness* 25 (1–2), 144–158.

Yeh, S.L., Chou, W.L. and Ho, P. (2017) Lexical processing of Chinese sub-character components: Semantic activation of phonetic radicals as revealed by the Stroop effect. *Scientific Reports* 7 (1), 15782. https://doi.org/10.1038/s41598-017-15536-w

Yoon, H.Y., Bond, K. and Walter, D.R (in preparation) A concept-based approach to teaching Korean verbal honorific morphology: A comparison of L2 and HL learners.

Yu, L. (2001) Communicative language teaching in China: Progress and resistance. *TESOL Quarterly* 35 (1), 194–198.

Zamri, E. and Azman, N. (2020) The role of parents in HL maintenance in Malaysia. *The 5th International Conference on Education, Islamic Studies and Social Sciences Research* (pp. 801–808). Ho Chi Minh, Vietnam: ICEISR 2020 Organizing Committee.

Zárate-Sández, G. (2019) Spanish pronunciation and teaching dialectal variation. In R. Rao (ed.) *Key Issues in the Teaching of Spanish Pronunciation: From Description to Pedagogy* (pp. 201–217). Abingdon: Routledge.

Zhang, D. and Slaughter-Defoe, D.T. (2009) Language attitudes and HL maintenance among Chinese immigrant families in the USA. *Language, Culture and Curriculum* 22 (2), 77–93.

Zhang, J. (2020) Family and HL maintenance: Parents' and children's attitudes over the years. Unpublished master's thesis. McGill University.

Zhang, H. and Roberts, L. (2021) The influence of L1 script directionality and L2 proficiency on Hanzi learning among Arabic and English learners of L2 Chinese. *International Review of Applied Linguistics in Language Teaching*.

Zhou, X., Marslen-Wilson, W., Taft, M. and Shu, H. (1999) Morphology, orthography, and phonology reading Chinese compound words. *Language and Cognitive Processes* 14 (5–6), 525–565.

Zieger, J.C., Jacobs, A.M. and Stone, G.O. (1996) Statistical analysis of the bidirectional inconsistency of spelling and sound in French. *Behavioral Research Methods, Instruments, and Computers* 28 (4), 504–515.

Ziegler, J.C. and Goswami, U. (2005) Reading acquisition, developmental dyslexia, and skilled reading across languages: A psycholinguistic grain size theory. *Psychological Bulletin* 131 (1), 3–29.

Zuengler, J. and Miller, E.R. (2006) Cognitive and sociocultural perspectives: Two parallel SLA worlds? *TESOL Quarterly* 40 (1), 35–58.

Zwaan, R.A. and Radvansky, G.A. (1998) Situation models in language comprehension and memory. *Psychological Bulletin* 123 (2), 162–185.

Zyzik, E. (2006) Learners' overgeneralization of dative clitics to accusative contexts: Evidence for prototype effects in SLA. In *Selected Proceedings of the 7th Conference on the Acquisition of Spanish and Portuguese as First and Second Languages* (pp. 122–134). Somerville, MA: Cascadilla Proceedings Project.

Index

accent 164, 166
accuracy 41, 72, 95, 98, 99, 127
accusative 65
activation 47, 63, 70, 72, 84
administrators 24, 46, 66, 118, 119, 121, 135, 140, 145
adolescents 20
adverbial 165
Africa 23, 24, 25, 114
agency 39, 72, 120
alcohol 72
alphabetic 44, 45, 82, 83, 85
amalgams 95
anxiety 136, 137, 167
apps 121, 128
artifacts 3, 5, 126, 127, 128, 143, 170, 174, 176
assessment 171
assimilation 45
attention 41, 51, 54-59, 64-72, 73, 75, 80, 88-89, 92, 95-96, 99, 104, 107-108, 112, 114, 125, 137, 152, 156-157, 165-166
audience 86, 97, 105, 108, 125, 166, 168
audiolingual 26-27
Australian 16
authentic 38, 64, 109, 111-112, 125, 127-128, 136, 142, 148, 162, 166, 171, 175
automatization 5, 75, 79, 91-92, 102-103
avoidance 29, 38, 109-111, 113

background
  educational 40
  family 149
  knowledge 47
  linguistic 76
  noise 42
  technological 121
backward design 145-147, 150, 171, 176-177
basal ganglia 103
behaviorism 26-27, 29
beliefs 9, 14, 19-21, 24, 66-68, 70, 76, 100, 118-119, 127-128, 132-133, 137, 149-150, 174
Bible 11-12
bifurcation 123-124
bilabial 48
bilingual 15-16, 38-39, 109, 112-113, 133, 141, 176
biological 3, 31, 51, 130
brain 32, 43, 48-49, 51-52, 103, 131, 178
breathing 72
business 15-17, 132, 174

Cantonese 67
case marking 47, 65, 93
characters 44-45, 83-84, 91
China 25
Christianity 8, 10
chunk (-s, -ing) 77-78, 81-82, 88, 91-96, 99-100, 110, 129, 164
classroom 7, 19, 21, 26, 35, 39, 46, 68, 78, 92, 112, 117-125, 129, 151, 153, 162
coda 45, 78
code-switching 76, 109-111, 113
cognate 78
cognitive processes 31, 36, 41, 68-69, 95-96
cognitive science 29, 31, 36

205

college 13, 56, 112, 131, 140-142, 149, 172, 174
collocation 159
colonialist 124
communication 17, 46, 93, 108, 110, 151, 160, 164, 171
communicative method/approach 10, 24-25, 33, 47, 99, 161, 172
community 11, 14, 17, 19, 21, 46, 76, 100, 118-119, 126, 130-131, 135-136, 138, 141, 171-175
competency 23, 79, 147, 152, 166
competition model 33
complex dynamic systems theory 28, 33, 36, 66, 106
complexity 53, 62-63, 65, 82, 90, 101-102, 108, 110, 146, 154, 161, 165
comprehension 37, 41, 48, 69-70, 77-79, 81-82, 85-86, 100, 107-108, 113, 150, 154-155, 163-164
concept-based language instruction (C-BLI) 35, 161-162
concepts 48, 54, 86-87, 90, 114, 149, 161-164
connectionism 31
consciousness 49-54, 56, 58, 60-62, 64, 67-72, 73-75, 81-82, 86, 92-93, 95-96, 107-108, 114-115, 119, 126, 143, 163, 165, 173, 178
consonant 48-49, 78, 83
construction grammar 33, 93
constructivist 22
contextual information 33, 46-47, 49, 59, 77, 101, 104, 165
corpus 160, 162, 169
critical period 130-131
crosslinguistic 85
cues 42-43, 75, 78-79, 86, 119
cultural context 24, 174
cultural knowledge 18, 84, 90, 114, 133, 136, 148, 155, 169
curriculum 13, 71-72, 98, 100, 103, 105, 109, 122-124, 127-128, 133-134, 145-155, 160, 162, 171-172, 176-178

dative 65
decoding 45, 82, 84-85

deductive 30
dialect 10, 16, 36, 43, 100, 142, 164, 166
dialogue 26-27, 32, 34, 57, 127
dictogloss 155
digital 121, 128
discourse 59, 80-82, 114, 155, 165, 171, 176
dynamic assessment 35, 157-158, 170

economics 19, 21
elementary school 10, 130, 133, 135, 176
embodied cognition 31-33, 166
embodiment 32-33
emergentism 33, 66, 171-172
emotion 48, 70, 82, 137, 167
empirical 24-26, 39, 102
employment 16, 19
enclave 16
encode 17, 46, 83-84
encourage 105-106, 161
enrollment 123, 138-140
environment 21, 23, 42-43, 56, 73, 75, 91, 109, 117-118, 120-122, 124-126, 130, 135, 141, 143, 158, 162, 167
episodic 48, 54, 69
epistemology 51
event-related potential (ERP) 69, 80, 107
evolution 10, 16, 46
explicit instruction 29, 63-64, 160
explicit knowledge 58, 73, 95, 104, 112, 157, 162, 164
extinction 18
extracurricular 131, 141-142

faith 13-14
family 11, 19-21, 112, 121, 131-132, 149, 162, 172
feedback 74, 100, 137, 147-149, 151, 157-158, 165, 167, 177
feminine 65
fetus 42
film 30, 76
first language (L1) 17, 27-28, 31, 34, 37, 40, 43, 56, 58, 60, 63, 70, 72, 74-93, 95-96, 100, 104, 106-117, 120, 130-131, 135-136, 139-140, 149-150, 154, 159, 162, 164, 166, 168-169, 174-175, 178

fluency 10, 24, 41, 62, 81-82, 98-100, 108-109, 164-165
focus on form 63, 154, 161
formality 75, 105, 162
formalization 7, 27
French 8, 20, 30, 45, 50
frequency 160, 172
functional magnetic resonance imaging (fMRI) 52, 166
future 110, 112, 140, 151, 156, 158, 160, 167

Gaelic 21
gender 49-50
generative 27, 75
genitive 65
genre 64, 86-87, 90, 108, 154, 166-169, 176
geography 20, 142
German 8-9, 15, 45, 50, 65, 67, 84, 124, 140, 142, 164, 173
gesture 43, 78, 80, 109, 152, 158
globalization 15-16
goal 7, 10, 14, 19, 22, 25-26, 34, 37, 49, 51, 56, 60, 66-70, 101, 118, 120, 122, 125, 130, 133, 137, 144, 149-151, 160, 175-177
grammar 8-32
grammatical gender 50, 65, 75, 93
grapheme 43-45, 59, 82-85, 89-91, 93, 96, 166-167
guessing 23, 77, 86

habits 26, 49, 86
hieroglyphs 43
high school 122-123, 129, 133, 135, 141-142, 149, 153, 176
hiragana 45, 83-84
history 28, 36-37, 57, 99, 124, 138
homework 99, 137, 156, 167, 172
homography 93
homophony 93

identity 19, 38-39, 76, 100, 111-112, 171-172, 178
idiomatic expressions 86, 159
immigration 126
implicature 105
implicit knowledge 73, 81, 96
implicit learning 1
implicit processes 86
incidental learning 56, 73, 105, 113-114, 125, 155
Indonesia 21
inductive 29
infant 42
inhibition 79
inhibitory 55, 137
innate 29, 61
input 28, 30, 33-35, 42-43, 47-48, 53-55, 58-59, 63, 66, 74, 79, 84, 91, 93, 96, 100, 105, 126, 160
input processing 33, 63
input-interaction-output 34
institutions 9-11, 14, 16-17, 118, 122-124, 132, 134, 137, 139-140, 147
instructed second language acquisition (ISLA) 4, 7-8, 17, 21, 25, 28, 37, 39-40, 41-43, 60-61, 65-66, 68, 70-71, 73, 92, 111-113, 117, 119, 122, 130, 143, 144
intercultural 10, 21
intercultural communication 7, 17, 106, 151-152
interdisciplinary 31, 33, 40, 51
interlocutor 26, 46, 75, 81-82, 92, 99, 102, 161, 176
internalization 108-109, 114, 160
internalize 57, 108
intervention 41, 43, 54, 74, 130, 143, 158, 161
Ireland 21
Islam 14, 22
isolation 88
Italian 8, 50

jobs 16
Judaism 14

K-12 14, 17, 122-123, 135, 138, 145
kanji 45-46, 84
katakana 46, 83-84

language education 9, 13, 16, 25, 73, 118, 135, 137-138
language play 127
Latin 8-12, 56

Latinx 20
learnability 115
learning context 33, 102
less commonly taught languages (LCTL) 139
linguistic context 45
linguistic knowledge 73, 75, 86-87, 90, 109, 112, 133, 135, 158
listening 26, 32, 76-80, 88, 97, 100, 120, 132, 148, 154-155, 164, 166
literacy 19, 64, 130, 148, 166
local context 35, 105
logographic 43-45, 82-84, 91
long term memory 53-54

machine learning 31
Mandarin 43
markedness 113
markets 15
masculine 65
materials 18-19, 30, 33, 39-40, 65, 118-119, 125-128, 132, 139, 146-148, 151, 162, 166, 176-177
McGurk effect 48
medieval 8-9
memorization 22-24, 26, 44, 95
memorize 22, 26, 45, 81, 90-91, 94-95, 103, 159
mental models 47, 75
metacognition 51, 56-57
metalanguage 64, 162-164
metalinguistic awareness 62
metalinguistic knowledge 57, 61, 86, 90, 112-114, 150, 162-164
methodology 32, 51, 150, 161
migration 16, 126
mind 29, 49, 51, 55, 60, 62, 65, 67, 70-71, 80, 98, 107, 112, 152, 159, 165
missionaries 11-13
modularity 61
money 16, 122
monitoring 23, 50, 80, 100, 108, 146
monolingualism 137
morphology 38, 50, 59, 62, 80-81, 84, 86, 89, 93, 95, 104-105, 159-160
morphosyllabic 44-45, 82, 84, 91
morphosyntax 115

motivation 7, 9, 16, 19, 21-22, 66-68, 71, 100, 118, 123, 125, 132-133, 135, 148-151, 167, 171
multilingual turn 29, 37-38, 113
multilingualism 105-106, 137, 172
multiliteracies 10, 168
multimodal 54
music 42, 153, 176

narrative 70, 135-136, 175
native 17, 34, 37, 58, 76, 106-107, 113, 121, 160, 164, 178
neuroscience 49-50
neuter 50, 65
nominative 65
nonalphabetic 85
nonnative 34
North America 19, 21, 112, 117
noticing 50, 54-56, 62-63, 105, 156, 161
noun 63, 75, 76, 81

object 26, 46, 63, 71, 92, 96
online 17, 48, 76, 121, 128
ontogenetic 24
organization 97, 101, 113, 118, 124, 137, 170
orthography 44, 84
output 34, 42, 53, 61, 155, 163, 166
output hypothesis 33-34
overgeneralization 74, 103

paralinguistic 46-57, 114
parents 14, 19-21, 46, 58, 97, 118, 131, 133, 137-138, 145, 149-150
passive 125, 163
pattern 8-9, 26, 28, 30-31, 42, 47, 58, 62-63, 74-75, 78, 81-82, 84, 88-89, 91-93, 95, 101, 103-104, 135, 145, 152, 158, 160, 166
pedagogy 7, 9, 21-22, 24-25, 29, 31, 33, 37, 39, 71-72, 98-99, 101, 109, 111, 113-114, 118-122, 124, 144-145, 159-161, 168,
perception 19-20, 113, 124, 138, 142
phonetics 10, 45, 90
phonological loop 53-54
pictograph 43
pitch 42
plagiarism 169

plural 65, 95, 159
politics 16
power 12, 14-15, 19, 50-51, 119-120, 129, 138, 164, 171, 178
pragmatics 28-29, 38, 46, 59, 86, 92, 97, 104-106, 144, 148, 161-162, 165, 167, 176
prediction 36, 79, 155
proceduralization 81, 91, 102, 104
processability theory 33
proficiency 17, 23, 45, 61, 66, 79-80, 82, 92-93, 96-99, 102, 105-108, 114, 118, 121, 125-126, 129, 132-134, 136-137, 141-142, 148-149, 154-155, 158, 163, 165-166, 171-173
pronunciation 26, 43, 45, 82, 100-101, 106, 165-166
prototype 103
purpose 8, 10, 13-15, 18-19, 22-23, 34, 37, 59, 66, 73, 83, 86-87, 90, 96, 98, 103, 106, 109-114, 119, 125, 131-132, 135, 142, 148-149, 155, 166, 168

qualitative 19
quantitative 19
Quran 13-14, 22

radical 44
readiness 66, 115, 131, 153, 170
reading 26, 32, 46, 48, 70, 76-77, 82, 84-86, 88-91, 97, 104-105, 115, 132, 145-146, 148, 150, 154-155, 159-161, 163, 166-169
reflection 22, 38, 48-49, 56, 67, 73, 76, 86, 100, 112, 115, 123, 138, 146, 155, 170
reflective practices 72
refugees 21, 125, 132
religion 8, 11-12
religious context 9, 14, 15, 21
repertoire 34, 66, 81-82, 89, 101-102, 157
repetition 30, 79, 81, 125, 148, 154, 157, 165
resources 9, 17, 20, 49, 55-56, 58-59, 62-63, 65, 67-68, 71, 74-75, 77-78, 86-90, 95, 99-105, 107-108, 112, 115, 119, 122, 125, 128, 135, 142, 169, 172, 174, 178
respect 51, 167
rote 95
routines 84, 162
rule 10, 29-31, 48, 61, 74, 81-82, 95, 107, 127, 158, 163

saliency 92
salient 92, 174
scaffolding 78, 148, 153-154, 167, 169-170
semantics 14, 29, 70
semitic 85
systemic functional linguistics (SFL) 63-64, 168
short term memory 63, 71
silent way 29-31
social 9-10, 12, 15, 18, 21, 34-37, 40, 56, 70, 92, 97, 101, 105-106, 108-109, 118, 120, 130-132, 137, 142-143, 144, 148, 151, 159, 162, 174
social context 18, 137, 144
social turn 28, 33-34, 36
socialization 36, 174
sociocultural 34-35, 52, 64, 108, 114, 148, 157, 177
sound 10, 42, 44-46, 48, 58, 75, 82-86, 89-91, 95-96, 101, 115, 164, 166-167
space 9, 11, 14, 38, 66, 68, 71-72, 78-79, 88, 110, 112-114, 117-122, 124-125, 128-130, 134, 141, 143, 152, 155-156, 172-174, 177
Spanish 8, 16, 19-20, 45, 50, 67, 93, 124, 139, 164
speaking 26, 30, 49, 62, 67, 74, 76, 80-82, 89, 91, 97, 99-100, 104, 108, 127, 132, 136-137, 150, 152, 164-165, 175
spectrograph 166
spelling 115, 170
spreading activation 47, 63
standards, 147, 170
storytelling 154
strategy 88, 90
students 119-126, 129, 130-132, 136-137, 141, 149-152, 171-174

study abroad context 126
subconscious 50, 60-63, 68-72, 106-108, 171
subject 92-93
subjunctive 63, 87
substrate 53
subvocal 81
syllabic 44-45, 82-83, 89
symbols 31, 45-46, 78, 80, 83-84, 86, 167
syntax 62-63, 86, 90, 111, 160

task-based language teaching (TBLT) 33, 62, 147, 161
teachers 122-125, 128-129, 132-137
technology 33, 119-121, 128-129, 148, 169
TESOL 11
test 11, 57, 80, 140-141
textbooks 38, 65, 127-129, 142, 146, 148, 163, 166
Thai 83
theology 50
tonal 75, 166
tone 26, 87, 92, 166
topicalization 75
total physical response (TPR) 32-33, 119, 178
transfer 22, 25, 28, 60, 63, 65, 75, 77-79, 82, 84, 87, 92-93, 95, 100, 104, 110, 114, 123, 150-153, 166, 168
translanguaging 113-114
translation 8, 15, 24, 76, 83, 107, 109, 114, 169
transparency 45, 83, 91

travel 9, 12, 135, 150-151, 175-176
turn-taking 101

unconscious 49, 55-57, 60, 64-65, 68-72, 73, 80, 89, 92, 95, 111, 115, 157
undergraduate 123
ungrammatical 80, 107
universal grammar (UG) 9, 28, 75, 131
university 10, 12-13, 118, 123-124, 131, 134, 136, 140-141, 172
usage-based 9, 33, 93
U-shaped learning 74, 104
utterance 26, 28, 37, 63, 80-81, 88-89, 92, 96, 111, 158

verb 63, 74, 76, 79, 81, 92-93, 96, 99, 169
vernacular 9, 11, 163
visuospatial sketchpatch 53-54
vocabulary 18, 25, 30, 32, 50, 57, 70, 74, 76, 78, 81, 84, 86, 89-91, 93, 96, 99-100, 106, 108, 110-111, 113, 115, 136, 154-155, 159-160, 162, 165-166, 168, 170, 176
volition 50, 53
vowel 78, 83, 85
(non-)Western context 21, 24-25

working memory 51, 53-54, 59, 68-69, 81, 93, 105, 115
writing 30-32, 74, 76-77
writing system 78, 82-84, 86-91, 97-98, 100, 108, 127, 132, 148, 150-151, 162, 167-170

Yiddish 14

For Product Safety Concerns and Information please contact our EU Authorised Representative:

Easy Access System Europe

Mustamäe tee 50

10621 Tallinn

Estonia

gpsr.requests@easproject.com

www.ingramcontent.com/pod-product-compliance
Ingram Content Group UK Ltd.
Pitfield, Milton Keynes, MK11 3LW, UK
UKHW021823220426
5349IPUK00003B/55